Aristocratic Government and Society in Eighteenth-Century England

Modern Scholarship on European History

HENRY A. TURNER, JR.
GENERAL EDITOR

Aristocratic Government and Society in Eighteenth-Century England

THE FOUNDATIONS OF STABILITY

Edited with an Introduction by

Daniel A. Baugh

NEW VIEWPOINTS

A Division of Franklin Watts, Inc. New York 1975

Library of Congress Cataloging in Publication
Data
Main entry under title:

Aristocratic government and society in
eighteenth-century England.

(Modern scholarship on European history)
Bibliography: p.
Includes index.
CONTENTS: Miege, G. The present state of
Great Britain: an eighteenth-century self-por-
trait.—Swift, J. The Examiner no. 14: a Tory
view of war and the moneyed interest.—
Wrigley, E. A. A simple model of London's im-
portance in changing English society and econ-
omy, 1650–1750. [etc.]
    1. Great Britain—Social conditions—18th
century—Addresses, essays, lectures. 2. Great
Britain—Politics and government—18th century
—Addresses, essays, lectures.
I. Baugh, Daniel A.

HN385.A72   309.1'42'07   75-5825
ISBN 0-531-05370-9
ISBN 0-531-05577-9 pbk.

Table of Contents

Preface

This book serves two purposes and may be used at two levels. One is to illustrate social realities and political relationships in eighteenth-century England; the other, to explore how these realities and relationships came about, and how they yielded the stability and apparent serenity that are the most striking features of the period.

Readers who are mainly interested in the former may begin with "An Eighteenth-Century Self-Portrait" from Miege's handbook and then skip to the essays by J. H. Plumb, Dame Lucy Sutherland, Edward Hughes, and Sir Lewis Namier. All provide materials and insights for making an imaginative leap backward to the England of two centuries ago. To afford such leaps of imagination, while keeping them within the bounds of truth, is one of history's main objects.

But history is also concerned with change. My introduction, the brief selection from *The Examiner* by Jonathan Swift, and the articles by E. A. Wrigley and H. J. Habakkuk are in one way or another concerned with the shaping of eighteenth-century England and the conditions upon which stability was established. For it is only by a historical approach that one can discover why certain institutional and customary peculiarities dominated the scene and held on so long. Historians will recognize that this portion of the book is inspired by J. H. Plumb's *The Growth of Political Stability in England, 1675–1725* (1967); and it is my hope that the presentation here will move readers to turn to Professor Plumb's book and will enrich their understanding of it.

Readers deserve a word of warning about repetition. Since the primary aim of this book is to assemble writings that will illuminate the relation between the government of eighteenth-century England and its social foundations, and since it was considered best to print each chapter or article of modern scholarship in its entirety, some repetition has been unavoidable. The editor hopes that readers will treat any matters that become overly familiar as indications of common ground and will move quickly through them with a sense of comfort rather than annoyance.

One last point. All of the modern historians represented here have habitually adhered to a broad outlook in their scholarship, yet done so without yielding to superficiality. Adhering to a broad outlook is becoming difficult for historical scholars in all fields, but especially in the field of eighteenth-century Britain. On the one hand there are the political historians, who are driven to master the complexities of the constitutional fabric and the intricacies of influence and connection, or perhaps are concerned to discover the roots of modern political forms. On the other hand there are the economic historians, who explore the territory for clues as to the nature of underdeveloped societies or the roots of the industrial revolution. Economic history was building a private edifice of economists' questions even before the advent of the new mathematical apparatus that has rendered much of it incomprehensible to most historians. These are all worthy enterprises, for it is undeniable that they encompass some of the best (as well as some of the worst) recent work in eighteenth-century British history. The new techniques are not to be dismissed as meretricious; good historians will, at the very least, have to master them sufficiently to assess their utility and significance. But a historian who commits himself to a single line of sight yields up his birthright. If this little book manages not only to serve the practical needs of students but also to help preserve the unity and scholarly health of the field, it will have achieved all of its aims.

My acknowledgment to the authors and publishers who gave me permission to reprint their publications is recorded in the prefaces to each chapter. It is a pleasure to record here my obligation to Peggy Daub and William Sheasgreen, as well as many Cornell colleagues for advice concerning the bibliographical note. I am especially grateful to my colleague, Clive Holmes, for his careful and critical reading of the introduction. Nearly all his suggestions were warmly welcomed, but of course responsibility for any faults that remain is mine. Finally, I would like to thank my wife for typing difficult texts, reading proof, and advancing the work in countless ways.

Ithaca, New York
March 1974
D.A.B.

I

Introduction:
The Social Basis of Stability

Whether a historian's concern is with the origins of the industrial revolution, of modern politics, or of the United States of America, eighteenth-century England cannot be ignored. It is a convenient starting point for modern history, a stable platform for launching the story of the revolutionary age. But for this very reason eighteenth-century England is often misrepresented and misunderstood. It has been made to serve symbolic ends by exemplifying what is "pre-industrial," "pre-revolutionary," or "traditional." Undeniably, eighteenth-century England retained a traditional social structure and a disjointed and rather archaic system of local administration, but from a comparative point of view it was a remarkably modern country.

With the possible exception of the Dutch provinces, it was the most modern country in the world. Its maritime and commercial supremacy and its financial institutions were the envy of Europe. Their strength was reflected in the surging growth of London. And London was linked to the countryside. For centuries it had enjoyed easy communication with the rest of England through coastal trade and river navigation. There were no administrative barriers to internal trade, and during the first half of the eighteenth century the old scheme of road maintenance, which failed most egregiously on the heavily used arteries radiating from the metropolis, was being replaced by the turnpike system.[1] Until the nineteenth century, England was to an unusual degree a single-city kingdom.

London was a modernizing force throughout England. Large as it was in the eighteenth century, it did not suffer from the problem of commanding a food supply. It was fed effortlessly through the mechanisms of market agriculture; and the desirability of marketable surpluses shaped the character of English estate management. By the eighteenth century practically the entire English peasantry was a rural proletariat, retaining Poor Law rights in the parish and rights in village common lands but no stake in the profits of agriculture. Most people lived on the land, and most industry was connected with the produce of the land. Yet the national market centered in London and the export markets as well were pushing industry to a high degree of specialization: It seemed possible that English manufacturing was approaching a point where no further economies could be gained by division of labor.[2]

The advantages and innovative features of English political arrangements were noticed throughout eighteenth-century Europe. The effectiveness of England's government as to certain functions, that is raising revenues and fighting wars, was second to none in Europe by 1715. Although the revolutions of the 1640s and of 1688 failed to achieve any permanent inversion of social forces, the turmoil of the seventeenth century did move politics outside the confines of the court and forced governmental leadership to respond to a wide range of interests. The electorate of the House of Commons became much enlarged;[3] the press was clamorous. And although the system of local government was archaic, it did leave a great deal of latitude to the local community and the individual subject.

The open, untidy, pragmatic character of politics and government reflected the tenor of English cultural values, and here perhaps it would be well to speak of "British," for none exhibited this pragmatic turn of mind more notably than the common-sensical Scots. "In England," Voltaire wrote in 1726, "one can think freely and nobly, without hesitations caused by servile fear. If I followed my inclinations that is where I would settle down, with the sole purpose of learning to think."[4] He particularly liked the Englishman's disposition to honor accomplishment as well as birth, noting that the "chief men of the nation contended for the honour of bearing" Newton's pall at his funeral. "Go into Westminster Abbey; admiration is not paid to the tombs of the kings, but to the monuments which the gratitude of the nation has erected to the greatest men who have contributed to its glory."[5] In foreign eyes, the people of Great Britain appeared to be utilitarians before the invention of the word.

Against these features of modernity the fact must be set that English government in the eighteenth century was dominated by an aristocracy of landowners. Elie Halévy's observation is sweeping, but substantially correct: "This aristocracy controlled all the machinery of government. It was supreme in both Houses of Parliament and disposed at pleasure of every government office."[6] Its influence over the Church of England was practically absolute. The irreverent view that by the end of the century the established church's key function was to support the aristocracy's lesser relations, reward political services, and provide pensions for household tutors and guardians was not without foundation. The revenue offices and military and naval establishments that had grown up since 1689 to contest with France the control of Europe and the world overseas, were invaded by sons of aristocrats at the top, and in due course influence was applied in appointments lower down. In addition, the bulk of local government was under aristocratic influence.

Modernity and aristocratic domination of government are two of the three most striking features of eighteenth-century England. The third is stability. The period from 1714 to 1760 "was an age of stability in politics, in religion, in literature, and in social observances."[7] Since modernity on the one hand and domination by a hereditary class of great landowners on the other do not appear to be compatible, this stability is at first glance puzzling, and it raises the most interesting question one can ask about eighteenth-century England: How were the modernizing elements, primed by moneyed wealth, accommodated by a traditional social system based on landholding? For it was upon this accommodation that England's remarkable unity and strength in the eighteenth century rested.

Stability and the Lower Orders

Public order is the bedrock of social stability. Under certain conditions it may be successfully maintained by savage and unremitting repression. This was the case in Ireland where the English Ascendancy isolated itself from the Catholic peasantry and ruled by force. But eighteenth-century England was ruled through tradition, influence, and sometimes reciprocity. The governing classes were not fearfully huddled together; their first thoughts were not of social inundation. Instead, their outlook was open, assured, and confident, and remained so until shaken by the French Revolution. It is true that the tranquillity of eighteenth-century England was far from perfect: Riots were frequent and sometimes got out of hand. But they rarely provoked much anxiety in governing circles. Public order rested essentially on the conservatism that has always dominated the behavior of the lower orders of pre-industrial societies so long as their means of subsistence, their relation to land and community, and their spiritual values are left undisturbed. During the first three-quarters of the eighteenth century the governing classes of England were careful to leave those things undisturbed.

It had not always been so. In Tudor and Stuart England the tranquillity of the lower orders was repeatedly broken by agrarian turmoil and religious conflict. Elizabeth's reign was beset by local agrarian rebellions, raised to the boiling point by enclosures, inflation, and dearth. "The years between 1500 and 1650 are the last great age of . . . peasant uprisings . . . , and hardly a generation in that stormy period elapsed without one."[8] Agrarian distress produced vagrancy. Dispossessed and distressed peasants took to the road, and the frightening numbers of "sturdy beggars" gave rise to the most remarkable body of social legislation enacted in pre-industrial England—the Elizabethan Poor Law. Its purpose was to keep poor people in their respective parishes and force their parishes to take care of them.

Taming the lower orders was not made easier by the religious fears of the sixteenth century and the fanaticism that broke loose in the seventeenth.[9] Fighting God's battle and ignoring the social consequences, Puritan divines and Puritan gentry produced a cleavage in society that the Civil War enlarged and fixed. Although the fire went out of Puritanism after the Restoration of 1660, most Englishmen remained rabidly anti-Catholic. English anti-Catholicism bore a heavy political accent and triggered a good deal of mob violence during the Revolution of 1688, particularly in London. On December 12 of that year, Londoners were gripped by a hysteria akin to "the great fear" of 1789 as rumors spread through the city "that disbanded Irish soldiers, numbering many thousands, were 'burning Towns, massacring the people, and marching directly for London to put the like in execution here.'" There seems no doubt that acceptance of William III and the Revolution Settlement was speeded by anxieties about popular unrest,[10] anxieties that recalled the social upheavals of the Interregnum. The quick decision was important. For, while the Revolution Settlement left the running battle between crown and Commons unresolved, it was a massive step toward removing the threat of the lower orders from politics.

Eighteenth-century tranquillity was, to a large extent, the deliberate aim of social policy. There was no massive repression. No effective police force existed, because the aristocracy, ever suspicious of royal bureaucracy and absolutism, did not want one. Instead, there was accommodation tempered with petty repression through local influence and local instruments of government, and, in extremis, enforced by use of the Riot Act, the militia, and the army. Since calling upon the militia or the army was a nuisance, matters were seldom allowed to get that far. Persistent troublemakers were shipped off to the Caribbean or the American colonies, either condemned to be transported or compelled to sign a servant's indenture. And yet it is astonishing how many rioters, even ringleaders, were left unpunished or, if punished, subsequently forgiven after having "made submission."

In the countryside and market towns popular disturbances were usually bread riots occasioned by high food prices, and normally the riots brought prices down.[11] Industrial strikes were not unknown—the authorities called them riots—and although every attempt was made to suppress them by force and to take ringleaders into custody, the usual outcome was a negotiated settlement followed eventually by pardons.[12] This is not to say that humanity was the unfailing guide in dealings with the lower orders. Poverty was taken as an indication of sin. "A breach of the law by the poor, therefore, was an aggravation of their already unsatisfactory moral state" and punished accordingly.[13] The law specified death for petty crimes against property, and although the penalty was seldom invoked, the pathetic cases of children being made to suffer it richly deserve their notoriety. But the common pattern was petty repression. The severity of the 1790s was not characteristic of most of the century.

Repression's distinguishing feature in the eighteenth century was its sensitivity to power. The weak were indifferently crushed, while those elements of the common people who seemed capable of pursuing their cause through violence or politics were handled with discretion. Nowhere is this more evident than in the English approach to that infallible disturber of internal peace, military recruiting. The principal weapons of the British recruiting sergeant, hemmed in as he was by law and custom, were alcohol and contrived good fellowship. The navy's press gangs did most of their dirty work at sea. Although gangs often provoked frays on land, it should be noticed that the governing authorities in many, and perhaps most, of the provincial ports of England actively obstructed the gangs in the execution of their duty. When war broke out and local magistrates were called on to help find recruits, they invariably used the occasion to sweep the riff-raff off the streets, people whose worthlessness was decried by army and navy officers alike. Even in the 1790s, when the services were hard-pressed for men and quotas were imposed on parishes, the common method of responding was to raise a bounty through the Poor Rate to purchase a volunteer or substitute outside the parish. No eighteenth-century British statesman, however great his concern for the safety of the realm, the shape of Europe, or the extension of empire, could ignore these endemic restraints on military manpower.

Besides the moderation of the authorities, there were three substantial foundations of public order in eighteenth-century England. One was religious toleration. The remembrance of seventeenth-century turmoil guaranteed a chilly reception for "enthusiasm," especially within the body of the Church of England. The importance of toleration is best exhibited by the fact that two great eighteenth-century riots erupted when religious passions were aroused: the Sacheverell riot of 1709, sparked by warnings of the church in danger, and the Gordon riots of 1780, where a mild proposal for the relief of Roman Catholics provided Lord George Gordon, a crackbrained agitator, with an opportunity for unleashing the ferocious anti-popery of the London mob. In neither case was popular feeling much different from that of their betters, and these explosions had no long-term significance. Thanks to the policy of toleration, they were not eruptions of segregated and oppressed groups. Certainly toleration was incomplete and uneven. Jews were denied the civil rights accorded to Protestants. A parliamentary act to improve their situation in 1753 was speedily repealed the same year by its Whig sponsors in the face of popular agitation and the threat of its becoming an election issue. Roman Catholics were subjected to a combination of penalties and restrictions that can only be called persecution. This affected a handful of Englishmen and a mass of Irishmen. In due course a terrible price was paid in Ireland, but in England the policy made for social peace, for the pattern of toleration's imperfections in England was broadly popular.

A second foundation of public order was the existence of a mobile agricultural surplus. Agricultural productivity was impressive, transportation was good, and marketing barriers were insignificant. The problem of feeding the metropolis seemed not to exist; there was a notable absence of food riots in eighteenth-century London when compared to Paris.[14] Of course prolonged bad weather caused dearth—particularly in 1709, 1740–41, 1767, 1795, 1800–01—but famine was virtually unknown. It is indeed ironical, as one authority has recently observed, that "Malthus's idea that population might outrun food supplies" should have "occurred to a man in a country where such a thing had not happened for at least five hundred years."[15]

Finally, public order was founded on the Poor and Settlement laws. The Poor Law not only dealt with hardships of widowhood and infirmity, but also provided a framework for relieving distress caused by dearth or unemployment. Together with the Settlement Law, it reduced the problem of vagrancy to the scale of a minor annoyance except in the vicinity of London. The Poor Law's role in insuring tranquillity and order in rural England can best be appreciated by noting the uprisings that occurred after 1815 when parish authorities became either unable or unwilling to pay the price of rescuing the workers in hard times.[16]

Summing up, it is obvious that the authorities in eighteenth-century England tailored policy to the needs of social control, but it must be granted that their way was partly paved by good fortune. It is almost certain (notwithstanding our lack of statistics) that agricultural products were not only more easily moved, but also more plentiful in, say, 1730 than in 1630. And while the civil impact of religious belief still troubled the public mind, the passion of righteousness and irreconcilable dogma was gone. Nor can we ignore England's geographical advantage over her continental neighbors. At bottom, it was her island situation that allowed discretion and restraint to be exercised in military recruiting. The lower orders were not completely banished from politics in the eighteenth century. The mob scored many local successes, and widespread popular agitation led by Londoners achieved three notable national successes: It forced the withdrawal of Walpole's excise scheme in 1733, rendered the Gin Act of 1736 nugatory, and forced the repeal of the "Jew Bill" in 1753. But, by and large, the greatest threat to stability came not from the bottom, but from contests near the top, between the traditional rulers of the land and the new men of commerce and finance.

Land and Money

Money confounds subordination, by overpowering the distinctions of rank and birth, and weakens authority by supplying power of resistance or expedients for escape. The feudal system is formed for a nation employed in agriculture, and has never long kept its hold where gold and silver have become common.[17]

Dr. Johnson's remark, as he pondered the consequence of paying rent in money rather than in kind, touched on one of the great problems of Western European society in the early modern period: the problem of incorporating a surging expansion of commercial wealth into a social system based on landed wealth. The astonishing growth of London is of itself sufficient evidence of the size of the problem in England. From the mid-sixteenth century "few of the gentry retained their estates intact unless they were enriched by marriage, trade or the practice of law." In Lincolnshire, for example, "hardly a family of old standing survived the middle of the seventeenth century, unless enriched by trade or marriage, while a number are said to have disappeared or become extinct through their inability to adapt themselves to the new order."[18] The influence of commercial wealth on landholding patterns was not always direct nor was it all-encompassing. Inflation, high-handed action by the crown or by rich privileged courtiers and officeholders, misfortunes at law, taxation, and civil war—all offered severe challenges to the old order. But behind the economic turmoil lay the growth of the great metropolis and its commerce, enhanced to an extent we cannot measure by the infusion of American gold and silver, as well as tropical products from East and West, into the European economy. The effects of this infusion seemed so pervasive to Adam Smith from his vantage point of the 1770s that he declared: "The discovery of America, and that of a passage to the East Indies by the Cape of Good Hope, are the two greatest and most important events recorded in the history of mankind."[19]

That many of England's landed families speedily accommodated themselves to the new wealth is one of the striking features of her history. The enthusiasm for investment in maritime and trans-oceanic enterprise that stirred the merchants of London and the lesser seaports in the late sixteenth and early seventeenth centuries infected some of the landed gentry as well.[20] And a century later it was considered normal for landowners to invest in East India stock, Bank of England stock, or government annuities. As for social mixing, the English aristocracy's lack of disdain for money, from whatever source, has often been remarked. A judicious "City" marriage was a standard remedy for a heavily mortgaged estate headed toward bankruptcy, and where remedies of this sort were not or could not be applied, a way was opened for wealthy merchant families to enter the aristocracy through purchase of an estate. In the latter circumstance, social acceptance was, by foreign standards, comprehensive and rapid, and for this reason a self-conscious *bourgeois* mentality could not flourish in the upper echelons of English mercantile society. Hence, the English aristocracy has rightly been regarded as open.

The openness was reinforced by two institutional features. One was primogeniture. While it preserved the landed estate intact upon inheritance, it tended to push younger sons socially downward, out of the landed aristocracy. If they were to remain in the fold, they would have to do it largely by their own efforts and, very likely, by amassing a fortune through professional or commercial skill. Connection could help them, and so could money, which they often inherited; but neither the blood nor the lands of their fathers could save them.

The other was the small number of aristocrats possessing bestowed or inherited titles. There were about 170 peers of England in 1700 (excluding a handful of royal dukes), and the number did not rise much for eighty years thereafter. The baronetage, which numbered about 775 in 1700, declined to 500 by 1755.[21] The number of knights was not growing either. While the membership of these formally titled ranks remained stable or diminished, the ranks of esquires and gentlemen grew. All sons of noblemen were automatically esquires, as were the eldest sons of knights. Some esquires were "created by the King, by putting about their Neck a Collar of SS's, and bestowing on them a Pair of Silver Spurs." But the majority became esquires informally: "Lastly, divers that are in superior public Office for King or State, are reputed Esquires, or equal to Esquires, . . . [various court] and other Officers of Rank and Quality; so Justices of the Peace, Mayors of Towns, Counsellors at Law, Bachelors of Divinity, Law, or Physic; though none of them are really so." As for gentlemen, the older families naturally stressed distinctions between armigerous gentry and the rest, but, although ancient lineage was given its due, formal distinctions were undermined by the ease with which heraldric trappings could be bought for cash. Chamberlayne's *Magnae Britanniae Notitia*, from which these quotations are taken, was fastidious on matters of honor ("in Propriety of Speech, no Man is a Gentleman who is not born so"), but acknowledged that: "All in England are accounted Gentlemen who maintain themselves without manual Labour." And he added that to be a merchant was "no Disparagement to a Gentleman born."[22] Because the titled nobility in England was small, it played a limited role in social aspirations. Sometimes Irish titles were acquired, but the main focus of English social advancement was the lower aristocracy, whose ranks were large and expanding. Most of its new members acquired their status informally on their own initiative.

The social mixing of landed and commercial wealth reflected

a developing recognition of their symbiotic relationship. English landlords and farmers, while they might take pleasure in nurturing an old prejudice against merchants, were becoming businessmen themselves. An age of great lords with their castles and armed retainers had given way in the sixteenth and seventeenth centuries to an age of professional land stewards, profit-minded farmers, and landless laborers.[23] Throughout the seventeenth century the trend was away from small peasant holdings and subsistence agriculture toward hired laborers, large farms, large estates, and a market orientation. The trend continued in the eighteenth century.[24] Thus the growing requirements of London reached farther and farther into the hinterland, overlaying local marketing networks with a national market and encouraging the development of large-scale agricultural enterprise. By the end of the eighteenth century English farmers had become, in Halévy's words, "intelligent capitalists—on the alert for any new method of making money."[25] And even at the beginning of the century the benefit to agriculture of a thriving financial community as a ready source of loans was widely felt.[26] As for trade, it was a commonplace of eighteenth-century economic thought, expressed by respected authorities as well as ordinary pamphleteers, that trade served to increase the value of land and its product.[27] Finally, English law concerning mineral rights gave many large landowners a direct interest in the coal trade and industrial development. "In Britain alone in Western Europe all minerals, save gold and silver, belonged by a judgment of 1568 . . . to the owner of the soil. The landowners, therefore, had a personal stake in their exploitation."[28] It is hardly surprising that textbook accounts of eighteenth-century English society have emphasized the harmony of the landed, commercial, and financial interests.

This picture of harmony, however, is overdrawn and can easily be misused.[29] From a comparative point of view the absorption of commercial and financial wealth by families of rank during the eighteenth century appears on close examination just as impressive in France as in England—some would say more impressive. "Could it be," Lawrence Stone has asked, "that English society closed ranks a century earlier than France, in the late seventeenth instead of the late eighteenth century, and the reputation enjoyed by pre-industrial England as an unusually mobile society is largely an illusion based on false assumptions and a dearth of statistical evidence?"[30]

There are numerous indications that English social mobility in the higher echelons was less vigorous at the beginning of the eighteenth century than a century earlier. We have seen that while the gentry expanded, the baronetage and knightage shrank. Of about 500 existing baronetcies in 1748 only 71 had been created since 1700; 144 had been created between 1661 and 1699, 65 in 1660, the year of Restoration, and the rest before that.[31] As for marriage, the attitude of Sir William Massingberd was probably typical. He urged his cousin, in 1703, to rescue his estate by finding "a discreet wife with five or six thousand pound (and if she have more 'tis the better still)," but cheered the passage of the Property Qualifications bill which was aimed at walling moneyed men out of Parliament.[32] And although landed men in financial straits took moneyed wives, they recoiled from socially diminishing their daughters by marrying them to mere money.[33] There are a number of reasons for accepting Habakkuk's conclusion that "though the connections between commercial capital and landowners were manifold they were not those of personnel. There was less interlocking of the two classes than there had been under Elizabeth and the early Stuarts."[34] But notwithstanding all this, there was no general pattern of social exclusion. Newly risen City gentlemen could join established London clubs; the ancient universities and Inns of Court were not barred to their sons. It is true that the land unmistakably reasserted its ancient monopoly of social dignity during the eighteenth century, but it is hard to see a situation of "closed ranks" before 1750.

Toward the end of the century the lines appear to harden. The apprenticing of younger sons to trade or finance fell into disfavor; it became a last resort of penurious families who lacked the connections to obtain socially acceptable employments in government, the Church of England, the army, navy, or law.[35] Possession of land—in quantity—remained the *sine qua non* of high social standing. One assumed that a successful lawyer or wealthy merchant, or naval officer who suddenly struck it rich with prize money, would be in the market for an estate. Moreover, that political power should ultimately rest in the hands of landowners was the accepted view, and the most influential political economist of the time endorsed the traditional suspicion of merchant wealth:

> *A merchant, it has been said very properly, is not necessarily the citizen of any particular country. It is in a great measure indifferent to him from what place he carries on his trade; and a very trifling disgust will make him remove his capital, and together with it all the industry which it supports, from one country to another. No part of it can be said to belong to any particular country. till it has been spread as it were over the face of that country, either in buildings, or in the lasting improvement of lands.*[36]

And so, while interaction between landed and moneyed wealth continued to play a significant economic role in the eighteenth century, the social membrane that separated the two was less permeable than in the century before. Where social intercourse was old and established, as between leading Yorkshire woolen merchants and the local squirearchy, it was not disrupted,[37] but new wealth normally had to follow the path of estate purchase.

Where does this leave the question of harmony? To dispel confusion we must recognize that there were really three important social elements in eighteenth-century England. Two were developing in the later seventeenth century: the "moneyed interest," centered in London; and the class of great landed aristocrats, whose ranks were enlarged, and influence increased, by the growth of large estates after 1680. Both challenged the influence of the third, the country gentry. The gentry were a class to be reckoned with.[38] Although the openness of aristocratic society restrained the development of a social gulf between money and land, the existence of this independently minded class gave political expression to the conflict of interests.

The problem of the origins and progress of this class of landed gentlemen—the gentry or squirearchy—has stirred a great controversy among historians.[39] That is not our concern here. For our purposes it is enough to recognize that this class, which Habakkuk describes as "a unique feature of English society . . . distinct from the great territorial aristocracy on the one hand and the smaller freeholder and tenant farmer on the other,"[40] was established by the end of the seventeenth century in a position of immense influence in the countryside. Resisting James II's electoral outrages in 1688 with a firm front, it was the tough political nut that the Stuart monarchy could not crack.[41] Its ranks supplied, and would continue to supply for the next hundred years, the bulk of the membership of the House of Commons. Equally important, the squirearchy, or gentry, ruled rural England. The squires occupied the county bench, served as local justices of the peace, and commonly maintained a firm paternal influence over parish administration.

And yet, after 1690 this class had reason to feel that its political and economic position was being undermined. Its income came almost entirely from agricultural rents. Few of these men could claim iron or coal mines, and their estates were seldom large enough to cushion the shocks of agricultural adversity. And much as they might need City money in a pinch, they resented and feared its encroachment on the land. To their long-standing hatred of the court and royal officeholders (assumed to be useless and predatory) they added, after 1690, a deep suspicion of the Bank of England, the national debt, the stock exchange—indeed, the entire apparatus of the "moneyed interest" that developed during the long wars against Louis XIV. They believed, with some justice, that war enriched the "moneyed interest" through speculation, privateering, insurance, and exchange dealings, while it impoverished landed gentlemen through the land tax. One of the striking contributions of J. H. Plumb's *The Growth of Political Stability in England* is the manner in which it forces us to recognize that the gentry, however much it contributed to continuity and tranquillity in the countryside, implied anarchy in national politics. Unquestionably it was the most numerous class in the House of Commons and ran the bulk of local government, so that England could not be peaceably governed without its cooperation, but at the same time it had no taste for strong central administration and was doubly suspicious of a government that favored and found support from the new rapidly growing financial institutions of the realm. "In 1688," Plumb writes, ". . . it seemed as if the forces of political instability had won, for the Revolution had been undertaken by those forces in society that were thoroughly opposed to strong executive government. For the Revolution of 1688 was a monument raised by the gentry to its own intractable sense of independence."[42] Thus the task of national politics was to reconcile or tame this uneasy and, on the whole, reactionary class to the new necessities of commerce and finance.

That task was made far more difficult by the increasing concentration of the country gentry in the Tory party. In 1690 the "country party" included both Whigs and Tories, but as conflict over the powers of monarchy receded and the strain of war took its toll, old principles of division were supplemented by new. By the beginning of the eighteenth century most country gentlemen were Tories.[43] "Living in increased isolation from their greater neighbours with more ample resources, and bitterly critical of City finance and government influence, they made up the strength of the Tory Party."[44] Unavoidably, the direct "confrontation of landed and commercial interests in Parliament" became a prime focus of party conflict,[45] and the long continuance of war in Queen Anne's reign raised the conflict to a fever pitch.[46] The Tory party was the peace party. Its leaders saw that, notwithstanding Marlborough's great victories, Whig objectives in Europe were probably beyond reach. Meanwhile, they argued, the war and the moneyed wealth it generated were submerging the old landed order.[47] When Whigs claimed that Tory supremacy would bring the destruction of public credit, Swift replied with characteristic sarcasm:

> *What people then, are these in a corner, to whom the constitution must truckle? If the whole nation's credit cannot supply funds for the war without humble application from the entire legislature to a few retailers of money, it is high time we should sue for a peace. What new maxims are these . . . ? Must our laws from hencefor-ward pass the Bank and East-India Company, or have their royal assent before they are in force?*[48]

Whatever private misgivings the Tory leaders may have had about the "country" view of public finance, they were prepared to make the most of it politically.

It is a fact that ten years after Anne's death the excitement was gone. Tory attitudes and resentments lived on, but the Tory party as a force in government had begun to disintegrate.[49] To understand the significance of this development we should consider a situation that did not arise, that is we should imagine what would have been the state of England if the Whig monopoly of government had not supervened.

Although peace had a calming effect, a conflict between land and money could have magnetized politics for decades if an effective Tory party had remained on the scene. The realities must be faced. The British government was irrevocably dependent on City finance; the Treasury, Admiralty, and other departments of state that had mushroomed between 1689 and 1714 were maintained to preserve Britain's new grandeur in Europe and to expand and defend the empire overseas; and the expense was met not only by the land tax but by excise taxes and customs duties as well, whose high yields depended on vigorous foreign commerce.[50] At the same time British attitudes were becoming more rational and speculative. Innovation, though habitually denounced, was accepted where it seemed promising, and in some circles noisily welcomed. New wealth, and with it political influence, was accumulating in the hands of people who were not communicants of the established church, and the Whig policy of religious toleration aimed not only at securing freedom of thought, but also at encompassing these people within the body politic. Against all this, Toryism offered a sort of gentlemen's populism in financial matters, an ingrained hostility to big government, a sincere belief that the fruit of Whig religious policies would be an unchristian and possibly godless society, a dogged nativism, and a deep suspicion that the whole of Whiggism was no more than a coordinated scheme to overthrow the traditional landed social order.[51] For eighteenth-century Tories the Church of England was more than the embodiment of the old comfortable religion; it was a symbol of the traditional order and provided an implement for social control and political exclusion.

Of course, a Tory government would have trimmed its policies to the wishes of the court and the demands of the City. Tories were not nearly as hostile to trade as to finance. And certainly the Tory inclination to avoid expensive European wars and keep taxes down was broadly popular. But the task of Tory leaders in office would have been beset with difficulties: The bulk of the Tory gentry was at bottom independent and unruly, and Tory religious policy was dangerously divisive. Moreover, the party's turbulent allies in the City of London, the lesser merchants and tradesmen who held "restrictionist economic views" and resented the power of the great financial institutions on which the government relied, were hardly a stable element in politics.[52] It is therefore easy to imagine a continuation of the party strife that marked Queen Anne's reign if the Tory party had remained organized as a potential force in government.

The Role of the Great Landed Aristocrats

In breaking the power of the landed gentry, the aristocracy of great landowners played a crucial role, for the solution of the problem they posed had to be political. It could not be administrative or constitutional because the Revolution of 1688 had confirmed the independence of local government from royal coercion and had established, in reaction to James II's energetic remodeling of borough charters,[53] the immutability of the electoral and representational system.

A political solution rested first and foremost on the destruction of the Tory party. This occurred with astonishing speed. Everyone knew that Queen Anne's death and the Hanoverian succession would hurt the Tory cause, but few foresaw the severity and permanence of the party's collapse. As events unfolded, Toryism's internal contradictions, particularly regarding the nature and power of monarchy, were strikingly manifested in the Jacobite treason of 1715. It was a crisis, and the party's leaders failed abysmally to meet it.[54] Afterward the Tory spirit lived on; Tory M. P.'s continued to be elected to the House of Commons;[55] but the Tory party as a potential force in government was finished. This of course left the field to the Whigs.

The solid base of Whig political power lay in the great aristocrats. By the end of the seventeenth century the landed magnates in much of Western Europe had been either subdued by despotism or financially overwhelmed, but in England they had managed to avoid falling into a servile relationship with the crown on the one hand, while taking nourishment from new sources of wealth on the other. J. H. Hexter has suggested that an organizing question of English social history ought to be: "How then did they do it?" How did these English magnates preserve their position of strength?[56] Indisputably, any answer must notice the fact that the English aristocracy was a working aristocracy. In England "armorial bearings . . . conferred social prestige," but "they did not convey privileges in respect of law, taxation, the ownership of land, or entry into the army and the church, nor, on the other hand, did they debar those who bore them from moving into trade and industry."[57] The English nobility had privileges, but they were, as Habakkuk says, trivial.[58] Therefore, the aristocracy secured its position not by social bulwarks embedded in the constitution, but by participating in politics and bearing responsibility in government. As it happened, it did dominate the army and the church in the eighteenth century and also contrived to have the laws affecting landownership written to its specifications. This was done by political influence. Although the aristocracy had had its moments of doubt and difficulty, especially in the early seventeenth century,[59] its strength was obviously growing at the beginning of the eighteenth century both politically and economically. We do not fully understand the reasons for its recovery, but Habakkuk's work is the best starting point.[60] Whatever the causes, the aristocracy's dominant position is the distinguishing feature of eighteenth-century political history.

This aristocracy was, to use Sir Lewis Namier's term, amphibious. It resided part of the year in London and part in its country houses. Though habituated to urban tastes and tolerant of urban modes of moneymaking, it never severed its direct connection with the land. It is true that the great Whig aristocrats of the eighteenth century accommodated the new financial interests, made their arrangements with the court, and discountenanced the old country persuasion; but they never lost touch with the network of political power in the counties and market towns, nor forgot the interests of landowners and the everyday economic concerns of agriculture. Thus the Whig aristocracy was ideally situated to mediate between city and country and to use its immense influence at court and in the countryside to tame the landed gentry.

To be politically effective, such influence had to be applied to the task of securing majority support in the House of Commons. This was known as management, chiefly a Whig art, and one whose methods Swift learned quickly to loathe: "I already imagine the present free Parliament dissolved, and another of a different Epithet met, by the Force of Money and Management."[61] Management constricted the political influence of the independent country members. Sir Robert Walpole, the greatest of eighteenth-century managers, elaborated the system. By melding the patronage of the court, the interests of the great financial institutions, and the influence of the aristocracy, he secured a corps of loyal M.P.'s, many of whom were gentlemen detached from the Tory cause. Understandably, the Tory faithful viewed this shameless and systematic bartering of favors, funds, and offices as not only ruinous to their party but to the constitution as well. Bolingbroke offered a sketch of its history in the 1730s that even contrived to lay at its door the rise of the "moneyed interest" and the great estates:

> *The notion of attaching men to the new government, by tempting them to embark their fortunes on the same bottom, was a reason of state to some: the notion of creating a new, that is, moneyed interest, in opposition to the landed interest or as a balance to it, and of acquiring a superior influence in the city of London at least by the establishment of great corporations, was a reason of party to others: and I make no doubt that the opportunity of amassing immense estates by the management of funds, by trafficking in paper, and by all the arts of jobbing, was a reason of private interest to those who supported and improved this scheme of iniquity, if not those who devised it. They looked no farther. Nay, we who came after them, and have long tasted the bitter fruits of the corruption they planted, were far from taking such an alarm at our distress and our danger, as they deserved; till the most remote and fatal effects of causes, laid by the last generation, was very near becoming an object of experience in this.[62]*

The loyal group of government supporters acquired by management did not, however, command a majority on occasions when issues flared up and attendance in the House was high. Walpole therefore aimed his policies at keeping the temperature down. He understood the mind of the country gentlemen—he was one himself—and thus he came "to accept what was essentially a Tory foreign policy" and bent every effort toward keeping the land tax low.[63] Although he concurred in the prevailing abhorrence of constitutional innovation, he did fight successfully on behalf of the Septennial Act of 1715, which lengthened the maximum time between general elections from three to seven years. But aside from this single constitutional measure, the methods by which royal government was sustained on terms acceptable to both the aristocracy and the City were political.

Management was an unlovely business, but, for all the popular revulsion, it worked. It solved the problem posed by the conflicting claims of crown and Parliament, and the resultant stability of government supplied the basis of Great Britain's naval power, imperial expansion, and diplomatic influence in the eighteenth century. Without it, no government could stay in office very long.

This political system had the interesting social effect of gradually unifying the aristocracy, of arraying it in a single hierarchy of subservience with the apex in London high society. Essentially this was a restoration of earlier conditions, before the alienation of the bulk of the gentry, but its degree and scope was quite unprecedented: The eighteenth-century Establishment's influence was felt throughout England and Wales and in much of Scotland and Ireland. Naturally, some disgruntled gentry remained alienated, but in the House of Commons there was very little fundamental social discord by mid-century. The stage was thus set for Edmund Burke's notion of aristocratic trusteeship: government by men above the battle, trained from birth to a nobler outlook and wealthy enough to avoid the temptation of tawdry economic interest, men who, while conversant with the varied interests of the realm, would never "work with low instruments for low ends."[64]

Sooner or later every oligarchy comes up with some such notion. In England, because the system of management joined crown and Parliament only in fact, not in theory, it was possible to argue that the aristocratic leadership of the kingdom should never be subservient to the executive. Burke argued this and went further. He held, as many did, that Parliament was as independent of the people as of the crown and argued with increasing firmness that changes in the electoral and representational structure would tend to destroy the moderating benefits of aristocratic leadership.

Burke's description of the constitution was highly fanciful, but it had some solid justification in the conditions and governing-class attitudes of the later eighteenth century. The important matter is that such arrangements could not have lasted. There are three reasons. First, the system of management narrowed political participation. In 1761 only 48 constituencies (out of 315) actually went to the point of polling votes, and "between 1715 and . . . 1784 the duration of three Parliaments only" was curtailed by political factors, and then only slightly; the rest ran the full seven years.[65] Hence, while during the turbulence of Queen Anne's reign, "tens of thousands . . . , a very significant proportion of the male population, had the right to choose their governors," by "the middle of the eighteenth century much of that birthright had been lost."[66] Second, in the course of time royal government became clogged with well-connected aristocrats and political appointees. Naturally, sinecures had been in such hands from the start, but by mid-century the pressures to place untrained, incompetent people in offices of business were intense. The effect on bureaucratic morale of conventions that allowed offices to be gained by connection and influence, exchanged through negotiation, and executed by deputy, though they did not apply to all offices, was probably more damaging than the actual incidence of useless officials. (The estrangement of the American colonists was partly owing to a bureaucratic carelessness that was a natural consequence of the priority given to patronage over policy.) Third, the system relied on personal acquaintance and face-to-face dealing. It could not cope with great issues and crises nor encompass the aspirations of broadly diffused wealth.

The later eighteenth century witnessed the emergence of both. Issues noisily returned to the political scene when controversy over the peace treaty with France, an issue of a traditional sort, was transformed into a debate over constitutional rights by the government's ill-advised attempts to punish and rebuff John Wilkes. The Wilkes affair forced "freeborn Englishmen" to reconsider the extent of their freedom, and the radical outlook that found expression was sustained in the 1770s by the claims of the American revolutionaries. At the same time that management was assaulted by popular radicalism it was being undermined at court. George I and George II had learned to believe in management—without enthusiasm, to be sure—because it provided for most of their desires. The young George III, who came to the throne in 1760, did not believe in it. But he was unable to find an effective substitute and hence had the worst of both worlds: Management carried on, but without adequate royal support. By 1780 the whole system was under challenge from all sides. The disastrous conduct of the American war exposed its frailties and it was attacked by the popular radicals, by the Yorkshire Association, which applied a radical twist to the old Tory notion of gentry independence, and by the Rockingham party, which sought through Economic Reform to diminish the force of crown patronage.[67]

As politics overflowed the boundaries of personal connection, alignments in the House of Commons were increasingly determined by issues rather than persons, and effectiveness became a prime test of government. Toward the end of the century the industrial revolution and the wars against revolutionary and Napoleonic France eliminated any possibility of reviving management as the key instrument of aristocratic domination.[68] As the industrial interest gained ground, wealth accumulated in new hands and new areas, and consequently the social and economic significance of certain traditional issues, particularly those involving the civil claims of the Church of England, became more sharply focussed. In such an atmosphere it was natural that the landed aristocracy should behave increasingly like an agricultural interest group.

These emerging political forces compelled reform of both the political structure and public administration. In the event, administrative reform preceded structural reform of Parliament, but only central administration was reformed. Local administration was left alone and remained structurally disconnected. Until the early nineteenth century English internal administration bore the imprint of the Revolution Settlement and the role of patronage. Its ties to central administration continued to be personal rather than bureaucratic.

This meant that, although England was ruled by the landed aristocracy, with almost its entire administration in the hands of the old order of society, free rein was given to the energies of the nation in business pursuits. Thus, the consequences of economic innovation and technological invention were practically unstoppable. The same legislative process that secured enclosure acts for landlords could be employed by other local interests to assist transportation, trade, and industrial development.[69] And the task of repressing industrial development would have been one for which the system of administration was extremely ill-suited.

It never came to that. The great landlords played the game of productive enterprise as eagerly as the industrialists. As Halévy observed: "To the large estate corresponded the large factory. In both were found the same spirit of enterprise, the same improvement of machinery, the same recourse to banking credit, the same growth of output, the same concentration of capital."[70] So, while embracing an attitude that favored economic growth, an attitude provided with structure and logic by a growing literature of political economy, the great landed aristocrats perpetuated a system of government that lacked administrative means to direct the growth. Both of these were bequeathed to the nineteenth century, and when the miseries of economic dislocation led to demands for governmental action, the attitude inhibited the development of the means.

But there were also bequeathed traditions that kept administration firmly under law, institutions that kept it under parliamentary control, and conventions that sustained consultation and reciprocity in local affairs. Lastly, there survived a small body of Whig aristocrats who believed that government ought to be directly answerable to the property of the nation and that its representative bodies should be reformed accordingly. They were not democrats, but they paved the way for democracy through parliamentary means.

NOTES

I. *Introduction*

[1] See William Albert, *The Turnpike Road System in England 1663–1840* (Cambridge, 1972), pp. 30–56, 224–229.

[2] E. A. Wrigley, "The Process of Modernization and the Industrial Revolution in England," *Journal of Interdisciplinary History*, III (1972), pp. 240–242.

[3] J. H. Plumb, "The Growth of the Electorate in England from 1600 to 1715," *Past and Present*, No. 45 (1969), pp. 90–116.

[4] Theodore Besterman, ed., *Select Letters of Voltaire* (Edinburgh, 1963), p. 26.

[5] Archibald Ballantyne, *Voltaire's Visit to England 1726–1729* (1893), p. 182.

[6] Elie Halévy, *History of the English People in the Nineteenth Century. I: England in 1815*, 2nd ed. (1949), p. 221.

[7] Basil Williams, *The Whig Supremacy 1714–1760*, 2nd ed. (Oxford, 1962), p. 1.

[8] R. H. Tawney, *The Agrarian Problem in the Sixteenth Century*, (1912; reprinted New York, 1967), p. 318.

[9] For an example of the role of the mob in the sixteenth century, see M. E. James, "Obedience and Dissent in Henrician England: The Lincolnshire Rebellion, 1536," *Past and Present*, No. 48 (1970), pp. 5–29.

[10] See William L. Sachse, "The Mob and the Revolution of 1688," *Journal of British Studies*, IV (1964–65), pp. 23–40.

[11] See R. B. Rose, "Eighteenth-Century Price Riots and Public Policy in England," *International Review of Social History*, VI (1961), pp. 283–290.

[12] *E.g.*, J. D. Chambers, *Nottinghamshire in the Eighteenth Century: A Study of Life and Labour under the Squirearchy*, 2nd ed. (1966), pp. 40–43; Daniel A. Baugh, *British Naval Administration in the Age of Walpole* (Princeton, 1965), p. 324.

[13] Chambers, *Nottinghamshire in the Eighteenth Century*, p. 48.

[14] George Rudé, *Paris and London in the Eighteenth Century* (1970), p. 55.

[15] T. H. Hollingsworth, in *Economic History Review*, 2nd ser. XXVI (1973), p. 529.

[16] See A. J. Peacock, *Bread or Blood: A Study of the Agrarian Riots in East Anglia in 1816* (1965); and E. J. Hobsbawm and George Rudé, *Captain Swing* (1969).

[17] Samuel Johnson, *A Journey to the Western Islands of Scotland*, ed. by Allan Wendt (Boston, 1965), p. 85.

[18] Chambers, *Nottinghamshire in the Eighteenth Century*, p. 9. In the first instance Chambers quotes Lord Ernle, *English Farming Past and Present*.

[19] Adam Smith, *The Wealth of Nations*, ed. Cannan, 6th ed. (1950), II, p. 141.

[20] See generally Theodore K. Rabb, *Enterprise and Empire: Merchant and Gentry Investment in the Expansion of England, 1575–1630* (Cambridge, Mass., 1967), pp. 19–101. For a moderating view see J. H. Hexter, *Doing History* (Bloomington and London, 1971), pp. 123–125.

[21] Edward Chamberlayne, *Angliae Notitia: or the Present State of England*, 19th ed. (1700), pp. 457–462, 563. John Chamberlayne, *Magnae Britanniae Notitia: or the Present State of Great-Britain*, 38th ed. (1755), Book III, pp. 36–45.

[22] John Chamberlayne, *op. cit.*, pp. 178–180.

[23] On the eclipse of private armies see the chapter on "Power" in Lawrence Stone, *The Crisis of the Aristocracy 1558–1641* (Oxford, 1965), pp. 199–270.

[24] See Alan Everitt's chapter in Joan Thirsk, ed., *The Agrarian History of England and Wales: Volume IV, 1500–1640* (Cambridge, 1967), esp. p. 462; Arthur H. Johnson, *The Disappearance of the Small Landowner* (Oxford, 1909, repr. 1963), pp. 75–82, and Joan Thirsk's introduction to the reprint edition, pp. vii–xii; G. E. Mingay, "The Size of Farms in the Eighteenth Century," *Economic History Review*, 2nd ser. XIV (1962), pp. 469–488. The size of estates is treated in H. J. Habakkuk, "English Landownership, 1680–1740," *Economic History Review*, X (1940), pp. 3–8.

[25] Halévy, *England in 1815*, p. 231.

[26] The point is made in J. H. Plumb, *The Growth of Political Stability in England 1675–1725* (1967), p. 8, published in U.S. as *The Origins of Political Stability, England, 1675–1725* (Boston, 1967).

[27] E.g., Malachy Postlethwayt, *The Universal Dictionary of Trade and Commerce*, 2 vols., 2nd ed. (1757), article on "Landed Interest."

[28] Harold Perkin, *The Origins of Modern English Society 1780–1880* (1969), p. 75. See also David Spring, "English Landowners and Nineteenth-Century Industrialism," in J. T. Ward and R. G. Wilson, eds., *Land and Industry* (Newton Abbot and New York, 1971), p. 17.

[29] It is overdrawn in Sir George Clark, *The Later Stuarts, 1660–1714*, 2nd ed. (Oxford, 1955), pp. 36–37.

[30] Lawrence Stone, "Social Mobility in England, 1500–1700," *Past and Present*, No. 33 (1966), p. 55.

[31] Guy Miege, *The Present State of Great Britain and Ireland*, 11th ed. (1748), Appendix, pp. 16–26.

[32] W. A. Speck, "Conflict in Society," in Geoffrey Holmes, ed., *Britain after the Glorious Revolution 1689–1714* (1969), pp. 145–146.

[33] *Ibid.*, pp. 146–147.

[34] Habakkuk, *loc. cit.*, p. 17. See also his essay "The English Land Market in the Eighteenth Century" in *Britain and the Netherlands*, ed. by J. S. Bromley and E. H. Kossmann (1960), pp. 170–173.

[35] The East India Company's service remained socially acceptable, but it should be noted that as the century wore on employment in India was becoming more governmental than mercantile in character.

[36] Adam Smith, *Wealth of Nations*, I, pp. 444–445.

[37] Richard G. Wilson, *Gentlemen Merchants: The Merchant Community in Leeds 1700–1830* (Manchester, 1971), pp. 161–236.

[38] See Lord Ernle, *English Farming Past and Present*, 6th ed. (1961), pp. 141, 144.

[39] For an introduction see Lawrence Stone, *Social Change and Revolution in England 1540–1640* (1965); and J. H. Hexter, "Storm over the Gentry," in *Reappraisals in History* (1961), pp. 117–162.

[40] *Economic History Review*, X (1940), p. 2.

[41] J. R. Jones, *The Revolution of 1688 in England* (1972), p. 174.

[42] Plumb, *Political Stability*, pp. 29–30.

[43] See Geoffrey Holmes, *British Politics in the Age of Anne* (1967), chaps. 4 and 5, and esp. p. 120. Swift wrote in *The Examiner*: "Besides, the Whigs themselves have always confessed, that the Bulk of Landed Men in England was generally of Tories." No. 25, from Jan. 11 to Jan. 18, 1710/11 (London, printed for John Morphew, 1710).

[44] Charles Wilson, *England's Apprenticeship, 1603–1763* (1965), p. 217.

[45] Holmes, *British Politics in the Age of Anne*, p. 164.

[46] The role of party conflict in the politics of this era is a disputed matter. Robert Walcott, in *English Politics in the Early Eighteenth Century* (Cambridge, Mass., 1956), showed that ministries did not come and go in Anne's reign according to the rules of a two-party parliamentary system. This led him to question whether parties in Anne's time played a much more significant role than they did in the early years of George III's reign. Walcott studied the behavior of M.P.'s. For an opposing view,

based on a study of electoral politics, see W. A. Speck, *Tory and Whig: The Struggle in the Constituencies 1701–1715* (1970).

[47] The full-blown argument may be found in Chapter III.

[48] *The Examiner*, No. 38, from April 12 to April 19, 1711.

[49] For a dissenting view see W. T. Laprade, "Plumb on the Origins of Political Stability in England," *South Atlantic Quarterly*, LXVII (1968), pp. 542–550. Laprade estimates that the Tory party had a "more effective apparatus than any previous party" and waged a "long, persistent, continuous campaign" against Walpole (p. 549). The grass-roots power of the Tory party is beyond dispute; the problem lies in whether one believes it had, after 1715, the kind of apparatus and leadership that could sustain it in office.

[50] See Ralph Davis, "The Rise of Protection in England, 1689–1786," *Economic History Review*, 2nd ser. XIX (1966), p. 317.

[51] See generally Swift's contributions to *The Examiner* in 1710 and 1711. Tory attitudes are analytically discussed by Isaac Kramnick, *Bolingbroke and His Circle: The Politics of Nostalgia in the Age of Walpole* (Cambridge, Mass., 1968); see especially Chapter 3 on the gentry and finance. Tory nativism came sharply into focus when issues of immigration and naturalization arose. These provided a clear indicator of Tory affiliation until well into the century. See Thomas W. Perry, *Public Opinion, Propaganda, and Politics in Eighteenth-Century England: A Study of the Jew Bill of 1753* (Cambridge, Mass., 1962), p. 191.

[52] *Ibid.*, p. 70; and see Dame Lucy Sutherland's treatment in Chapter VII.

[53] For a detailed history of this see Jones, *Revolution of 1688*, Chap. 6.

[54] See Plumb, *Political Stability*, pp. 161–172.

[55] See Sir Lewis Namier, "Country Gentlemen in Parliament, 1750–84," in *Crossroads of Power: Essays on England in the Eighteenth Century* (1962), pp. 30–45.

[56] Hexter, *Reappraisals in History*, p. 19.

[57] See H. J. Habakkuk, "England" in Albert Goodwin, ed., *The European Nobility in the Eighteenth Century*, rev. ed. (New York, 1967), pp. 1–21.

[58] *Ibid.* These are summarized below, pp. 44–45.

[59] See Lawrence Stone's massive work on this subject, *The Crisis of the Aristocracy 1558–1641*.

[60] See Habakkuk's articles cited in notes 24 and 34, and also his "Marriage Settlements in the Eighteenth Century," *Transactions of the Royal Historical Society*, 4th ser. XXXII (1950), pp. 15–30.

[61] Swift, *The Examiner*, No. 26, from Jan. 18 to Jan. 25, 1710/11.

[62] Bolingbroke, *Letters on the Study and Use of History*, Letter 2; in Isaac Kramnick, ed., *Lord Bolingbroke: Historical Writings* (Chicago, 1972), p. 21.

[63] Plumb, *Political Stability*, p. 177, and see generally pp. 173–189.

[64] Edmund Burke, *Reflections on the French Revolution* (New York, 1961), p. 60.

[65] Sir Lewis Namier, *The Structure of Politics at the Accession of George III* (2nd ed., 1957), p. 159. The House of Commons had 558 members from 315 constituencies.

[66] Plumb, "Growth of the Electorate," *loc. cit.*, p. 116. In the borough of Westminster where voters were numerous, however, politics remained turbulent; see Nicholas Rogers, "Aristocratic Clientage, Trade and Independency: Popular Politics in Pre-Radical Westminster," *Past and Present*, No. 61 (1973), pp. 70–106.

[67] For the relation of the Rockingham Whigs to the Yorkshire Association see N. C. Phillips, "Edmund Burke and the County Movement, 1779–1780," repr. in Rosalind Mitchison, ed., *Essays in Eighteenth-Century History from the English Historical Review* (1966), pp. 301–325.

[68] The pioneering work on the declining weight of patronage is Archibald S. Foord, "The Waning of 'The Influence of the Crown'" in Mitchison, *op. cit.*, pp. 171–194.

[69] See J. M. Norris, "Samuel Garbett and the Early Development of Industrial Lobbying in Great Britain," *Economic History Review*, 2nd ser. X (1958), pp. 450–460 for the way in which industrial lobbying improved its methods during the later eighteenth century.

[70] Halévy, *England in 1815*, p. 204.

The Present State of Great Britain, *by Guy Miege, a native of Switzerland who emigrated to England in 1661, was a revision and continuation of* The New State of England, *which went through six editions from 1691.* The Present State of Great Britain *went through eleven editions from 1707 to 1748. It was one of two popular handbooks of the time. The other, entitled* Magnae Britanniae Notitia: or the Present State of Great-Britain, *was begun, as* Angliae Notitia, *by Edward Chamberlayne in 1669 and continued by his son, John; it went through thirty-six editions, the last in 1755. Chamberlayne's is deservedly far better known. Its formal matter is fuller and more authoritative, its lists more reliable.*

It appears that Miege stole both the title and overall plan from Chamberlayne, and some of his chapters are as full of plagiarism as a dictionary. But Miege's work has certain merits. Whereas Chamberlayne's book emits a Tory aroma of the Establishment—its treatment of religious dissent, for instance, is pretty narrowly confined to conditions of toleration and points of doctrine, betraying as to the latter a trace of abhorrence—Miege's is somewhat Whiggish and less dignified. Miege's book is also more compressed. Its chapters on national character and customs are lively and incisive, and its remarks on institutions are more given to social commentary.

The portrait of England Miege provides is plainly self-congratulatory. No one should put complete faith in the accuracy of his facts and observations, for in this respect the work is no better, nor worse, than most guidebooks. Inaccuracy is a modest price we pay for having a guide speak to us from the eighteenth century. These selections are taken from the last edition, 1748, which was revised, insignificantly as far as these chapters are concerned, by Samuel Bolton. Spelling and punctuation have been modernized.[1]

II

The Present State of Great Britain: An Eighteenth-Century Self-Portrait

BY GUY MIEGE

CHAPTER X

The origin of the English Britons. Their language, complexion, constitution, temper, genius, and their famous men in former ages.

As Great Britain is divided into England, Scotland, and Wales, so its inhabitants (especially since the Union) may be divided into English, Scotch, and Welsh Britons.

The English Britons are an aggregate body of several nations; but chiefly of Saxons, Danes, and French-Normans, not without some mixture of British and Roman blood.

Their speech is likewise a compound of several languages, but chiefly the Saxon, Latin, and French; the first being properly the stock on which the others are ingrafted.

When the Romans were possessed of England, they caused the Latin tongue to be generally used in this country, and all court-rolls, records, charters, patents, commissions, writs, and bonds were in Latin until the Act of George II [in 1731].

The Saxons next introduced their language (a dialect of the Teutonic) wherever they settled. Such are to this day: most English monosyllables, surnames, counties, towns, and the body of our language.

The Normans, afterward getting possession of England, caused the Norman or French tongue to be learned at school by the Saxons. And until the thirty-sixth year of Edward III, the English laws, pleadings, sermons, and writings were in Norman. The same has been hitherto the language of our common law, all moots and law exercises, pleadings and reports being made in Norman, which puts our young students of the law upon the necessity of learning it. The royal assent and dissent to bills in Parliament is still expressed in the Norman tongue. As for our terms in heraldry, dancing, cards, dice, cookery, hunting, hawking, and the art of war, they are mostly French. On the other hand, learned men have introduced a great many Latin and Greek words by which the English tongue is very much improved and refined, wonderfully copious, expressive, and significant. It even exceeds the Latin in a peculiar grace of making compounds and derivatives, one of the greatest beauties of a language. In point of sweetness, it is true, the French and Italian run smoother. But they want strength; whereas the English is both harmonious and manly and very agreeable to the ear when spoken by the fair sex.

Their complexion answers to their climate, for they are neither sunburnt as in hot countries, nor weather-beaten as in cold regions. And I venture to say that no kingdom in Europe can outdo England for charmingness of youth, comely stature and graceful countenance in men, or delicate form and beauty in women—the fair sex being one of those remarkable things for which England is noted. According to the old Latin verse:

Anglia mons, pons, fons, ecclesia, femina, lana.

England for women, and its wool is named,
For springs, fine bridges, hills and churches famed.

The English are generally of a strong constitution, but it is often spoiled by education. For when they want their usual food, good bread and meat especially, they are presently to seek [*i.e.*, at a loss] and cannot shift as other nations. Therefore it is commonly said that a Scotsman will soon starve an Englishman. And it is observed, the English lose more soldiers in their first campaign if they are short of provisions than any other nation in Europe.

Their temper is naturally suitable to their climate: not so fiery as the French, nor so cold as the northern people.

They are for the most part reserved, less communicative, and not like the French, vain and boasting. And as their friendship is not easily gained, so when once got, not easily lost.

Their thoughtfulness is of great use to cool that fire which renders men volatile and prompts them to rashness. It makes them studious to improve inventions and to fathom the depth of all arts and sciences. It is observed that an ingenious Frenchman who has breathed for some years the air of England and imbibed its phlegmatic quality is an excellent compound.

So great is the respect and tenderness of Englishmen for the fair sex in general that out of civility they always give them the upper hand and put them, the least of any nation, to hardship and drudgery. Women are not shut up as in Italy and Spain, but have here more liberty allowed them than anywhere else. In short, such is their complaisance for the sex in general that it is not to be paralleled, and has given birth to the proverb that England is a paradise for women.

Valor is a peculiar character of the English, who never draw the sword in vain, and their conduct answers to their courage. Witness their conquest of Wales and Ireland, but especially that of France in the reigns of those renowned kings, Edward III and Henry V. The monarchy of Spain has also severely experienced the English valor in Queen Elizabeth's reign. Nor was Queen Anne less glorious, who, in conjunction with her allies, conducted by the Duke of Marlborough, stopped an insolent aspiring monarch in his full career toward the sovereignty of all Christendom.

I conclude with the English genius, wherein they yield to no nation in Europe. None has more improved the mechanic arts; and the world to this day is obliged to England for many useful inventions and discoveries. Here are made the best clocks, watches, barometers, thermometers, air pumps, and all sorts of mathematical instruments; clocks, with all the motions of the celestial bodies; and various musical automata, in which a very agreeable concert is performed by clock-work; watches of 50 or 60 pounds a piece; locks of iron and brass of 50 pounds. They have found out the way to polish the insides of great iron guns and to weigh up ships that are sunk to the bottom of the sea. They have invented the use of cane chairs and several engines for printing stuffs and linen, etc. Glass, tin, copper, brass, earthen and horn ware they have improved to admiration. They make the best woolen cloth, stockings, knives, and outdo France itself in all sorts of rich silks. They excell all nations in polishing iron and making many useful and bright utensils thereof. For merchandise and navigation, except the Hollanders, none come near them, and their surprising wealth arising from trade is a plain demonstration of it. For building geometrical staircases with neat and convenient houses upon a little spot of ground, they have a singular talent. And in the art of scaffolding they surpass all people.

As to liberal arts, where shall one find a people so generally knowing? Here experimental philosophy is improved to a wonder, and no foreign church is so well stocked with divines as England's, which makes their learned works so much in request abroad. It is well known how they baffled and silenced the popish clergy in Charles II's and his brother's reigns.

To educate great men in all professions England has the advantage of the best universities, an infinite number of learned men, and a vast variety of public and private libraries. And the English generally are such lovers of learning that among people of any substance a closet of choice books is very frequently seen. In short, there are few of the common people but what can read, write, and cast accounts.

CHAPTER XI
Of the religion in Great Britain.

[The chapter begins with a brief historical account of English religion.]

The doctrinal points, consisting of thirty-nine articles, being the confession of faith of the Church of England and a summary of her doctrine, not only the episcopal government is thereby retained, but also such rites and ceremonies as are for decency. Such is the surplice, the bowing and kneeling before the altar, the sign of the cross in baptism, and a few others. A great number of papists nevertheless kept to their religion, and those extrinsicals proved such a stumbling block to others of the reformed party, as made at last a schism in the church. For many, at that time called Puritans, rather than comply with those ceremonies, separated themselves from the church, keeping her fundamentals but renouncing both her discipline and rites. From hence called dissenters, nonconformists, or separatists: some of them Presbyterians, others Independents, and some Anabaptists. All which together make a numerous party.

The most considerable are the Presbyterians, so called from their ecclesiastical government by presbyters or elders. These come nearest, in point of doctrine, to the Church of England.

The Independents are so called because each congregation among them governs itself independently of all others.

The Baptists, or Anabaptists, from their rebaptizing such as join in their communion who were baptized in their infancy. For they are against baptizing of children, and therefore called also Anti-pedobaptists.

These sects, however, agree in fundamentals with all the Protestant churches but come nearest to Calvin. It is true they use no liturgy, as the Calvinists do, but only extemporary prayer, the Lord's Prayer being used only by some of them.

There is another particular sect we call Quakers, from their original way of quaking and groaning at their meetings when they wait for the spirit. They were a sort of enthusiasts, pretending to inspiration, but now much more rational than formerly. It is true they own the Trinity, and that the writers of the Old and New Testament were divinely inspired. But they reject all ministerial ordinances, use no sacrament, and follow a light within that leads them to the way of truth.

In civil matters they would have all men equal and think all oaths unlawful. Therefore they only use yea or no to affirm or deny a thing; and in courts of justice, the government has indulged them so far that their affirmation is taken in lieu of an oath. They ridicule the civility of the hat; and their way is thee and thou to all men without distinction. Their dress, especially that of the women, is very neat and plain. They keep all their own poor and manage their churches or meetings with a wonderful exact order. So that all over the British dominions they are as one brotherhood, which things are laudable and worthy of imitation.

The strictness of discipline used by dissenters is that which has kept up their party in a great measure. And it is observable how much the Church of England men and dissenters differ, not only in their behavior but even in their countenances. The first have generally a free, affable way with them. The dissenters on the contrary are much upon the reserve. One side is generally open-handed and the other close-fisted. I wish the first less guilty of public immoralities, while the last keeps a fair and decent outside, however it is within. In short, of all Protestants, the dissenters are the strictest keepers of the Lord's Day and fall little short of the Jews in their Sabbath.

To prevent the growth of dissenters and bring them into the pale of the Church, severe laws were made against them, which sometimes were strictly put into execution. This created high feuds among Churchmen and dissenters and lasted until the happy revolution, when the dissenters, joining with the Churchmen against the illegal proceedings of King James II, obtained a license for their separate meetings, called the Toleration Act.

I come now to the Romans, commonly called papists, and by the law, popish recusants, who grew so formidable in the reign of James II. There are divers laws in force against them, but seldom put in execution. If they keep within bounds without endeavoring to make converts and live peaceably, they need not fear being molested. Nor has the government any cause to fear them, their party being very inconsiderable since the extinction of the family of Stuart.

As for Jews, they are tolerated by royal permission. They were formerly banished [from] England, but Cromwell readmitted them. Then they were inconsiderable, but now they are so increased that within the City they have three or four synagogues. They govern the exchange of money throughout the world and are without doubt a great benefit to such a busy mercantile nation as this is.

In point of morals the English have their share in the corruptions of the age, and vices as well as virtues. As they live generally at ease and in plenty, so luxury seems to predominate with them. It is the unhappy effect of the loose and licentious reigns of Charles and James II. But if good examples could make as strong an impression as bad, the religion and morals of the court are surely altered much for the better since the Protestant settlement in the house of Hanover.

But whatever be the corruption of manners in this depraved

age among the English, virtue is not yet banished [from] the land. So far from it, that there are persons of both sexes (and I hope good numbers of them) temperate in their way of living, just to their neighbors, kindhearted to their friends, inoffensive to their enemies, charitable to the poor, and sincere in the practice of all Christian duties.

CHAPTER XII

Of the English way of living, as to lodging, food, raiment and fuel; exercises and recreations, fasts and festivals, with some particular customs. Their computation of time and most common diseases.

The English nation is vastly improved in architecture of all kinds; particularly that of houses, which in the modern way are very neat, with light staircases, lofty ceilings, closets in most rooms, and sash-windows, all pleasant and conducive to health. And such is their compactness and uniformity that the same quantity of ground will afford double the conveniences of an old-built house.

The use of hangings, whether tapestry or any other, is generally left off, since wainscoting came into fashion, which is fitter for a moist country and prevents the danger of damp walls.

For diet the English choose butchers' meat as the most proper nourishment for this country; and all edible roots and herbs are used only as a supplement. They are indeed great flesh-eaters, and that without kitchen sophistry, plain boiled, roasted, or baked being the general way of dressing it. French mixtures, compound dishes, venison, good fish and fowl are seldom eaten but by the better sort. In pastry work and chiefly venison pasties, they excell all nations. Their variety of puddings and, at Christmas, their plum porridge, rich Christmas pies, and brawn [boar's meat] are properly English dishes, hardly known to other nations.

It is not many years since a little bread served their turn, and some did scarce eat any. But now they eat more, though not so much as the French.

Though malt liquor be their usual drink, yet vast quantities of wine are consumed here, notwithstanding the dearness of it by reason of the custom. Before the war with France at the late revolution, French claret was the wine mostly used. But the scarcity of that is now supplied by the Florence and Portugal wines.

For fineness of color, strength, and taste, they have beer and ale, little inferior to wine; besides, cider, punch, and other liquors.

In former ages they used to eat three or four meals a day, and supper was a principal one. But that custom being much disused, they now chiefly confine themselves to a dinner, making up the rest with slight things. So less time is spent in eating, and the more saved for business. Besides, this way is found to be more healthy, especially at London.

Coffee and tea, two sober liquors, are of common use in England, of which last there is a vast consumption; and mixed with cream or milk [it] is a pleasant, cooling, wholesome drink. But punch is much in vogue, especially since rum and brandy are now entirely a British manufacture.

The use of tobacco is almost universal and indeed not improper for so moist a climate.

For raiment, the common wear among men is plain cloth without much of costly trimming.

But the fair sex spare for nothing to make the best appearance. Those who are able in the richest silks, of 8 or 10 pounds a yard, with all the gay ornaments that art can invent.

England is too temperate a country to use stoves as in colder climates, a chimney-fire, of wood or pit coal, being much better to warm and cheer the spirits.

From these necessary things for human life I proceed to the English exercises and recreations.

I pass by such as are common with other nations as hunting, fowling, fishing, shooting with bow and arrows, dancing, music, stage plays, etc.

Playing at mall,[2] so frequent in France, is out of date in England, and playing at tennis not so common.

But bowling is much used, for which there are bowling greens kept very neat and smooth as velvet, peculiar to the English. And so is the recreation of paddock courses, horse races, cock fighting, cricket. And with the common people, leaping, wrestling, bull baiting, prizefighting, cudgeling, boxing, and in frosty weather, football. Among which, the races show the wonderful swiftness of English horses; cock fighting the inimitable spirit of their cocks; bear and bull baiting that of their dogs; and prizes, the dexterity and courage of some men in the use of sharp weapons.

The art of ringing bells is peculiar to the English, whence this island is called by the French the ringing island.

I proceed to give an account of the English festival days, particularly at Christmas, Easter, and Whitsuntide. The first continue from Christmas day, December 25th, to twelfth day, January 6th, being days of entertainment among friends and relations in which also landlords generally treat their tenants. As for the holidays at Easter and Whitsuntide, they are each of three days continuance.

They have also public days of rejoicing upon a civil account, particularly the King's birthday, Proclamation and Coronation Day, when the Tower guns go off, the bells ring, and in the evening there are illuminations and bonfires. The 5th of November, being Gunpowder-Treason Day, is a thanksgiving for the wonderful deliverance of James I and the Parliament then sitting, as is also May 29th for the restoration of monarchy and the royal family.

Many societies likewise have their feasting days; but none to be compared, in this point, to the Inns of Court for state and magnificence when they keep their Readings.

In families of the better sort it is usual to celebrate their birth and wedding days with particular friends.

As to fasting days, the Church of England has indeed appointed Lent as a particular time of fasting and humiliation, but not (as the Roman Church) wholly to abstain from flesh all that time. However, many of the Church of England abstain from flesh on Wednesdays and Fridays in Lent; but Good Friday, particularly, is observed with fasting until the evening.

The 30th of January, called the Martyrdom of King Charles I, is appointed by law to be as a fast observed in detestation of that horrid act. And the 2nd of September, being the day when the City was burnt in 1666, has been yearly observed as a fast ever since by the Londoners.

To avert God's displeasure, and implore his mercy, the sovereign appoints solemn fasts when he thinks proper, as he does public thanksgivings for signal blessings.

On the 1st of March, being St. David's Day (the Patron of Wales), the Welsh wear a leek on their hats to perpetuate, as they say, the memory of a signal victory they obtained upon that day when each soldier put a leek in his cap to know their friends from their foes. The common sort wear garden leeks, but the better sort, those made of silk. The King himself wears one.

November 30th being St. Andrew's Day, the Patron of Scotland, the Scots wear a blue cross on the forepart of their hats.

As to the English computation of time, the natural day begins with them, as in most parts of Europe, at midnight; counting twelve hours from that time to noon, and twelve hours more, beginning at one o'clock, until the next midnight.

But the year begins properly and legally with them on Lady Day, March 25th, according to which they date all their public transactions, writings, and records, though they allow the year, by the cycles of the sun and moon, to begin January 1 and commonly call it New Year's Day. To distinguish therefore the time from the 1st of January to the 25th of March, it is a practice with some to set down both years in the date of letters thus, 1744–45.

Lastly, the English epoch is from the time of the birth of Christ. But they keep the old or Julian style; whereas all popish and some Protestant states go by the new, otherwise called the Gregorian style, from Pope Gregory XIII, who corrected the calendar by the advice and direction of Lilly and other great mathematicians in the year 1582. By this new style they count eleven days before us.[3]

The diseases common to the English are the rickets, the scurvy, and consumption. The first is incident to children, the second to the majority of the people, and the third to many. The rickets may proceed from the moisture of the air. But the other two might be greatly prevented by eating less flesh, particularly unwholesome salt provisions.

There is no country where rheums and coughs are more predominant in the winter, which are best cured by keeping within.

Augues and rheumatisms are common in the fen counties. But fevers are not so frequent as in hotter climates.

The gout, stone, gravel, colick, and other diseases are in England as well as other nations. But surfeits are more frequent, the English being sometimes apt to indulge their appetites. . . .

CHAPTER XIII
Of the vast trade of Great Britain both at home and abroad

The British trade is carried on two ways: first at home, both by land and water.

By land all provisions and commodities are conveyed in wagons and upon pack horses; by water, either by sea or upon navigable rivers.

This vast transport of provisions and commodities, both by land and water, employs a world of wagoners, seamen, and watermen. And whereas London is in a manner the center of this trade, hence comes that great concourse of carts and wagons by land, of ships and barges by water. To receive what comes by land we may reckon 150 inns at London, where the wagons come to unload, and from whence they return at set times, with London commodities. By which means, a vast number of porters are employed to load and unload the wagons and carry the parcels where they are directed. But among the inns aforesaid, I do not reckon such as take in coaches only, or others that keep horses at livery.

As to the conveyance by water, one may judge of the vast number of ships, mariners, and watermen employed in England by the sea-coal trade only, which requires yearly a thousand great vessels between London and Newcastle, whose seamen are counted some of the best in England. This trade therefore is kept up, though at a great distance, in order to encourage navigation and preserve a supply of able seamen for the service of the state.

But if the carriage only employs so many people both by sea and land, how great must the number be of such as are employed in manufactures, both in city and country? London swarms with them, and there are many towns in the country full of manufactures of several sorts.

The difference between the trade carried on at home and abroad lies in this, that the first makes the money circulate, whereas the other is carried on chiefly by the bartering of commodities.

Though the home trade be so prodigious, and of so great benefit to the nation, yet we may reasonably conclude the foreign trade to be infinitely greater.

Not but that Britain can subsist without it. For the island yields all things necessary for life and could very well shift without the help of other countries, which cannot be said of Holland, her rival in merchandise. But as foreign trade is very useful to employ artists, set the poor to work, and improve manufactures, so it is an effectual means to enrich the nation, to strengthen the state, and to make it formidable. England therefore trades in all parts of the world; nor does any nation whatever drive such a commerce with her own commodities. This makes her strong in shipping, multiplies the number of her mariners, enriches the kingdom, and procures her whatever the whole world can afford, to gratify the fancy or please the appetite. In short, it is by foreign trade that Britain has become a support to her friends and a terror to her enemies. And whereas the Dutch trade chiefly consists in the transportation of foreign commodities from one country to another, the English principally export their own goods, not only over all Europe, but also to Asia, Africa, and America. Though the English consume more farfetched goods than any other nation, yet they keep not only the balance of trade even by the excellency and quantity of their own commodities, but also come off great gainers by transporting into other countries what they cannot consume at home. With France only they were formerly losers, when that Crown laid exorbitant customs upon English goods, and England was so kind to France as to pass it by without any retaliation. It was so while the family of Stuart was upon the British throne, but the case is otherwise now.

The principal commodities of the growth of Great Britain are first, her wool, of which vast quantities of cloth and stuffs are made, to the sum of two million sterling per annum and sometimes more. Her tin, lead, copper, pit-coal, great guns, bombs, carcasses [shells thrown by a mortar], etc., for one million. Moreover, she exports great quantities of corn, red herrings, pilchards, and salmon, besides abundance of leather and saffron. Many of her manufactures are also in great request, particularly satin, damask, velvet, silk stockings, plush, locks, pendulums, and watches; barometers, thermometers, spectacles, looking glasses, prospective glasses [field glasses], telescopes, microscopes, and all sorts of mathematical instruments, great quantities of which are exported, etc.

Besides the great consumption England makes of the products of her vast countries in the new world, particularly sugar, indigo, cocoa nuts, tobacco, etc., she spares [*i.e.*, does without them] to the sum of half a million a year for other parts of Europe. Her trade with Ireland and fishery with Newfoundland is also very beneficial to her: with Ireland, by exporting her wool, beef, hides, tallow, butter, and fish.

It has been already observed that Holland has the advantage of England in point of transportation, but Holland being a small narrow country, full of water, her merchants find there but little room to settle and little land to purchase. Whereas England being a spacious, beautiful, and fruitful country, her merchants have opportunities enough to buy estates for themselves and their heirs, where they go to enjoy the fruits of their industry and take their ease, when tired with the hurry and concern of trade.

The foreign commerce is regulated chiefly at London by several companies or societies of merchants, empowered by royal charter to make, from time to time, such regulations for the improvement of their trade as they shall think convenient. By which companies the poor are set to work, many great ships are built, and a vast number of seamen continually employed.

[The remainder of the chapter gives some details concerning the foreign trading companies: East India, Levant, Russia, Eastland, Africa, Hamburg, Greenland, and Hudson's Bay.]

CHAPTER XVI
Of the several orders and degrees in England.
And first of the nobility.

The people of England are generally divided into laity and clergy, and the first subdivided into nobility, gentry, and commonalty.

I begin with the laity, not out of any disrespect to the clergy, but because the greatest honors conferred upon the laity are hereditary, which is not so with the clergy.

By the nobility I mean only the temporal peers of the realm, being Lords of Parliament; of whom there are five degrees, distinguished by the several titles of Duke, Marquis, Earl, Viscount, and Baron.

A duke is created by patent, cincture of sword, mantle of state, imposition of a cap and coronet of gold on his head, and a verge of gold put into his hand. He is girt with a sword, to put him in mind that he is bound to defend the King and kingdom in time of war. And his head is adorned with a crown of gold as a token that he is councillor to the King and kingdom in time of peace.

A duke's coronet has leaves without pearls, and his mantle of state four gards [trimmings] faced with ermine. He is called His Grace, a title formerly given to the Kings of England, before they took that of Majesty.

A duke's eldest son is called Marquis by courtesy; the younger sons by their Christian names, with the title of Lord prefixed: Lord Thomas, Lord William, etc.; and all a duke's daughters are Ladies.

A marquis and an earl are created, as a duke, by cincture of sword, etc., but with this difference in their coronets, that a marquis's has a pearl and a strawberry leaf round, of equal height; and an earl's has the pearls raised upon points. Their mantles of state are (as a duke's) faced with ermine. But whereas a duke's has four gards, a marquis's mantle has but three and a half, and an earl's, three.

All the sons of a marquis are Lords by the courtesy of England, and all his daughters Ladies. And as a duke's eldest son bears the title of Marquis, so an earl's bears that of Viscount. But the younger sons of an earl are only Esquires, although all his daughters are Ladies.

Viscounts and barons are made by patent. The difference in their coronets is that a viscount's has a circle of pearls without a set number; and a baron's six pearls upon the circle. Their mantles are both faced with plain white fur.

None of their sons bear the title of Lord, nor any of their daughters that of Lady. Therefore the eldest son of the first viscount is the First Gentleman, and his eldest daughter the First Gentlewoman, without a title in England.

But the title of Lord is given to all the sons of dukes and marquises and the eldest sons of earls; and the title of Lady to all their daughters. Moreover, the sovereign may call up to the House of Lords by writ the eldest son of any peer above a viscount. And though a Scots peer cannot be created an English peer, which was the case of Hamilton and Queensberry just after the Union [in

1707], yet the eldest son of any Scots peer above a viscount may be made English, as were the eldest sons of Montrose and Roxburgh by George I.

All peers and baronets keep rank according to the date of their patents; their ladies the same. But the wives of all knights, judges, bishops, etc., keep rank otherwise.

A Scots nobleman takes place next to the English of his rank; and an Irish nobleman, after a Scots peer of his rank.

But there are some high officers, who by virtue of their office precede even all dukes that are not of the royal blood, whatever be their quality, *viz.*, the Lord Chancellor, or Lord Keeper, the Lord High Treasurer, the Lord President of the Council, and the Lord Privy Seal. And others that take place only of all that are of their degree, particularly the Lord Great Chamberlain of England, the Earl Marshal, the Lord High Admiral, the Lord Steward, and Lord Chamberlain of the King's household, and the Secretaries of State.

Guillim in his heraldry has determined that colonels, by the law of the Earl Marshal's Court, are to precede knights bachelors; meaning thereby all field officers as well as flag officers.

THE PRIVILEGES OF THE NOBILITY

The British nobles enjoy many great privileges, the principal of which are these:

1. That they are free from all arrests for debt, as being the King's hereditary councillors. Therefore a peer cannot be outlawed in any civil action, and no attachment lies against his person. But execution may be taken upon his lands and goods.

For the same reason they are free from all attendance at courts-leet, or sheriffs turns. Or in case of a riot, from attending the service of the *posse comitatus*.

2. In criminal causes they are only tried by their peers, who give in their verdict, not upon oath, as other juries, but only upon their honor. And then a court is built on purpose in the middle of Westminster Hall, at the King's charge, which is pulled down again when their trials are over.

3. To secure the honor of, and prevent the spreading of any scandal upon peers or any great officer of the realm, by reports, there is an express law, called *scandalum magnatum*, by which any

man convicted of making a scandalous report against a peer of the realm (though true) is condemned to an arbitrary fine and remains in prison till it be paid.

4. Upon any great trial in a court of justice, a peer may come in to court and sit covered.

They have other privileges, which I pass by for brevity's sake. Yet none has that of the grandees of Spain, to be covered in the King's presence; neither is it decent or fit that they should, for it is a diminution to the sovereign, whatever honor it be to the subject. In short, it is a privilege to be unmannerly.

CHAPTER XVIII
Of the gentry and inferior sort of people.

Next to the peers of the realm, dukes, marquises, earls, viscounts, and barons, who properly are the nobles of England, I come to what we call the gentry, consisting of knights, esquires, and gentlemen without title.

Besides the aforesaid Knights of the Garter [discussed in preceding chapter, omitted], here are three other sorts: *viz.*, Baronets, Knights of the Bath, and Knights Bachelors, all distinguished from the rest of the gentry by the title of Sir before their Christian names.

Baronets are the first of Gentry, and the only honor among them that is hereditary. It was first instituted in 1611 by King James I, who limited their number to two hundred. But his successors did not keep to that rule, so that now there are many more, a catalogue of which is among the Lists [appended to the original volume]. To be qualified for it, a man must be born a gentleman, of good reputation, and have an estate. He must pay to the Exchequer as much as will maintain thirty foot-soldiers 3 years at 8 *d.* a day in the province of Ulster in Ireland; which amounts to near £1100, the whole of which is now remitted by the Crown and has been ever since the Restoration.

Knights of the Bath are so called from their bathing, used before they were created. Henry IV was the founder of this order in 1399, when to grace his coronation he made forty-six of these knights, who were bathed in the Tower; which order was established by King George I in the year 1725 and made a military order forever, for thirty-six knights besides the sovereign. The gentleman receiving this honor kneels before the King, who knights him in the usual manner, and then puts a crimson riband over his right shoulder, producing it under the left arm, at the ends of which thus meeting hangs the badge or symbol of the order. . . . The symbol is a scepter, three imperial crowns with a rose and thistle in a circle of gold, and this motto: *tria juncta in uno*; which badge and riband is daily worn, as the Knights of the Garter do theirs.

Knights Bachelors are now less esteemed, though it is the first foundation of all honor and military dignity. It was given formerly to noblemen's sons and great commanders for eminent service. Then they were knighted and girt with a sword having gilt spurs put on, whence they were called in Latin: *equites aurati*. But of later times this honor has been given to lawyers, physicians, merchants, painters, and others, though perhaps men of very good fortune. The manner of making these knights is much altered from what it was. The King bids the gentleman (calling him by his name as a gentleman) to kneel down, upon which he lightly touches his left shoulder with a naked sword, then bids him rise up by the title of Sir to his Christian name. Note that all knights' wives bear the title of Lady, which gives them precedence of esquires' and gentlemen's wives.

Esquires, from the French word *escuyers*, called in Latin *armigeri*, are properly the younger sons of earls, the sons of viscounts and barons, the eldest sons of the younger sons of peers, and the eldest sons of baronets and knights.

There are also esquires created by the King, who put round their necks a collar of SS, and giving them a pair of silver spurs. And at the King's court there were formerly two considerable officers, called Esquires of the Body.

Those that are in public offices, or in any eminent station, such as justices of the peace, members of Parliament, mayors of towns, serjeants of the several offices in the King's court, and many other officers are properly Esquires; sheriffs also, and admirals; captains in the army and navy, councillors or any gentleman that has two or three hundred a year in land.

Gentlemen (in Latin *generosi*) are those properly who, being descended of a good family, bear a coat of arms, without any particular title. Of these such as are of a good family and live without trade, are as much regarded as knights and esquires. For in England all noblemen are gentlemen, though all gentlemen are not noblemen.

We reckon in England ten thousand gentlemen, one with another, at £500 a year, beside twenty thousand younger brothers, who having but a small estate get preferments one way or other.

Formerly, trading degraded a gentleman. But now a thriving tradesman, when he leaves off trade, becomes a gentleman.

As to merchants, the founders of trade and of the nation's wealth, they deserve indeed to be ranked among gentlemen. For by their means land is improved and inbred commodities exported. They employ a world of artificers and seamen and procure a good livelihood to a vast number of tradesmen and retailers. Therefore many, gentlemen born, some of them younger sons of noblemen, take upon them this profession as they do likewise in France, without any hurt or blemish to their birth and family.

In short, the title of Gentleman is commonly given in England to all that distinguish themselves from the common sort of people by a genteel dress and carriage, good education, learning, or an independent station.

As the gentry of England is very numerous, so their wealth, upon the whole, far exceeds that of the nobility, though most of these have great estates and some of them beyond sovereign princes. Here we have many knights and esquires, who have each, two, three or four thousand pounds a year; some from five to ten thousand a year, and some to much more.

By the inferior sort of people I mean such as get their livelihood either in a mechanic, or servile way, as tradesmen, mariners, husbandmen, servants, and laborers.

But there is a middle sort between the degree of a gentleman and these, *viz.*, yeomen and copyholders.

Those are called Yeomen, or Freeholders, that have land of their own to a good value and husband it themselves. Great is their number in England, many of them having land that yields them forty or fifty pounds a year, some one hundred or two hundred. Nay there are yeomen in Kent that have one thousand pounds, and some more, per annum, the like not to be found anywhere else in Europe.

The copyholders are much of the same nature, a copyhold being a sure inheritance. For though the hold be void at the tenant's death, yet the next of blood, paying the customary fine, takes possession.

Not to insist upon the meaner sort, I shall only observe that they are the happiest people in Europe, and by the laws of the land the least liable to oppression from the sovereign.

[A table of precedence concludes the chapter.]

CHAPTER XXII
Of the British government.

The laws of Great Britain are the foundation of its monarchy. They are the rule of the King's government and the people's obedience.

I begin with the common law, that is, the common customs of the nation, which in process of time have obtained the force of laws. It is a summary of the laws of the Saxons and Danes, to which William I, having added some of the good customs of Normandy, he caused them all to be written in the Norman dialect, and so they have continued hitherto.

We have also the statute law; that is, laws made from time to time by King and Parliament, as occasion requires, and where the common law is deficient, or thought to be so.

The martial law: which concerns only soldiers and mariners in time of actual war.

The forfeit law: concerning forfeits, by which the will is reputed for the fact, so that a man hunting of a deer may be arrested, as if he had taken it.

The civil law: made use of in the court of admiralty, the two universities, all spiritual courts, the Earl Marshal's court, and in royal treaties abroad. This is the law of nations, looked upon as the product of the common reason of mankind and made use of where common and statute law takes no cognizance.

The laws of Rhodes and Oleron, concerning maritime affairs, have been long since incorporated into the volumes of the civil law. Rhodes is an island in the Mediterranean, now belonging to the

Turks, whose ancient inhabitants, being great traders at sea, made such regulations in all maritime concerns that the very Romans left their sea affairs, and all debates and differences of that kind, to the decision of the Rhodian laws.

Oleron [is] an island of Aquitaine, not far from Rochelle, where Richard I made such excellent laws relating to sea affairs that they were almost in as great repute in these western parts of Europe as the Rhodian laws were in the Mediterranean.

There have been maritime laws made by King Edward III, at Queenborough, and by other princes and states in France, Italy, and Spain. But the Rhodian laws still extant have the preference.

The canon law: which takes place in things relating merely to religion, and is so called from such canons or rules of general councils and of English synods as are received by the Church of England, by which she exercises her jurisdiction, so far as the said canons are consonant to the Holy Scripture and the laws of the realm.

But there are other laws, called municipal, or by-laws, proper to corporations, such as the magistrates of a town or city may make by virtue of the King's charter for the benefit of their corporation, provided they are not inconsistent with the laws of the land.

By their own laws all Britons are free, because no law can be made or repealed without their own consent by their representatives in Parliament, so that their subjection to laws is not forced, but voluntary.

By the same laws, no English subject ought to be imprisoned without cause shown. Nor may he be denied a writ of habeas corpus, if desired, to bring him speedily to his trial. And if upon an habeas corpus no cause of imprisonment is alleged, the prisoner must be set at liberty.

No racks are used to force confession from a prisoner, and nothing but clear evidence, upon oath, can convict him.

None can be tried but by a jury of his peers, or condemned but by the laws of the land, or an Act of Parliament passed on purpose. Nor ought any to be fined, but according to the merit of the offense, or ability of the offender.

No taxes or loans can be levied in England without consent of the people by their representatives in Parliament. Nor are any to be prest for soldiers but such as Acts of Parliament in great emergencies direct.

In times of peace or war (unless upon an invasion) no soldiers can be quartered on a private housekeeper against his will, though they pay for their quarters.

As to women, when a woman marries, she gives herself over, and what she brings with her, to her husband's power. She parts with her very surname and assumes her husband's. If she has any tenure, it is all in capite. That is, she holds it of and by her husband, who is the head of his wife. She can make no contract, nor give away, nor alienate anything without her husband's consent. In short, a married woman can call nothing her own, unless it be otherwise settled before marriage.

If she offends, her husband may correct [punish] her. But if she wrong another by her tongue, or trespass, her husband answers for the fault and must make satisfaction because the law makes her subject to him. If she takes things upon trust, unknown to her husband, and so runs him in debt, he is liable to pay it, unless he has cried her down in the market.

A woman that has killed her husband is, by law, to be burnt alive, for the offense is accounted petty treason; that is, as great a crime as parricide.

If a wife brings forth a child begotten before marriage by another man, the husband is bound to own it as his child, and the child shall be his heir at law.

If she brings forth a child after a long absence of her husband, and he lived all that while within the four seas, he must father that child. And if it be her first-born son, and the husband's estate entailed or left without will, that child shall be heir to it.

A wife that has no jointure settled before marriage, may challenge after her husband's death the third part of his yearly rents (if land) during her life, and within the city of London, a third part of her husband's personal estate forever.

If a wife, being an heiress, brings to her husband an estate in land, it descends to her eldest son. And if she has no son, but only daughters, it is divided among them. But if she dies without issue, the land goes to the heir at law. Only the husband shall enjoy the profits thereof during his life.

As to contracts or covenants made before marriage, they take place and are of force according to the tenor thereof.

In short, as the husband and wife are accounted but one, so she cannot be produced as a witness for or against him. Nor can they be wholly separated by law but upon a nullity of marriage, precontract, consanguinity within the degrees forbidden, impotency, or such like. In which cases this is called separation *a vinculo matrimonii* from the bond of matrimony, by which each party is free to remarry. But in case of adultery, the law of England does not allow of this plenary divorce; only a separation *a mensa et thoro*, that is, living asunder without liberty to remarry while either party is alive. Yet it has been allowed by Act of Parliament in some particular cases.

I come now to noblewomen, who are so by descent, creation, or marriage. We call them noble by descent or birthright upon whom the honor of peerage is devolved for want of male issue, as it falls out sometimes, according to the settlement of the title in the patent. Others are noble by creation, being a particular favor from the sovereign, or to continue a particular title.

But the greatest part of English noblewomen are so by marriage, all being accounted noble that [are] noblemen's wives.

A noblewoman by descent, or creation, marrying a second husband not noble, keeps her honor by law and is still called by her title. Though her new husband becomes, by marriage, master of her goods and chattels, yet she adds no honor to him. But both her honor and estate descend to the next heir.

A noblewoman by marriage, who marries another husband of lower estate, loses her honor by law. However she is by the courtesy of England still respected as noble and called by her former title.

A noblewoman by birth, married to a baron, takes place only as baroness, though she be a duke's daughter. But if she marry one under a nobleman, the courtesy of England gives her place according to her birth and not her husband's condition.

A knight's widow marrying below herself is still called Lady by the courtesy of England with her first surname.

Titular honor without fortune being but a shadow, the eldest son of a family is, by the custom of England, provided for beyond all other children, and succeeds both in the title and estate, that he may bear up the honor of the family. He inherits all lands, and younger children the personal estate. But if there be no son, both the real and personal estate are equally divided among the daughters.

When the estate is not entailed, the father may leave it to what child he pleases, or give it away from his children, which keeps them in awe and within the bonds of filial obedience.

An orphan at the age of fourteen may choose his guardian, consent to marriage, and by will dispose of goods and chattels. At twenty-one he is of age and can make contracts.

A daughter may consent to marriage at seven years of age and at twelve may retract or confirm it.

Servants are commonly hired for one year, at the end whereof they may leave their masters, after a month's warning. It is unlawful to take another man's servant without his leave or certificate, and the penalty is five pounds.

The law considering the condition of a servant, how by going to service he loses his liberty and subjects his will to another, has wisely provided for the payment of his wages. For if a servant's wages be not paid, it is but complaining to a justice of the peace upon oath; and if he is an upright magistrate, he will cause justice to be done.

However, a master may by law correct his servant for a just cause, and resistance in a servant is liable to a severe penalty. If he kills his master, it is petty treason, that is, a crime next to high treason. But if a servant is turned away without notice, the master or mistress in such a case must allow a month's wages.

Apprentices are another sort of servants who, to learn a trade, are bound to serve seven years, and all that time bare-headed in open shop. Whereas in other countries they go later, and serve about half the time, and learn their trades as well; which way, I confess, is not so much for the master's advantage.

An apprentice is bound by his indenture not to marry during his servitude. But if a maiden apprentice do marry, she is free, of course, and may go to her husband.

Black slaves, brought into England and baptized, are free from slavery, though not from common service. That is, they are free from being bought and sold.

NOTES

II. *The Present State of Great Britain*

[1] I have relied on Michael Jolliffe's note on Miege's handbooks in the *Bulletin of the Institute of Historical Research*, Vol. XVII, No. 51 (1940), pp. 130–131.

[2] Pall-mall, a game involving elements of croquet, hockey, and golf.

[3] Three years after this was published, Britain adopted the Gregorian calendar by Act of Parliament (1751). Eleven days were wiped off the calendar in September 1752—to the consternation of the common people—and the official year in England was thereafter marked, as it had been for a century and a half in Scotland, from January 1st.

*E*nglish politics were turbulent at the beginning of the eighteenth century. Their most prominent feature was the noisy struggle between the Whig and Tory parties. These parties should be seen as focal points of affiliation rather than as organized institutions, but their importance was no less for that. By 1710, England had been at war with Louis XIV for twenty years with only a slight respite, and war-weariness was beginning to dominate political discourse. Late in that year Jonathan Swift, with A Tale of a Tub *(1704)* behind him and Gulliver's Travels *(1726)* still in the future, enlisted his pen in Tory service by writing The Examiner, *a weekly political tract;* he wrote, all in all, about thirty numbers, until June 1711.[1] In No. 14, his first effort (No. 13 in some later editions), he assailed the methods by which the moneyed interest used the war to surpass the landed interest. It must be granted that Toryism was concerned with much more than this: It had a particular outlook on inheritance, legitimacy, monarchy, the place of the established church in civil life, and other matters, as Swift's subsequent contributions amply illustrated. But the suspicion and resentment of moneyed men's politics that are expressed here bring into focus the economic tensions in English society during the early eighteenth century; and they continued to find expression for the next half century whenever war broke out. This passage is taken from the original edition, printed for John Morphew, near Stationers-Hall, London, 1710.

III

The Examiner No. 14:
A Tory View of War and the
Moneyed Interests *

BY JONATHAN SWIFT

. . . The late revolutions at court have given room to some specious
objections, which I have heard repeated by well-meaning men, just
as they had taken them up on the credit of others who have worse
designs. They wonder the Queen would choose to change her ministry at this juncture, and thereby give uneasiness to a general
[Marlborough] who has been so long successful abroad, and might
think himself injured if the entire ministry were not of his own
nomination. That there were few complaints of any consequence
against the late men in power, and none at all in Parliament, which,
on the contrary, passed votes in favor of the chief minister. That if
Her Majesty had a mind to introduce the other party, it would have
been more seasonable after a peace, which now we have made desperate, by spiriting the French, who rejoice at these changes, and by
the fall of our credit, which unqualifies us for continuing the war.
That the Parliament, so untimely dissolved, had been diligent in their
supplies and dutiful in their behavior. That one consequence of these
changes appears already in the fall of the stocks; that we may soon
expect more and worse; and lastly, that all this naturally tends to
break the settlement of the Crown and call over the Pretender.

* *The Examiner*, No. 14, October 26 to November 2, 1710.

These and the like notions are plentifully scattered abroad by the malice of a ruined party, to render the Queen and her administration odious, and to inflame the nation. And these are what, upon occasion, I shall endeavor to overthrow, by discovering the falsehood and absurdity of them.

It is a great unhappiness when, in a government constituted like ours, it should be so brought about that the continuance of a war must be for the interest of vast numbers (peaceable as well as military) who would otherwise have been as unknown as their original. I think our present condition of affairs is admirably described by two verses in Lucan:

Hinc usura vorax, avidumque in tempore faenus,
Hinc concussa fides, & multis utile bellum.

Which without any great force upon the words may thus be translated:

Hence are derived those exorbitant interests and annuities;
hence those large discounts for advances and prompt payment; hence public credit is shaken, and hence great numbers
find their profit in prolonging the war.

It is odd that among a free trading people, as we take ourselves to be, there should so many be found to close in with those councils who have been ever averse from all overtures towards a peace. But yet there is no great mystery in the matter. Let any man observe the equipages in this town; he shall find the greater number of those who make a figure to be a species of men quite different from any that were ever known before the Revolution, consisting either of generals and colonels, or of such whose whole fortunes lie in funds and stocks: so that power, which according to the old maxim was used to follow land, is now gone over to money, and the country gentleman is in the condition of a young heir, out of whose estate a scrivener receives half the rents for interest, and has a mortgage on the whole, and is therefore always ready to feed his vices and extravagancies while there is anything left. So that if the war continues some years longer, a landed man will be little better than a farmer at a rack rent, to the army, and to the public funds.

It may perhaps be worth inquiring from what beginnings, and

by what steps, we have been brought into this desperate condition. And in search of this we must run up as high as the Revolution.

Most of the nobility and gentry who invited over the Prince of Orange, or attended him in his expedition, were true lovers of their country and its constitution in church and state, and were brought to yield to those breaches in the succession of the Crown, out of a regard to the necessity of the kingdom and the safety of the people, which did, and could only, make them lawful; but without intention of drawing such a practice into precedent, or making it a standing measure by which to proceed in all times to come; and therefore we find their councils ever tended to keep things as much as possible in the old course. But soon after, an underset of men, who had nothing to lose, and had neither born the burden nor heat of the day, found means to whisper in the King's ear that the principles of loyalty in the Church of England were wholly inconsistent with the Revolution. Hence began the early practice of caressing the dissenters, reviling the universities as maintainers of arbitrary power, and reproaching the clergy with the doctrines of divine right, passive obedience, and non-resistance. At the same time, in order to fasten wealthy people to the new government, they proposed those pernicious expedients of borrowing money by vast premiums and at exorbitant interest: a practice as old as Eumenes, one of Alexander's captains who, setting up for himself after the death of his master, persuaded his principal officers to lend him great sums, after which they were forced to follow him for their own security.

This introduced a number of new dextrous men into business and credit. It was argued that the war could not last above two or three campaigns, and that it was easier for the subject to raise a fund for paying interest than to tax them annually to the full expense of the war. Several persons who had small or encumbered estates sold them and turned their money into those funds to great advantage. Merchants, as well as other moneyed men, finding trade was dangerous, pursued the same method. But the war continuing, and growing more expensive, taxes were increased, and funds multiplied every year till they have arrived at the monstrous height we now behold them. And that which was at first a corruption is at last grown necessary and what every good subject must now fall in with, though he may be allowed to wish it might soon have an end: because it is

with a kingdom as with a private fortune, where every new
incumbrance adds a double weight. By this means the wealth of the
nation, that used to be reckoned by the value of land, is now com-
puted by the rise and fall of stocks. And although the foundation of
credit be still the same, and upon a bottom that can never be shaken,
and though all interest be duly paid by the public, yet through the
contrivance and cunning of stock-jobbers, there has been brought in
such a complication of knavery and cozenage, such a mystery of
iniquity, and such an unintelligible jargon of terms to involve it in,
as were never known in any other age or country of the world. I
have heard it affirmed by persons skilled in these calculations, that if
the funds appropriated to the payment of interest and annuities were
added to the yearly taxes, and the four-shilling aid [land tax] strictly
exacted in all counties of the kingdom, it would very near, if not
fully, supply the occasions of the war, at least such a part as in the
opinion of very able persons had been at that time prudent not to
exceed. For I make it a question, whether any wise prince or state, in
the continuance of a war which was not purely defensive, or immediately at his own door, did ever propose that his expense should
perpetually exceed what he was able to impose annually upon his
subjects? Neither if the war lasts many years longer, do I see how
the next generation will be able to begin another; which in the
course of human affairs, and according to the various interests and
ambition of princes, may be as necessary for them as it has been for
us. And had our fathers left us as deeply involved as we are like to
leave our children, I appeal to any man what sort of figure we
should have been able to make these twenty years past. Besides, neither our enemies nor allies are upon the same foot with us in this
particular. France and Holland, our nearest neighbors, and the far-
thest engaged, will much sooner recover themselves after a war. The
first, by the absolute power of the prince, who, being master of the
lives and fortunes of his subjects, will quickly find expedients to pay
his debts. And so will the other, by their prudent administration, the
greatness of their trade, their wonderful parsimony, the willingness
of their people to undergo all kind of taxes, and their justice in
applotting as well as collecting them.[2] But above all, we are to consider that France and Holland fight in the continent, either upon or
near their own territories, and the greatest part of the money circu-

lates among themselves, whereas ours crosses the sea, either to Flanders, Spain, or Portugal, and every penny of it, whether in specie or returns, is so much lost to the nation forever.

Upon these considerations alone, it was the most prudent course imaginable in the Queen to lay hold of the disposition of the people for changing the Parliament and ministry at this juncture, and extricating herself, as soon as possible, out of the pupilage of those who found their accounts only in perpetuating the war. Neither have we the least reason to doubt but the ensuing Parliament will assist Her Majesty with the utmost vigor, till her enemies again be brought to sue for peace, and again offer such terms as will make it both honorable and lasting; only with this difference, that the ministry perhaps will not again refuse them.

> *Audiet pugnas vitio parentum,*
> *Rara juventus.*[3]

NOTES

III. *A Tory View of War and the Moneyed Interest*

[1] For further background see Richard I. Cook, *Jonathan Swift as a Tory Pamphleteer* (Seattle and London, 1967).

[2] Swift's crystal ball completely failed him here.

[3] Perhaps: "Young men (of military age) who would hear of battles, made scarce by fault of their parents." The lines are from Horace's *Odes*, Book I, 2nd ode.

E. *A. Wrigley is a Fellow and Senior Bursar of Peterhouse, Cambridge University and co-founder and member of the Cambridge Group for the History of Population and Social Structure. He is author of* Industrial Growth and Population Change: A Regional Study of the Coalfield Areas of North-west Europe in the Later Nineteenth Century *(Cambridge, 1961), but is best known for his detailed work on family limitation and mortality in pre-industrial England, based on the parish registers of Colyton in Devon. Precise references to his articles on Colyton may be found in the bibliography of his recent survey,* Population and History *(New York, 1969), a book that anyone interested in historical demography will find readable and rewarding. The consistent aim of Wrigley's demographic research has been to expose the deeper causes of social and economic change. Nowhere is this more evident than in this article on London. It is an imaginative, yet well-grounded and disciplined assessment of London's role as a modernizing force in England before the industrial revolution. This article is reprinted with the permission of the Past and Present Society and the author from* Past and Present, A Journal of Historical Studies, *No. 37 (July 1967). World copyright: The Past and Present Society, Corpus Christi College, Oxford, England.*

IV

A Simple Model of London's Importance in Changing English Society and Economy 1650–1750*

BY E. A. WRIGLEY

"Soon London will be all England": James I

Toward the end of the seventeenth century London became the largest city in Europe. The population of Paris had reached about 400,000 by the beginning of the seventeenth century and was nearing 500,000 toward its end, but thereafter grew very little for a further century. At the time of the 1801 census its population was still just less than 550,000. London, on the other hand, grew rapidly throughout the seventeenth and eighteenth centuries. Its exact population at any time before the first census is a matter for argument, but in round figures it appears to have grown from about 200,000 in 1600 to perhaps 400,000 in 1650, 575,000 by the end of the century, 675,000 in 1750 and 900,000 in 1800.[1] London and Paris were much larger than other cities in Europe during these two centuries and

* I am greatly indebted to Dr. P. Abrams, Professor T. C. Barker, Mr. P. Laslett and Dr. R. S. Schofield for their comments on an earlier draft of this paper.

each was very much larger than any rival in the same country. The contrast between the size and rates of growth of the two cities is particularly striking when it is borne in mind that until the last half of the eighteenth century, when the rate of growth of population in England increased sharply, the total population of France was about four times as large as that of England. In 1650 about 2.5 percent of the population of France lived in Paris; in 1750 the figure was little changed. London, on the other hand, housed about 7 percent of England's total population in 1650 and about 11 percent in 1750. Only in Holland does any one city appear to have contained such a high percentage of the total national population. Amsterdam in 1650 was already a city of about 150,000 people and contained 8 percent of the Dutch total. But Amsterdam by this time had ceased to grow quickly and a century later had increased only to about 200,000, or 9 percent of the total.[2]

These rough facts suggest immediately that it may be valuable to look more closely at the rapid growth of London between 1650 and 1750. Anything which distinguished England from other parts of Europe during the century preceding the industrial revolution is necessarily a subject of particular interest since it may help to throw light on the origins of that extraordinary and momentous period of rapid change which has transformed country after country across the face of the globe.

I

It is convenient to begin by examining first some demographic aspects of the rapid growth of population which took place in London. The implications of London's growth can be seen from a very simple model. The rates and quantities embodied in the model are at best approximations, and it is probable that within the next five years work already in train will make it possible to give much more precise estimates than can be made as yet; but it would require a radical revision of the assumptions used here to upset the general argument.

We may note first that since the population of London rose by about 275,000 between 1650 and 1750 it will, on an average, have been increasing annually by 2,750. Secondly, it seems clear that the crude death rate in London was substantially higher than the crude birth rate over the period as a whole. The gap between the two rates is difficult to estimate accurately and varied considerably during the hundred years in question, being apparently much higher in the last three or four decades of the period than earlier. The difference between the two rates is most unlikely to have been less than 10 per 1,000 per annum over the century as a whole, however, and may well have been considerably larger.[3] For the purpose of illustrating the implications of the model we may assume that this figure held throughout. Thus at the time when the population of London was, say, 500,000, the shortfall of births each year is assumed to be 5,000. At that time to make good this shortfall and to permit an annual increase of the total population of 2,750, the net immigration into London must have been about 8,000 per annum. Toward the end of the period, when the population of London was well above half a million and the gap between birth and death rates was at its greatest, the net figure must have been considerably larger than this. At other times it may have been rather less.

In any population it is normally the young and single who migrate most readily. There is a growing volume of evidence that in England in the seventeenth and eighteenth centuries mobility before marriage was very high but was reduced once marriage had taken place.[4] In view of this, let us assume, as a part of the demographic model of London's growth, that the mean age of those migrating into London was twenty years. Given the mortality conditions of the day any large group of twenty-year-olds coming into London would represent the survivors of a birth population at least half as large again.[5] Some 12,000 births, therefore, in the rest of England and elsewhere were earmarked, as it were, each year to make it possible for London's population to grow as it did during this period. Once again this is a very rough figure, too high for a part of the century, too low for the later decades, but useful as a means of illustrating the nature of the general demographic relationship between London and the rest of the country.

One further assumption will make the significance of this relationship clearer. If the average surplus of births over deaths in provincial England was 5 per 1,000 per annum (and assuming for the moment that London grew by immigration from England alone), then it follows that London's growth was absorbing the natural increase of a population of some 2.5 million.[6] The total population of England excluding London was only about 5 million (varying, of course, a little over the century in question), and there were some areas, especially in the west and north, in which for much of this century there was either no natural increase or even a natural decrease of population.

In view of the general demographic history of England at this time London's demographic characteristics assume a singular importance. For there are some surprising features in English demographic history in the century 1650–1750. Family reconstitution studies show that in some parts of the country at least this was a time of very late first marriage for women. And the reduced fertility which is usually associated with a rise in the average age of women at first marriage appears to have been still further diminished in places by the practice of family limitation. Moreover, there is some evidence that age-specific mortality rates, especially of young children, were higher at this time than either earlier or later, so that natural increase was much reduced or was replaced by a surplus of deaths over births.[7]

The preliminary results of a large-scale survey of parish register material using straightforward aggregative methods[8] suggest that these trends were least evident in the home counties and the Midlands, the areas from which access to London was easiest, and it may prove to be the case that a substantial surplus of births continued to be characteristic of these counties throughout the century 1650–1750, but that instead of building up local populations the surplus was siphoned off into London to counterbalance the burial surplus there and to enable it to continue to grow quickly at a time when the rest of the country was barely holding its own.[9] The absence of any great upward press of numbers in England as a whole in this century meant that population growth did not frustrate a slow rise in real incomes, in contrast with the preceding hundred years.[10] Yet this did not prevent a very marked growth in the country's largest city.

One further implication of the demography of London's growth is worth stressing. Let us assume that there was a time when the population of London was 500,000 and the population of the rest of the kingdom was 5 million. Let it further be assumed that the birth rate was uniformly at a rate of 34 per 1,000 (this is an arbitrary assumption, but too little is known of the age and sex structure of these populations and of the prevailing age-specific fertility rates to provide substantially more accurate figures; and in any case the main line of the argument would be unaffected except by radical adjustments). If this were so, then the number of births taking place annually in London would be 17,000 and in the rest of the country 170,000. If we assume that all the children born in London remained in London, and if to the figure of 17,000 children born each year in London is added the 12,000 born in the provinces and needed to maintain London's growth, then it is apparent that the survivors to adult years of almost one sixth of all the births taking place in the country (29,000 out of a total of 187,000) would be living in London twenty years or so after the arrival of the birth cohort used as an illustration.

It does not, of course, follow from this that a sixth of the national total of adults lived in London. The infant and child mortality rates of those born in London were far higher than elsewhere, so that many fewer of these children survived to adult years. Indeed, the fact that this was so is one of the main reasons for the large inflow of migrants from outside London. The calculation assumes, moreover, that immigrants to London came only from England, whereas there was also, of course, a steady stream of young Scots, Welsh, and Irish into the capital. Nor should it be forgotten that London was a great international center with substantial Dutch, French, and German communities.

On the other hand, all the calculations made above are based on figures of *net* immigration into London. The gross figures must certainly have been considerably higher since there was at all times a flow of migrants out of London as well as a heavier flow inward. If therefore one were attempting to estimate the proportion of the total adult population of England who had at some stage in their lives had direct experience of life in the great city, a sixth or an even higher fraction is as plausible a guess as any other.[11]

II

If it is fair to assume that one adult in six in England in this period had had direct experience of London life, it is probably also fair to assume that this must have acted as a powerful solvent of the customs, prejudices, and modes of action of traditional, rural England. The leaven of change would have a much better chance of transforming the lump than in, say, France, even if living in Paris produced the same change of attitude and action as living in London, since there were proportionately four or five times fewer Frenchmen caught up in Parisian life than Englishmen in London life. Possibly there is a threshold level in a situation of this type, beneath which the values and attitudes of a traditional, rural society are very little affected by the existence of a large city, but above which a sufficiently large proportion of the population is exposed to a different way of life to effect a slow transformation in rural society. Too little is known of the sociological differences between life in London and life in provincial England to afford a clear perception of the impact of London's growth upon the country as a whole. Some things, however, are already known, and other points can be adumbrated in the hope that more research will resolve present uncertainties.

London was so very much bigger than any other town in the country that the lives of the inhabitants of London were inevitably very different from the lives of men living in the middle rank of towns, such as Leicester or Derby, where local landed society could continue to dominate many aspects of town life and the ties with the surrounding countryside were ancient and intimate. Family life in London, at least for the very large number who had come to London from elsewhere, was necessarily different from the family life of those who lived within five or ten miles of their birthplace all their lives. Near relatives were less likely to live close at hand. Households in the central parts of London were larger on average than those in provincial England. And this was not because the conjugal families contained more children but because other members of the households were more numerous. There were many more lodgers than in the countryside, as well as servants, apprentices, and other kin in varying proportions according to the social type of the parish.[12]

Outside the household, moreover, a far higher proportion of day-to-day contacts was inevitably casual. Urban sociologists describe the characteristic tendency of modern city life to cause individuals in these circumstances to be treated not as occupying an invariable status position in the community, but in terms of the role associated with the particular transaction which gave rise to the fleeting contact. They stress the encouragement which city life gives to what Weber called "rational" as opposed to "traditional" patterns of action and the tendency for contract to replace custom. The "'aping' of one's betters," which often attracted unfavorable comment at the time and which has sometimes been seen as a powerful influence in establishing new patterns of consumption, is a common product of social situations like that in which the inhabitants of London found themselves at this period. Coleman has recently suggested that in the seventeenth century there was probably a backward-sloping supply curve for labor.[13] It would be fascinating to know how far the new patterns of consumption behavior established in London may have helped to reduce any preference for leisure rather than high earnings. There is much literary evidence of the shiftless and disorderly behavior of many members of London's population at this time, but there were important countervailing influences at work upon the bulk of the population. The shop, a most important, new influence upon consumer behavior, was a normal feature of the London scene by the latter half of the seventeenth century.[14] Sugar, tea, and tobacco had become articles of mass consumption by the early eighteenth century. Life in London probably encouraged a certain educational achievement in a wider spectrum of the population than might be expected. In 1838–39 fewer men and women were unable to sign their names on marriage than anywhere else in the country (marks were made as a substitute for signatures by only 12 percent of grooms and 24 percent of brides, whereas the national averages were 33 percent and 49 percent respectively). How long this differential had existed is not yet known, but if it proves to have been true of earlier periods in London's history also, it suggests that the London environment put a high premium on at least a minimum degree of literacy.[15]

There were many ways in which seventeenth-century London differed from a modern city. Glass, for example, notes that in 1695 the proportion of wealthy and substantial households was highest near the center of London and tended to fall with distance from the center, being very low outside the city walls (apart from

St. Dunstan in the West). "This kind of gradient is in contrast to that found in the modern city, in which the centrifugal movement of population has occurred particularly among the middle classes."[16] In this respect London was still in 1695 a pre-industrial city, but in general London was far removed from the classical type of pre-industrial city. Sjoberg's account of the typical pre-industrial city may serve as a means of underlining the "modernity" of London at this period. He draws illustrative material not only from the cities of Asia today, from ancient Mesopotamia and the Near East, and from the classical cultures of the Mediterranean, but also from medieval Europe.

Sjoberg's pre-industrial city is fed because the city houses the ruling elite. The elite "induces the peasantry to increase its production and relinquish some of its harvest to the urban community." It "must persuade many persons subsisting, relative to industrial standards, on the very margins of existence, under conditions of near starvation or malnutrition, to surrender food and other items that they themselves could readily use."[17] The farmer "brings his produce to the urban centers at irregular intervals and in varying amounts."[18] Within the city the merchants, those responsible for the organization of much of its economic life, are "ideally excluded from membership of the elite." A few manage to achieve high status under sufferance, but "most are unequivocally in the lower class or outcaste groups."[19] The chief reason for excluding merchants is that they necessarily meet all types of people, making casual contacts with men in all positions, and are therefore a menace to the stability of the existing societal arrangements.[20] Men are largely indifferent to the discipline of the clock and only half attentive to the passage of time. Almost all transactions, however trivial, are concluded only after long haggling.[21] There is little specialization of function in craft industrial production, though a good deal of product specialization.[22]

In the pre-industrial city the dominant type of family is the extended family, though necessity may prevent it developing so fully in the lower classes as in the elite.[23] Marriage takes place early, and before marriage a man does not reach full adult status.[24] On marriage the bride normally expects to move into the household of her husband's family.[25] "However, as industrial-urbanization becomes firmly entrenched, the large extended household is no longer the ideal toward which people strive. The conjugal family system now becomes the accepted and often the preferred norm." This occurs because "a fluid, flexible, small family unit is necessarily the dominant form in a social order characterized by extensive social and spatial mobility."[26]

In his anxiety to correct the naive assumptions of some sociologists about cities in the past and in the developing world today, Sjoberg may well have been tempted to straitjacket his material at times in a way which does violence to history. At all events, not only London but all England had moved far from his archetypal pre-industrial society by the seventeenth century. The conjugal family system was firmly established in England at that time. On marriage a man and his wife set up a new household.[27] And both sexes married late, later than in England today, and far later than in extra-European societies in which marriage, for women at least, almost invariably occurred at or even before puberty.[28] Where three generations did live together in the same household this was not usually because a son on marriage brought his wife to his parents' home, but because a grandparent came to live in the household of a married son or daughter when no longer able to look after himself or herself, for example on the death of a spouse.

London shared these sociological and demographic characteristics with the rest of the country. Three-generational households were possibly rather commoner in the wealthier parts of London than was usual elsewhere,[29] but everywhere the conjugal family appears to have been the dominant form. The status of merchants in London varied with their wealth, but it would be difficult to argue that they were largely excluded from the ruling elite. The provisioning of London was secured by an elaborate and sophisticated set of economic institutions and activities, and many of the farmers who sent their produce to the London market geared their land to commodity production in a thoroughly "modern" fashion.[30] In short, whereas pre-industrial cities might grow large and powerful without in any way undermining the structure of traditional society, a city like London in the later seventeenth century was so constituted sociologically, demographically, and economically that it could well reinforce and accelerate incipient change.

What might be called the demonstration effect of London's wealth and growth, for instance, played an important part in engendering changes elsewhere. London contained many men of great wealth and power whose sources of wealth did not lie in the land and who found it possible to maintain power and status without acquiring large landed estates.[31] Indeed in as much as it was the backing of London which assured the parliamentary armies of success in their struggle with the King, London could be said at the beginning of the century 1650–1750 to have shown that it possessed the power necessary to sway the rest of the country to its will. In the provinces in the later seventeenth and early eighteenth centuries there were increasingly large numbers of men of wealth and position who stood outside the traditional landed system. These were the group whom Everitt has recently termed the "pseudo-gentry." They formed "that class of leisured and predominantly urban families who, by their manner of life, were commonly regarded as gentry, though they were not supported by a landed estate."[32] Their links with London were close and their journeys thither frequent. They were urban in their habit of life but would have been powerless to protect their position in society if London had not existed. London both provided them with a pattern of behavior, and, because of its immense economic strength and prestige, protected them from any hostility on the part of the traditional elements in society. London was, as it were, both their normative reference group[33] and their guarantee against the withdrawal of status respect.

III

The social and economic changes of the seventeenth and eighteenth centuries reached their culmination in the industrial revolution. Although this was far more than simply an economic phenomenon, economic change was what defined it. It is natural, therefore, to consider the strictly economic effects of London's rapid growth as well as the demographic and sociological changes which accompanied it.

The importance of the London food market in promoting change in the agriculture of Kent and East Anglia from an early date has long been recognized. Fisher showed how even during the century before 1650 London was large enough to exercise a great influ-

ence upon the agriculture of the surrounding counties, causing a
rapid spread of market gardening, increasing local specialization, and
encouraging the wholesalers to move back up the chain of production and exchange to engage directly in the production of food or to
sink capital in the improvement of productive facilities. The influence of the London food market was "not merely in the direction of
increased production, but also in that of specialization, and in that
direction lay agricultural progress"—"Poulterers made loans to war-
reners and themselves bred poultry. Fruiterers helped to establish
orchards and leased them when established. Butchers themselves
became graziers." Between 1650 and 1750 it is reasonable to suppose
that the demand for food in the London market must have increased
by about three-quarters since population increased roughly in that
proportion. The increased demand was met from home sources
rather than by import, and it follows that all those changes which
Fisher observed in the preceding century were spread over a larger
area and intensified.[34]

Once more it is interesting to work initially in terms of a very
crude model and review its implications, though in this case the
orders of magnitude assumed are even more open to question than
those embodied in the demographic model used earlier. Suppose,
firstly, that in 1650 the population of London was 400,000 and the
population of the rest of the country 5,100,000 and that in the country outside the metropolis the proportion of the male labor force
engaged in agriculture was 60 percent.[35] This would imply that
3,060,000 were dependent on agriculture (those directly employed
plus their families), and that every 100 farming families supported a
total of 80 families who earned their living in other ways. If in the
next century the population of London rose to 675,000 and that of
the whole country to 6,140,000[36] but the proportion engaged in
agriculture outside the capital remained the same, then the agricultural population in 1750 would have numbered 3,279,000 and every
100 farming families would have supported 87 other families.[37] This
in turn would imply a rise in agricultural productivity per head of
about 4 percent. This figure is certainly too low, however, since this
was a century of rising exports of grain, especially after 1700. By
1750 exports formed about 6 percent of total grain production; at
the beginning of the century they were only a little over 1

percent.[38] Grain was not, of course, the only product of agriculture, but there were parallel movements in some other agricultural products. Imports of wool, for example, fell markedly in the early eighteenth century, while domestic production rose. There was a sharp rise in the production of mutton, though not of beef, and some minor agricultural products, notably hops, were grown in greater quantities.[39] All in all, it is reasonable to suppose that these changes represent a rise of not less than 5 percent in agricultural productivity per head. This, in combination with the rise which must have occurred in meeting London's demands, suggests a rise of about 10 percent in agricultural productivity per head.

A rise of 10 percent in productivity is far from trivial. It could have released a substantial amount of purchasing power into other channels as the price of foodstuffs fell and at the same time have made it possible for a substantially higher proportion of the population to be drawn into secondary and tertiary employment. The rise, however, is almost certainly understated at 10 percent, since the percentage of the total labor force outside the capital engaged in agriculture probably fell somewhat, implying a still steeper rise in agricultural productivity per head. It has been suggested, indeed, that the numbers engaged in agriculture actually fell in the first half of the eighteenth century.[40] This is an extreme hypothesis. Suppose, however, that the population dependent on agriculture rose only from 3,060,000 to 3,150,000 between 1650 and 1750, and not to 3,279,000 as in the first variant of the model (that is, the proportion engaged in agriculture fell over the century from 60 to 57.5 percent of the total population outside London). If this were the case, and making the suggested allowance also for growing exports and declining imports, then the rise in agricultural productivity per head would be about 13 percent during the century. This is not an extreme figure. Indeed it is very probably too low. Deane and Cole suggest that the rise may have been as high as 25 percent in the first half of the eighteenth century alone.[41] But a rise in agricultural productivity even of this magnitude is a formidable achievement and goes far to suggesting how a pre-industrial economy can slowly lever itself up by its own bootstraps to the point where a rapid growth of secondary industry can occur. The fact that income elasticity of demand for food is substantially less than unity makes it

easy to understand how grain prices might sag in these circumstances and how considerable the diversion of purchasing power into
the products of secondary industry may have been.

It does not follow from the above, of course, that the considerable rise in agricultural productivity per head which appears to
have taken place was due to London's growth in its entirety. What
can be said is that the steady growth in demand for food in London
as population there increased, necessarily caused great changes in the
methods used on farms over a wider and wider area, in the commercial organization of the food market, and in the transport of food. It
must also have tended to increase the proportion of people living
outside London who were not engaged directly in agriculture, since
tertiary employment was sure to increase in these circumstances.
Drovers, carters, badgers, brokers, cattle dealers, corn chandlers, hos-
tlers, innkeepers, and the like grew more and more numerous as
larger and larger fractions of the year's flocks and crops were consumed at a distance from the areas in which they were produced. As
yet it is difficult to quantify the changes in employment structure
satisfactorily, but many parish registers began regularly to record
occupations from the later seventeenth or early eighteenth centuries
onward,[42] and it is therefore a fairly straightforward matter to produce a picture of changing employment structure for this period for
many parts of the country, given sufficient time and effort. Such an
exercise may well reveal not only a slow fall in the proportion of
men directly employed on the land, but also differences in the
timing and speed of change related to the accessibility of the market.

There were other ways in which the immense demands of the
London market helped to promote economic and technological
changes in the structure of English production during this period.
The inhabitants of London needed fuel as well as food, and before
the end of the sixteenth century they were beginning to abandon
wood for coal as the chief source of domestic fuel. The annual shipment of coal south along the coast from Tyneside and Wearside had
reached about 650,000 tons by 1750, having doubled in the preceding
hundred years.[43] This represented a very substantial fraction of the
total production of coal in the northeast, and perhaps as much as a
sixth of the total national production. Coal production in England
was on a much larger scale during these years than in any other

country in Europe, and the coal industry was the forcing house for many of the technical improvements which were to come to a fuller fruition during the classical years of the industrial revolution. Newcomen's engine was developed largely to meet the drainage problem in coal mines and found its largest sale among mine owners. And it was in the Newcastle area that the first railways were constructed to enable horses to pull much heavier loads from the pitheads to the coal staithes. The first beginnings of the new technology of the steam engine and the railway lay in the eighteenth-century coal mining industry, and one of its chief supports in turn was the large and steadily growing demand for coal afforded by the London coal market.[44]

Furthermore, the increased shipment of coal down the east coast to the Thames required a major expansion in shipping capacity. Nef estimated that during this period about half the total tonnage of the English merchant marine was engaged in the Newcastle coal trade.

> *When we add, to the ships employed by the coal trade from Durham and Northumberland, the ships employed by that from Scottish and west-coast ports, it seems likely that, at the time of the Restoration, the tonnage of colliers had come to exceed the tonnage of all other British merchantmen. The coal trade from Newcastle to London was relatively no less important in the late seventeenth century than in the late eighteenth century, when, Adam Smith observes, it "Employs more shipping than all the carrying trades of England."*[45]

Apart from serving as an important reservoir of trained seamen in time of war, the growth of the coal trade played a notable part in the expansion of the English shipbuilding industry and the development of vessels which could be worked by far fewer hands per ton of cargo.[46]

The crude quantification of the importance of the London coal trade can be approached in a different way. If output per man-year of coal miners at this time was about 200 tons in favorable circumstances,[47] then by 1750 some 3,500 men must have been engaged in digging London's coal. Gregory King supposed that about 50,000 men were employed in his day as common seamen,[48] and it is therefore probable that at least a further 10,000 men[49] were employed on the colliers easing their way up and down the east coast (though the ships were laid up in the winter so that the employment was heavily seasonal). In addition the movement of coal to the staithes must have been the livelihood of hundreds of carters, wagoners and coal heavers.[50] In all the total employment afforded by the London coal trade outside London (except in as much as the sailors were Londoners) may well have risen from about 8,000 in the mid-seventeenth century to 15,000 a century later. Including their families increases the numbers directly dependent on the coal trade to about 25,000 and 50,000 people respectively. The multiplier effect of the presence and growth of London is well illustrated by this example. Secondary and tertiary employment increased considerably at a distance as well as in London itself.[51] No doubt the flourishing state of the mines around Newcastle and the consequent local demand for food produced in miniature in that area the sort of changes in agriculture which London had already produced in the home counties at an earlier date.

London's importance as a center of consumption, which prompted Defoe in 1724 to write of the "general dependence of the whole country upon the city of London . . . for the consumption of its produce,"[52] sprang not only from its size but also from the relatively high level of wages prevailing there. Gilboy's work on eighteenth-century wage rates provides evidence of this. "The London laborer had the highest wages of any group we have examined. In the first part of the century, at least, he had surplus income to spend and there is every indication that real wages improved as the century progressed."[53] When George remarked that "as early as 1751 it was said that the shoes sold in London were chiefly made in the country where labor was cheaper,"[54] she was touching upon a general phenomenon. Men and women were put in work over much of the home counties and Midlands because their labor was much cheaper than the labor of London artisans and journeymen. The existence of a mass of relatively well paid labor in London played a major part in creating new levels of real wages and new standards of consumption in the century after the Restoration, when "there was a rise in internal demand which permanently affected the level of expectation of most classes in English society."[55]

Access to the London market was the making of many a manufacturer and a forcing house of change in methods of manufacture, in marketing techniques, and in systems of distribution. Josiah Wedgwood was drawn thither.

> [He] was quick to realize the value of a warehouse in London. For high quality goods he needed a market accustomed to "fine prices." He was not likely to find it in the annual market fairs of Stafford-shire—the time-honored entrepôt of their county's pots—nor among the country folk who haggled over their wares straight from the crateman's back or the hawker's basket, and to whom expense was the controlling factor in deciding their custom.⁵⁶

But this did not isolate him from mass markets. Once having secured the custom of the London elite he was able also to sell his less expensive lines to the middle and lower classes. He studied closely the idiosyncracies of each group at home and abroad and produced goods designed to appeal peculiarly to each of them.

> By these means Wedgwood had created an enormous demand for his ware both ornamental and useful. The upper classes bought both, but mainly the expensive ornamental wares, and in imitation of their social superiors the lower classes bought the useful.⁵⁷

Moreover, his efforts to command a countrywide market drew him into canal construction and the promotion of turnpike trusts.⁵⁸

Wedgwood was one of the most original and successful entre-preneurs of his age. The actions of his fellows seldom show the same appreciation of the opportunities for new methods. And his product may have lent itself more than most to illustrating the sense in which a triumph in London opened up the markets of the whole country. Yet it is reasonable to quote his example, for his success hinged upon an economic and social fact of importance before Wedgwood's time —through the London market the whole country might be won.

> For a fashionable appeal in London had a vital influence even in the depths of the provinces. The woman in Newcastle upon Tyne who insisted on a dinner service of "Arabesque Border" before her local shopkeeper had even heard of it wanted it because it was "much used in London at present," and she steadfastly "declin'd taking any till she had seen that pattern."⁵⁹

The London market, of course, supported many industries within the city itself. Silk weaving at Spitalfields, brewing, gin manufacture, watch and clock making, cabinet making, the manufacture of soap, glass and furniture, and a wide range of luxury industries have all received notice. They all added to the economic weight of London and furthered its growth, though few of them produced striking technological advances or were transformed into path-breaking industries during the industrial revolution. They were impressive in their range but were not for the most part greatly different in kind from the industries to be found in large cities elsewhere in Europe.

London's prime economic foundation, however, had long been her trade rather than her industry. English trade expanded greatly during the century and London enjoyed the lion's share of it. It has been estimated that a quarter of the population depended directly on employment in port trades in 1700 and, allowing for the multiplier effect of this employment, "it is clear that the greatness of London depended, before everything else, on the activity in the port of London."[60] London's merchants, not her manufacturers, dominated her activities economically and politically, and it has long been a momentous question how best to conceive the mechanism by which the large fortunes made in London from commerce helped to transform the national economy.

Many London merchants bought land in the country. Some in doing so hastened agricultural change. The banking and general commercial facilities of London were available to men throughout England and played some part in financing the agricultural and industrial changes which occurred in many parts of the country. The success of the London merchants fostered a change of attitude toward trade. It helped to fulfill one of the necessary conditions of rapid economic growth in Leibenstein's analysis—that "the rate of growth of the new entrepreneurial class must be sufficiently rapid and its success, power, and importance sufficiently evident so that entrepreneurship, in some form or other, becomes an 'honorific' mode of life in men's minds."[61] But it is doubtful whether the prime connection between the growth of London and the great changes going forward outside London is to be sought in points of this type. London's trading pre-eminence is perhaps better conceived as acting more powerfully at one remove. It was the fact that the growth of her trading wealth enabled London herself to grow, to develop as a center of consumption, and to dominate English society which formed her greatest contribution to the total process of change in the country as a whole. The relationship between rising trading wealth and economic and social change outside London was primarily, as it were, indirect, springing from the changes which the steady growth of London provoked elsewhere in ways already discussed. While other big European cities during this century could do little more than maintain their population size, London almost doubled her population. Already as large as any other European city in 1650, it was much larger than any rival a century later. In order to meet the food and fuel requirements of a city of this size old methods in many cases were simply inadequate. And the new methods developed often produced those substantial increases in productivity per head which form the most promising base for a continuing beneficent spiral of economic activity.

IV

It is always well to be chary of accepting explanations which explain too much. The industrial revolution in England was a vastly complex congerie of changes so diverse that it would be absurd to suppose that any one development of earlier times can serve to explain more than a part of it. It will not do to pyramid everything upon changes in the supply of capital, or the burgeoning of nonconformist entrepreneurship, or an increase in upward social mobility. Complicated results had, in this case at least, complicated origins. It is therefore no part of this argument that the growth of London in the century before 1750 was the sole engine of change in the country, to which all the chief preconditions of the industrial revolution can be traced. But London's growth is a fine vantage point from which to review much that was happening. The period between the rapid rise in population and economic activity which ended early in the seventeenth century and the onset of renewed rapid growth of population and production in the last third of the eighteenth century has remained something of an enigma in economic history. It was a period in which population grew little if at all over the country as a whole. In some areas for long periods it was probably falling. Many of the chief indices of production, when estimates of them are possible, show comparatively little change and

certainly grew much less spectacularly than either before or after.[62]
There was a slow, if cumulatively important, improvement in agricultural productivity because of the introduction of new crops like
roots and clover, and because there was both a slow drift of land
into enclosure and increasing flexiblity of land use in the champaign
areas. Trade and industry expanded but in general at a modest rate.

How then should this period be understood? It was immediately followed by a period which saw the birth of a radically new
economic system, the transition from the pre-industrial to the
industrial world. Was England in 1750 greatly improved when compared with the England of the Commonwealth as a springboard for
rapid economic and social change? Was the triggering off of the
period of rapid growth connected, as it were, in great depth with
the preceding period, or could it have occurred almost equally readily at a considerably earlier period? It is against a background of
questions of this type that the growth of London appears so strategi-
cally important.

There were a number of developments tending to promote
economic change and growth in the hundred years 1650–1750.
Apart from the growth of London, for example, there were the agricultural advances which improved animal husbandry and lay behind
the secular tendency of grain prices to fall (thus helping real wages
to rise where money wages were unchanged or improved). Or again
there is the probability that because of stable numbers and a modest
increase in production the national product/population ratio rose
significantly. The idea of critical mass has been invoked recently as a
concept of value in conveying the nature of the importance of
cumulative slow change in the period immediately preceding rapid
industrialization.[63] It could be used appropriately of any of these
progressive changes, but is particularly telling when related to London's growth. It is not so much that London's growth was independently more important than the other major changes which modified
English economy and society during the century, as that it is a most
convenient point of entry into the study of the whole range of
changes which took place, especially since some aspects of London's
growth can be quantified fairly satisfactorily. Both the changes in
agriculture which took place and the failure of national population
to increase are closely intertwined with the growth of London, but

not with each other. Demographically the existence of London counterbalanced any "natural" growth of population in much of the rest of the country, and the necessity of feeding London created market conditions over great tracts of England which fostered agricultural improvement and reduced economic regionalism. The absence or slightness of population growth overall, had it not been for London's expansion, might well have inhibited agricultural change.

V

It is possible to write out a check-list of changes which by their occurrence in a traditional and predominantly agricultural society tend to promote social and economic change and may succeed in engendering the magic "take-off." On any such list the following items are likely to appear (the list is far from being exhaustive).

A. Economic changes

1. The creation of a single national market (or at least very much larger regional markets) for a wide range of goods and services, so that specialization of function may be developed and economies of scale exploited.

2. The fostering of changes in agricultural methods which increase the productivity of those engaged in agriculture so that the cost of foodstuffs will fall and real wages rise; so that a rising proportion of the work force can find employment in secondary and tertiary activities without prejudicing the supply of food or raising its price inordinately; and possibly so that a larger export income can be derived from the sale of surplus food supplies abroad.

3. The development of new sources of raw material supply which are not subject to the problem of rising marginal costs of production in the manner characteristic of raw materials in pre-industrial economies.[64] This occurs when mineral raw materials are substituted for animal or vegetable products (for example, coal for wood) and may well be accompanied by important technological changes contrived to overcome novel production problems (for example, the Newcomen engine or the coke-fired blast furnace).

4. The provision of a wider range of commercial and credit facilities so that the latent strengths of the economy can be more

expertly, quickly, and cheaply mobilized. Under this head might fall, for example, the cluster of changes accompanying and reflected in the establishment and development of the Bank of England.

5. The creation of a better transport network to reduce the cost of moving goods from place to place; to make it possible for goods to move freely at all seasons of the year in spite of inclement weather; to shorten the time involved and so to economize in the capital locked up in goods in transit; and more generally to foster all the changes of the type mentioned in (1) above.

6. The securing of a steady rise in real incomes so that the volume of effective demand rises *in toto* and its composition changes with the diversion of an increased fraction of the total purchasing power into the market for the products of industry. This is closely connected with (2) above.

B. *Demographic changes*

7. The interplay between fertility, mortality, and nuptiality must be such that population does not expand too rapidly and this must hold true for some time after real incomes per head have begun to trend upward. If this is not so, the cycle of events which is often termed Malthusian can hardly be avoided—there is a great danger that real incomes will be depressed and economic growth will peter out. This happened often enough before the industrial revolution. Leibenstein remarks with justice that ". . . historical evidence would seem to suggest . . . [that] it was the rate of population growth, whether or not induced by economic expansion, that ate up the fruits of expansion and resulted in expansion in the aggregate sense without much improvement per head."[65] Too rapid population growth can, of course, be avoided by the existence of areas of surplus mortality which counterbalance those of surplus fertility as well as by the existence of a rough balance of births and deaths in each area throughout the country.

C. *Sociological changes*

8. The steady spread of environments in which the socialization process produces individuals "rationally" rather than "tradition-ally" oriented in their values and patterns of action.

9. The establishment of conditions in which upward social mobility need not necessarily lead to what might be called the recir-culation of ability within traditional society but can also produce a

steady strengthening of new groups who do not subscribe to the
same priorities or use their wealth and status in the same ways as the
upper levels of traditional society.

10. The spread of the practice of aping one's betters. When
consumption habits become more fluid and the new styles and wants
of the upper ranks are rapidly suffused throughout the lower ranks
of society, men experience a stronger spur to improve their incomes,
and the first steps are taken toward the era of uniform, mass consumption. To be aware that a change in one's pattern of life is possible and to consider it desirable is a vital first step to the securing of
the change itself. No doubt this awareness is never wholly absent,
but it may be present in widely varying intensities and its increase is
an important stimulant to economic change.[66]

This check-list is, of course, also a catalogue of the ways in
which the growth of London may have promoted social and economic change in England in the period between the dying away of
the economic upthrust of Elizabethan and early Stuart times and the
sharp acceleration at the end of the eighteenth century. It may also
be represented diagrammatically in a form which enables the interconnection between some of the items on the list to be appreciated
more concisely.

Many of the changes are connected with the growth of
London in two directions, at once produced or emphasized by London's growth and serving in turn to reinforce the growth process, a
typical positive feedback situation, to borrow a term from communication engineering. In some cases growth was possible only because
of this mutual relationship. For example, the growth of London
could not have gone very far if it had not produced substantial
change in agriculture over large areas and brought about sufficient
improvements in the transport system to make it feasible to maintain
a reliable and moderately cheap movement of food surpluses from
the home counties and East Anglia into London. In other cases there
is no return connection between London and one of the aspects of
social and economic change promoted by its growth. For example,
the continued growth of London had much to do with the slightness
of population growth over the country as a whole, but it would be
difficult to argue that the reverse was also true. And in still other
cases, even though no arrow is drawn in on the diagram, it is obvious

that some degree of connection must have existed. A link may be presumed, for instance, between higher real wages (6) and improved transport (5), or between new consumption patterns (10) and agricultural change (2). Only those connections which appear more direct and more important have been shown—though, of course, a connection between any two boxes can be shown by moving around the network: for example, there is no direct link shown between improved transport (5) and higher real incomes (6), but an indirect link exists via agricultural change (2) and by other more circuitous routes.

Sometimes, where a connection is shown only in one direction, the absence of a return arrow may seem arbitrary: for example in the case of new forms of social mobility (9) and "rational" not "traditional" behavior (8). In several of these cases there was certainly some return effect, and with equal propriety but on different assumptions a return arrow might have been drawn. The act of judgment involved here demands careful scrutiny because the relationships which are expressed by a single arrow are of particular interest. Where there are arrows in both directions this implies an interconnection so intimate that in some ways it will prove pointless to distinguish between them. They are jointly parts of a larger situation which it is convenient to record separately for clarity's sake and for some analytic purposes. Where an arrow in only one direction exists, however, a clearer distinction, a lack of interdependence, and in some cases a causal sequence is implied. For example, the diagram suggests that the growth of London stimulated the development of "rational" modes of behavior (8), but that this in turn did not have any important direct return effect on London's growth (though very soon an indirect path is opened up via (4), better commercial facilities). This is a different type of relationship from that between London and improved land and water communication (5) which is represented as facilitating the growth of London directly. The latter is shown as a chicken and egg situation, as it were; the former is not. In the one case the positive feedback is direct; in the other this is not so.

A special interest attaches to boxes (6), higher real incomes, (2), agricultural change, and (8), "rational" rather than "traditional" behavior. They are key nodes in the system, connected to more

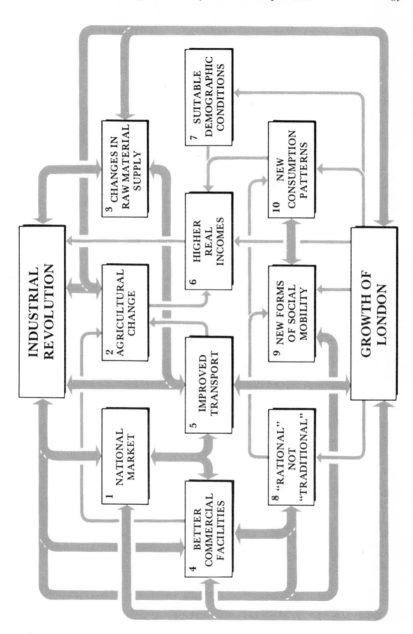

boxes than others and tied into the system by single as well as double arrows. If the relationships are correctly stated it is these aspects of the total social and economic situation which should prove most repaying to future analyses (and possibly also (5), improved transport). Unhappily the system embodies far too many subjective judgments to justify any but conditional statements about it in its present form.

The diagram underlines the poverty of our knowledge of many things which it is important to know. Sometimes the absence of an arrow betrays simple ignorance as much as an act of judgment. For example, it is impossible to feel sure as yet about the nature of the relationship between the demographic situation in the period 1650–1750 and economic and social change. Some points seem clear. It is reasonable to suppose that the relationship indicated in the diagram between population balance and higher real incomes is accurate. But other points are far from clear. It is very uncertain whether the reverse relationship holds good—that is to say whether higher real incomes tended to retard population growth, and in what ways this effect, if it existed (and it would certainly be premature to rule out this possibility), was produced.

This model is, like all models, intended as an aid to further thought. It is not more than this. It may be noted, incidentally, that some lines leading to the industrial revolution box, and more particularly those leading back from the industrial revolution box, should be viewed in a different light from other connections. The industrial revolution did not get fully into its stride until after the period discussed in this essay. Arrows pointing to it, therefore, show circumstances tending to promote its occurrence. Those in the opposite direction, on the other hand, cannot have existed before the event itself, if its place in time is strictly defined. In a more general sense, however, they simply underline the positive feedback elements in the situation which grew stronger as time passed but were present from an early date. In contrast with this, the period of economic growth in the sixteenth and early seventeenth centuries produced relationships between major variables which might be termed typically those of negative feedback. The very growth of industry and population, by increasing the demand for food and industrial raw materials in circumstances where there were increasing marginal costs of production, and by oversupplying the labor market, drove up food prices, forced wages down, and increased the difficulties of industrial production, thus throttling back the growth process.

VI

The comparative neglect of London as a potent engine working toward change in England in the century 1650–1750[67] is the more paradoxical in that the dominance of Paris within France has long been a familiar notion in political history. Yet London was larger than Paris, was growing much faster, and contained a far higher fraction of the national population. All leavens do not, of course, work equally effectively in their lumps; and political dominance connotes different issues from economic and social change, but the irony remains.[68] A just appreciation of London's importance must await a fuller knowledge of many points which are still obscure. Meanwhile this short sketch of a possible model of London's relationship with the rest of the country will have served its purpose if it helps to promote further interest in the complexities of the changes to which no doubt it does only the roughest of justice.

NOTES

IV. *A Simple Model of London's Importance*

[1] There is a very useful compilation of estimates of the size of towns and cities in western Europe chiefly for the period 1500–1800 in E. Hélin, *La démographie de Liège aux XVIIe et XVIIIe siècles* (Brussels, 1963), Annexe I, pp. 238–252. N. G. Brett-James summarizes the calculations of contemporaries and later scholars in *The Growth of Stuart London* (London, 1935), esp. pp. 496–512. He himself suggests figures of 250,000 in 1603 and 320,000 in 1625 (p. 512). John Graunt estimated the population of the capital to be 460,000 in about 1660: *Natural and Political Observations*, reprinted in C. H. Hull, ed., *The Economic Writings of Sir William Petty*, 2 vols. (New York, 1963 and 1964), ii, p. 371. Petty himself concluded that in 1682 London's population was already 670,000: *The Growth of the City of London*, in Hull, ed., *Sir William Petty*, ii, p. 460. Gregory King made a calculation of London's population in 1695 from the number of households arriving at a figure of 527,560: G. E. Barnett, ed., *Two Tracts by Gregory King* (Baltimore, 1936), p. 18. Creighton's estimates of London's population for 1603, 1625, and 1665 agree very closely with those of Brett-James and Graunt for the same periods: C. Creighton, *History of Epidemics in Britain*, 2 vols. (Cambridge, 1891 and 1894), i, p. 660. Mrs. George accepts figures of 674,500 for 1700 and 676,750 for 1750 based on the number of baptisms in the London parish registers: M. D. George, *London Life in the Eighteenth Century* (London, 1930), pp. 24 and 329–330. See also P. E. Jones and A. V. Judges, "London Population in the late Seventeenth Century," *Economic History Review*, vi (1935–36), pp. 45–63. The figures used in this text are rounded for convenience and are probably of the right order of magnitude, but nothing more can be claimed for them.

[2] See Hélin, *La démographie de Liège*, p. 242, and J. A. Faber, H. K. Roessingh, B. H. Slicher van Bath, A. M. van der Woude, and H.J. van Xanten, "Population Changes and Economic Developments in the Netherlands: a Historical Survey," *A. A. G. Bijdragen*, xii (Wageningen, 1965), pp. 58 and 110. It should perhaps be said that only in countries like England, France, and the Netherlands, if anywhere, does it make sense to relate city and national population totals. In areas like Germany, Italy, or Spain, political or economic fragmentation makes this a pointless

exercise. The only cities in Europe with populations of 100,000 or more *c*. 1650 apart from London, Paris, and Amsterdam were Naples, which was a very large city (250,000–300,000), and Palermo, Venice, Rome, and Lisbon (all 100,000–125,000); none of these grew much in the following century. By the mid-eighteenth century Vienna and Berlin were in this size class (*c*. 175,000 and 110,000 respectively) and perhaps Lyons. See Hélin, *La démographie de Liège*, pp. 244, 247, 249, and 251.

³ The uncertainty arises because of the problem of under-registration. Jones and Judges underlined this heavily in their examination of London's population at the end of the seventeenth century. They were able to show wide discrepancies between totals of baptisms and burials drawn from the three available sources: the returns made under the Marriage Duty Act of 1694, the Bills of Mortality, and the counts made in parish registers at Rickman's behest in 1801. See Jones and Judges, *Economic History Review*, vi (1935–36). Glass has made estimates of the degree of under-registration of baptisms and burials in the parish registers and the collector's returns under the 1694 Act for two city parishes: see introduction by D. V. Glass to "London Inhabitants within the Walls, 1695," *London Record Society Publications*, ii (London, 1966), pp. xxxv–xxxvii. There is a convenient summary of some of the available data in George, *London Life in the Eighteenth Century*, App. 1, pp. 405–410. Gregory King made estimates based on a notional time of peace which imply only a rather small burial surplus in the capital (about 4 per 1,000); however, elsewhere he produced figures for the year 1695 which suggest a much larger shortfall of baptisms: *Two Tracts by Gregory King*, esp. pp. 27 and 43. It is worth noting that Deane and Cole suggest a rate of natural increase for London in the period 1701–50 of −10.8 per 1,000 per annum and envisage an annual average net immigration into London of 10–12,000 (it should be added that they regard London's population as stationary in number during this half century): P. Deane and W. A. Cole, *British Economic Growth 1688–1959* (Cambridge, 1962), table 26, p. 115 and p. 111. William Farr thought the London death rate in the later seventeenth century was 80 per 1,000, declining to 50 per 1,000 in the eighteenth century: W. Farr, *Vital Statistics* (London, 1885), p. 131. Buer estimated that between 1700 and 1750 London needed an average immigration of 10,200 a year to maintain her population, and that during this period the ratio of deaths to births was 3:2: M. C. Buer, *Health, Wealth and Population in Eighteenth Century England* (London, 1926), p. 33.

⁴ This appears very clearly in family reconstitution work based on parish registers. The analysis of successive nominal listings of inhabitants

supports the same conclusion. See Peter Laslett and John Harrison "Clayworth and Cogenhoe" in *Historial Essays 1600–1750, presented to David Ogg*, ed., H. E. Bell and R. L. Ollard (London, 1963).

[5] The United Nations specimen life tables suggest that a birth population will fall to two-thirds its original number by the age of twenty when expectation of life at birth is forty: *Methods for Population Projections by Sex and Age*, United Nations, ST/SOA/Series A, Population Studies, No. 25 (New York, 1956). If expectation of life was substantially below this at this period (as it was at Colyton, for example, as I hope to show in a later publication), then a larger birth population would be needed to produce any given number of twenty-year-old immigrants into London.

[6] A rate of increase of 5 per 1,000 is a generous estimate for this period. Gregory King supposed that the annual number of births in England excluding London was 170,000 and of burials 148,000. Assuming the population of England without London to have been 4.9 million, this suggests a difference between the two rates of about 4.5 per 1,000. But King uses different assumptions elsewhere and presents material which implies a rate of increase less than half as high. See *Two Tracts by Gregory King*, pp. 25 and 27.

[7] On these points see E. A. Wrigley, "Family Limitation in Pre-Industrial England," *Economic History Review*, 2nd ser., xix (1966), pp. 82–109. This article was based on work done on the parish registers of Colyton in Devon. Preliminary work on reconstituted families of Hartland (Devon) also shows a late age of first marriage for women in the late seventeenth century. W. G. Howson has found the same phenomenon in parishes in the Lune Valley (personal communication).

[8] The survey is being carried out by the *Cambridge Group for the History of Population and Social Structure*. More than two hundred local historians have been kind enough to help in this work.

[9] The London apprenticeship records show that the proportion of apprentices coming from the north and west fell dramatically during the seventeenth century, while the proportion from the home counties rose. One reason for this may well have been the disappearance of a surplus of births in the north and west and its continuance nearer London. See L. Stone, "Social Mobility in England, 1500–1700," *Past and Present*, No. 33 (April 1966), pp. 31–32. Marshall noted that the great bulk of the inter-county movement from Bedfordshire was to London: L. M. Marshall "The Rural Population of Bedfordshire, 1671–1921," *Bedfordshire Historical Recording Society*, xvi (1934), p. 45.

[10] See Wrigley, *Economic History Review*, xix (1966), pp. 106–108.

[11] See George, *London Life in the Eighteenth Century*, pp. 109–110 for an interesting discussion of the chief types of migrants into and out of London. She suggests that the settlement laws tended to encourage rather than prevent migration and that London exercised a strong attraction upon those dislodged from their original settlement. She also quotes a contemporary, Burrington, writing in 1757, who thought that two-thirds of London's adult population came "from distant parts." The records of the Westminster General Dispensary between 1774 and 1781 reveal that only a quarter (824 out of 3,236) of the married people served were London born. Of the rest, 209 were born in Scotland, 280 in Ireland, and 53 abroad, a total of 542 in the three categories, or 17 percent. The balance were born elsewhere in England or Wales (George, *op. cit.*, p. 111).

[12] The characteristic English provincial situation is becoming clear from work now being carried out by the *Cambridge Group for the History of Population and Social Structure* on listings of inhabitants of English parishes. This work includes the analysis of London returns compiled in 1695 under the Marriage Duty Act. Glass's analysis of some of these London parish listings, though only a first survey of the material, provides much valuable information about the city: Glass, *London Record Society Publications*, vol. ii.

[13] D. C. Coleman, "Labour in the English Economy of the Seventeenth Century," reprinted from *Economic History Review*, 2nd ser., viii (1955–56), in *Essays in Economic History*, ed. E. M. Carus-Wilson, ii (London, 1962), p. 303.

[14] See A. H. John, "Aspects of English Economic Growth in the First Half of the Eighteenth Century," reprinted from *Economica* (1961), in *Essays in Economic History*, ed. Carus-Wilson, ii, pp. 366 and 369.

[15] See Registrar-General, *First Annual Report of Births, Deaths and Marriages* (London, 1839), pp. 8–9. Dr. R. S. Schofield is engaged in a study of inability to sign based on a random sample of suitable source materials from the sixteenth century onward. This will provide *inter alia* firm evidence about London in earlier centuries.

[16] Glass, *London Record Society Publications*, ii, p. xxi.

[17] G. Sjoberg, *The Preindustrial City* (New York, 1960), p. 118.

[18] *Ibid.*, p. 207.

[19] *Ibid.*, pp. 120 and 121.

[20] *Ibid.*, p. 136.

[21] *Ibid.*, pp. 204–205, 209–210.

[22] *Ibid.*, p. 197.

[23] *Ibid.*, pp. 157–159.

[24] *Ibid.*, pp. 145–146.

[25] *Ibid.*, p. 157.

[26] *Ibid.*, p. 162.

[27] See P. Laslett, *The World We Have Lost* (London, 1965), pp. 90–92.

[28] See J. Hajnal, "European Marriage Patterns in Perspective," in *Population in History*, ed. D. V. Glass and D. E. C. Eversley (London, 1965). Also Wrigley, *Economic History Review* (1966) and, more generally, W. J. Goode, *World Revolution and Family Patterns* (New York, 1963).

[29] See Glass, *London Record Society Publications*, ii, pp. xxxii–xxxiv.

[30] See Section III below.

[31] Stone in discussing the wealth generated by the great commercial expansion of the late seventeenth century remarks: "The closing down of the land market suggests that, however it was distributed, less of this wealth than before was being converted into social status by the purchase of an estate, and more of it was being reinvested in long-term mortgages, commerce, and banking." One reason for less money being invested in land was perhaps simply that rich Londoners no longer felt moved to use money in this way if their status did not suffer by refraining from acquiring land. See L. Stone, "Social Mobility in England, 1500–1700," *Past and Present*, No. 33 (April 1966), p. 34.

[32] A. Everitt, "Social Mobility in Early Modern England," *Past and Present*, No. 33 (April 1966), p. 71.

[33] To use the term employed by Runciman in a very lucid exposition of the concept of the reference group generally: W. G. Runciman, *Relative Deprivation and Social Justice* (London, 1966), chap. ii.

[34] F. J. Fisher, "The Development of the London Food Market, 1540–1640," *Economic History Review*, v (1934–35), pp. 56 and 63. The steady spread of the influence of London is well illustrated by the remark of a contemporary, John Houghton, who wrote *à propos* meat production for the London market, "The bigness and great consumption of London doth not only encourage the breeders of provisions and higglers thirty miles off but even to four score miles. Wherefore I think it will necessarily follow . . . that if London should consume as much again country for eighty miles around would have greater employment or else those that are further off would have some of it": J. Houghton, *A Collection of Letters for the Improvement of Husbandry* (London, 1681), pp. 165–166. I owe this reference to the kindness of Dr. J. Thirsk.

[35] This is once more rather an arbitrary figure. Different assumptions about its size produce slightly higher or lower estimates of increase

in agricultural production per head. A higher percentage engaged in agriculture will result in a lower figure of increased productivity and vice versa. The Tawneys' analysis of the Gloucestershire Muster Roll of 1608 suggests that a rather lower figure might have been appropriate: A. J. and R. H. Tawney "An Occupational Census of the Seventeenth Century," *Economic History Review*, v (1934–35), pp. 25–64 and esp. p. 39. Gregory King's work does not lend itself to a breakdown along these lines but is consistent with a figure of 60 percent or slightly higher. This is true also of the analyses of listings of inhabitants being carried out by Mr. P. Laslett in Cambridge. Some of the listings give details of occupations. Stone's assumption, based partly on King, that 90 percent of the population (presumptively in the mid-seventeenth century) were manual workers on the land is very difficult to accept. Even at the peak of the harvest period when men normally engaged in other pursuits might work on the land this would be an extraordinarily high figure. See Stone, *Past and Present*, No. 33 (April 1966), p. 20.

[36] Brownlee's estimate, supported by Deane and Cole: Deane and Cole, *British Economic Growth*, pp. 5–6.

[37] This assumes that farming and non-farming families were of the same average size, but could be rephrased without damaging the sense of the passage if this assumption is denied.

[38] Deane and Cole, *British Economic Growth*, table 17, p. 65.

[39] For wool, see Deane and Cole, *British Economic Growth*, p. 68, and B. R. Mitchell and P. Deane, *British Historical Statistics* (Cambridge, 1962), pp. 190–191. For mutton and beef, see Deane and Cole, *op. cit.*, pp. 68–71. For hops, see T. S. Ashton, *An Economic History of England: the Eighteenth Century* (London, 1955), p. 240.

[40] Deane and Cole, *British Economic Growth*, p. 75.

[41] Deane and Cole, *British Economic Growth*, p. 75.

[42] In the case of marriages, the occupation of the groom was given; in baptism and burial entries, the occupation of the head of the household in which the birth or death had occurred. Frequently occupations were noted in only one or two of the series rather than in all three.

[43] J. U. Nef, *The Rise of the British Coal Industry* (London, 1932), ii, pp. 381–382.

[44] I have discussed these changes from a different viewpoint and at greater length elsewhere: E. A. Wrigley, "The Supply of Raw Materials in the Industrial Revolution," *Economic History Review*, 2nd ser., xv (1962–63), pp. 1–16.

[45] Nef, *op. cit.*, i, pp. 239–240.

[46] It is interesting to remember John's comment on the growth of the export trade in corn at this time: "Grain became a major bulk cargo

and between 1730 and 1763 about 110,000–130,000 tons were, on an average, carried annually from English ports in ships which only occasionally exceeded a hundred tons burthen. This had its effect upon the more efficient use of shipping, upon investment in shipbuilding and upon the employment of dockside labor." Coal shipments along the coast at this time were running at about five times the level of corn shipments by tonnage. John, *Essays in Economic History*, ed. Carus-Wilson, ii, p. 364.

[47] Nef, *op. cit.*, ii, p. 138.

[48] *Two Tracts by Gregory King*, p. 31.

[49] The problem of moving coal in bulk by sea brought about a substantial saving in men employed per ton of cargo moved during the seventeenth century. For this reason it is likely that fewer men were employed on colliers than might be expected in view of their large share in the tonnage of the English merchant marine. See Nef, *op. cit.*, i, pp. 390–392.

[50] Nef, *op. cit.*, ii, p. 142.

[51] This is true of a wide range of manufacturing and service industries. Fisher, for example, noted that London had no malting facilities and few corn mills: "Consequently, a number of country towns found their major employment in the processing of the city's corn, and their inhabitants a regular occupation as middlemen": Fisher, *Economic History Review*, v (1934–35), p. 60.

[52] Fisher, *Economic History Review*, v (1934–35), p. 51.

[53] E. W. Gilboy, *Wages in Eighteenth Century England* (Cambridge, Mass., 1934), p. 241. See also chaps. i and ii.

[54] George, *London Life in the Eighteenth Century*, p. 198.

[55] John, *Essays in Economic History*, ed. Carus-Wilson, ii, p. 373.

[56] N. McKendrick, "Josiah Wedgwood: an Eighteenth Century Entrepreneur in Salesmanship and Marketing Techniques," *Economic History Review*, 2nd ser., xii (1959–60), pp. 418–419.

[57] *Ibid.*, p. 429.

[58] *Ibid.*, p. 429.

[59] *Ibid.*, p. 420.

[60] R. Davis, *The Rise of the English Shipping Industry* (London, 1962), p. 390. See also pp. 34–35 on the rapid growth of English commerce and London's predominance among English ports.

[61] H. Leibenstein, *Economic Backwardness and Economic Growth* (New York, 1963), p. 129.

[62] For the second half of the period there is a good summary of available quantitative evidence in Deane and Cole, *British Economic Growth*, pp. 50–82.

[63] See D. S. Landes, "Encore le problème de la révolution indus-

trielle en Angleterre," *Bulletin de la Société d'Histoire Moderne*, 12th ser., No. 18. This concept is discussed also in an article by F. Crouzet which clearly owes much to the idea, "Croissances comparées de l'Angleterre et de la France au XVIIIe siècle," *Annales, E.S.C.*, xxi (1966), esp. pp. 290–291.

[64] For a fuller discussion of the point see Wrigley, *Economic History Review*, xv (1962–63), esp. pp. 1–6.

[65] H. Leibenstein, "Population Growth and the Take-off Hypothesis," in W. W. Rostow, ed., *The Economics of Take-off into Sustained Growth* (London, 1963), p. 173.

[66] George quotes Defoe's description of the "topping workmen" to be found in England, ". . . who only by their handy labor as journeymen can earn from fifteen to fifty shillings per week wages as thousands of artisans in England can . . . 'Tis plain the dearness of wages forms our people into more classes than other nations can show. These men live better in England than the masters and employers in foreign countries can, and you have a class of your topping workmen in England, who, being only journeymen under manufacturers, are yet very substantial fellows, maintain their families very well . . .": George, *London Life in the Eighteenth Century*, p. 157.

[67] See P. Laslett, "The Numerical Study of English Society," in *An Introduction to English Historical Demography*, ed., E. A. Wrigley (London, 1966), pp. 11–12 for a brief discussion of much the same point.

[68] It is symptomatic of the neglect of this topic that a work as perceptive and authoritative as Deane and Cole's recent analysis of British economic growth from the late seventeenth century onward passes over the growth of London almost completely. Where London is mentioned at all it is incidental to some other main line of argument.

H.J. Habakkuk became Principal of Jesus College, Oxford, in 1967 and Vice-Chancellor of Oxford University in 1973. His university career is one of great distinction. A Cambridge graduate, he taught there until 1950 when he took up the Chichele professorship of economic history at Oxford. Professor Habakkuk's best-known work is American and British Technology in the Nineteenth Century *(Cambridge, 1962). His important work on the eighteenth century has appeared largely in the form of articles. Recently he has been concerned with the role of population in economic change; his latest book,* Population Growth and Economic Development since 1750 *(Leicester, 1972), reflects this interest. In his earlier work he explored patterns of landownership and exchange, and their relation to economic conditions and social and legal arrangements. This essay on England's nobility is inspired by that earlier work. It bears the characteristic features of his writings—clarity, brevity, authority. It originally appeared in* The European Nobility in the Eighteenth Century, *edited by Albert Goodwin, and is reprinted with the permission of Professor Habakkuk and the publishers: A & C Black, London, and Harper & Row, New York.*

V

England's Nobility*

BY H. J. HABAKKUK

In continental countries, nobility was usually a status. The rights attaching to it varied from country to country, but it was reasonably clear in any particular country what the rights of a noble were and who was entitled to enjoy them. The outlines of the class were distinct and visible. In England there was no nobility in this strict sense. The nearest analogy was, perhaps, the class of families entitled to use armorial bearings, but while such bearings conferred social prestige, they did not convey privileges in respect of law, taxation, the ownership of land, or entry into the army and the church, nor, on the other hand, did they debar those who bore them from moving into trade and industry. These families were not marked off from their neighbors by a barrier of specific and identifiable privilege. And though, in some sense, they formed a social class, the outline of the class was, as de Tocqueville said, indistinct, and its limit unknown. Within this class there was, indeed, a group—the peers—distinguished by the right to sit in the House of Lords, and by certain

* H. J. Habakkuk, "England," in Albert Goodwin, ed., *The European Nobility in the Eighteenth Century* (London: A & C Black, New York: Harper & Row, 1953), pp. 1–21. Reprinted by permission of the publishers.

privileges in law; and, in English usage, the word nobility became commonly restricted to the peers, as contrasted with the gentry. But the privileges of even this group were trivial: the right, for example, in criminal matters to be tried by their peers, or freedom from arrest upon mean process; they related only to the peer himself, and not to the members of his family; and they were much less important in distinguishing the peer from the commoner than the greater social prestige of the peer. Moreover, the group which enjoyed these privileges was much smaller than any continental nobility. In default of a precise counterpart, what class shall we examine? To accept what has become the normal usage and confine this essay to the aristocracy alone would be to sever a single, if not very homogeneous, social class, at a point which is not significant for the present purpose. I propose, therefore, to consider both the aristocracy and the gentry.

The basis of this class was the family estate, which provided the family not only with its revenue and its residence, but with its sense of identity from generation to generation. What was it that gave a landowner more general consequence than a moneyed man of equal wealth? Not only the visible fact of the rolling acres, the psychic ease which ownership of an estate conferred, the greater security of land, the control of tenantry at election times, but the fact that land could be made the vehicle of family purpose; its ownership could be determined for long periods ahead by the exercise of the general will of the family, in a way which was not true of other forms of property. What a merchant did with his money was primarily a matter for him alone. What a landowner did with his land was determined by a complex of decisions, in origin reaching far back into the family history, in effect stretching forward to his grandchildren yet unborn.

The descent of the typical English estate in the eighteenth century was governed by arrangements of immense complexity known as the strict settlement. These arrangements were most commonly made at the marriage of the heir, and they secured that the estate, or the greater part of it, descended intact to him, but descended on terms which greatly limited his power to sell and mortgage it. Once the deed of settlement was signed, the descent of the estate was settled for a generation ahead. Except by promoting a private act of Parliament to break the settlement, there was no way by which the owner could obtain complete control of the estate until the eldest son of the marriage came of age. As a corollary, the settlement provided that the younger children of the marriage should receive annuities or capital sums charged upon the estate.

"A class which wishes to preserve its special powers and privileges," wrote J. L. and Barbara Hammond, "has to discover some way of protecting its corporate interests from the misdemeanours and follies of individual members." This function the strict settlement performed for the English landowners; in the long-term interests of the family it limited the immediate interests of its representative for the time being. Its role was, in some respects, analogous to that of the *fidei commissum* in the history of certain continental nobilities. It was, of course, less rigorous and binding than the *fidei commissum*, for it had to be repeated every generation: when the eldest son of the marriage came of age, it was open to him, in theory, to refuse to enter into another strict settlement, and though in fact he usually did so, the repetition depended on the recurrent exercise of the family will. Moreover, some of the smaller gentry did not adopt this form of settlement as a regular practice. Even families which normally settled their estates often excluded a substantial part from the settlement, and on occasion the whole estate might, by the accidents of family history, remain unsettled for considerable periods. But, loose and flexible as it was in comparison with the *fidei commissum*, the strict settlement did impede the sale or dispersion of estates, and certainly provided a more precise and uniform legal basis for the English landowning class than had existed in the century before 1640.

With the family estate went the family house, the physical expression of the standing of the family and the tangible repository of its traditions. When the founder of a new family replaced or rebuilt an adequate existing mansion, it was not solely because of changing taste or want of room, but because building a family home was an integral part of the founding of a family. There was no market in second-hand mansions in eighteenth-century England. The great house was also the center of much of the life of the localities. The long corridors and enormous rooms were not mere ostentation; they were built to accommodate large households and the swarms of guests which descended on them at frequent intervals. "We used to sit down to dinner," wrote Lord Hervey, in July 1731, of the company at Houghton, "a little snug party of about thirty odd, up to the chin in beef, venison, geese, turkeys, etc.; and generally over the chin in claret, strong beer and punch. We had Lords Spiritual and Temporal, besides commoners, parsons and freeholders innumerable." From some eighteenth-century memoirs one might suppose that England was a federation of country houses.

Their families, houses, and estates provided the daily routines of most English landowners. Many of them—but we do not know how many—went to London or to some provincial capital for the "season." The season indeed ranks with the strict settlement as a primary institution of the class, for it linked the country house, rural, patriarchal, and sometimes parochial, with the more elegant and diversified life of the urban drawing-room, refining the one and invigorating the other. But early in June, when the season was over, they went back to the country, to hunting and drinking, but not less to the absorbing minutiae of estate and household management. And it was in the country that even the greatest of them spent most of their time. If among the most rural of the country gentry there were few mere country bumpkins, even among the greater aristocracy there was none whose life was entirely divorced from the soil. Discussing with the steward the merits of tenants, rents, repairs, and the management of timber was not a particularly strenuous occupation, but it gave landowners some real business to do. And country life gave them that stamina and bucolic vigor which they still exhibit in their portraits.

The largest item in the income of the aristocracy and gentry consisted of payments from tenant farmers, annual rack-rents, or sometimes, in the southwest and north, periodical lump sums called fines, which were calculated on the basis of the rack-rent value. Though several had home-farms, English landowners did not, like landowners east of the Elbe, depend on the profits of direct farming; they were and had long been rentiers. On the other hand they did not rely, as did some continental nobilities, on feudal dues; and the profits of manorial courts, quit-rents and copyhold rents provided a very small part of total income. Thus, in a sense, they had the best of both worlds. They were not farmers and therefore, like the

French nobility and unlike the Junkers, they were a leisured class. Nonetheless they were highly sensitive to changes in the fortunes of agriculture, they had an incentive to improve their estates—an incentive to which many responded—and their interests were directly and visibly linked with the prosperity of England's most important economic activity.

At what period these landowners began to draw a significant part of their income from urban and mining property is a question to which at present no satisfactory answer can be given. One of the few families which has been investigated in detail happens to have owned a great London estate. Miss Scott-Thomson has shown that the Bloomsbury estate of the Dukes of Bedford, which in 1732 yielded a gross return of thirty-seven hundred pounds, by 1771 yielded about eight thousand pounds, contributing, perhaps, between a third and a quarter of the family income. Other owners of London property, the Dukes of Portland, the Grosvenor family, the Pratts, the Comptons—possibly, too, owners of land in some provincial towns—must have profited in a similar way. In England common minerals were the property of the landowner, and several families owned mines. Some, like the Dudleys, worked them directly; others leased them to industrialists for long terms, and, as a class of men appeared who were capable of taking leases, this probably became the most usual method. It is easy enough to point to particular landed families who supplemented their incomes from the town and the mine, but difficult to judge how representative they were, since there were great variations from family to family and region to region. We know that in some regions, Durham, Stafford, and Cornwall for example, the composition and fortunes of the class we are considering were greatly influenced by mineral wealth. But if I had to venture an opinion it would be that landowners who drew a significant part of their income from urban rents and minerals were still exceptional, and that most of even these landowners probably drew the greater part of their incomes from agriculture.

Probably a more important and certainly a more widely diffused supplement to landed incomes was income from offices. It was one of the main charges of the writers who in the early nineteenth century attacked the whole aristocratic system that the governing class had farmed itself out on the public revenue. No one has yet

examined systematically the contribution which political and administrative office made to landed incomes, and indeed no precise estimate would be possible since a large part of the emoluments often
consisted of fees which fluctuated with the business of the office. But
clearly, the emoluments of the major government posts were considerable, particularly in time of war. It was estimated that from 1747
to 1753 the clear profits of the office of Secretary of State amounted
to an average of five thousand seven hundred eighty pounds a year.
The value of the office in 1762 was put at eight thousand pounds or
nine thousand pounds a year. Nor need gains cease with office. In
1756 the Earl of Waldegrave, refusing a pension of two thousand
pounds a year for life, asked for the reversion of one of the very
lucrative Tellerships of the Exchequer. When Lord Holderness was
turned out of the office of Secretary of State in 1761, he was given
the reversion of the Wardenship of the Cinque Ports, and a pension
of four thousand pounds a year in the meantime. Several peers,
moreover, held court offices, the salaries of which were often supplemented by pensions and annuities; and salaries, while less permanent
than incomes from land, were subject to far fewer deductions. What
the net gains really were we do not know. Much of the money from
offices, no doubt, went to maintain the style of life appropriate to
the office; but some sometimes went to promote the long-term interests of the family. A friend observed of George Grenville that it was
his unvaried practice "in all situations . . . to live on his own private
fortune, and save the emoluments of whatever office he possessed."

What a teller's place was for a family of importance, a minor
post in the Customs, the Excise, or the Tax Office might be for a
lesser one. But in calculating what official incomes meant to landed
families, whether great or small, it is not only the direct addition to
the income of the head of the family which is relevant. Offices were,
par excellence, a way of providing for the younger sons. This indeed
was the crux of the attack. "The aristocracy, usurping the power of
the state, have the means under various pretexts of extorting for the
junior branches of their families a forced subsistence." And when
one looks at the Walpole family, one is not disposed to write off
such language as baseless rhetoric. At Walpole's death, his eldest son
held among other offices the Auditorship of the Exchequer, valued
at seven thousand pounds a year. His second son, Edward, was Clerk

of the Pells, and derived from this office three thousand pounds a year. Horace Walpole held offices which, Mr. Ketton-Cremer has estimated, were worth, after his father died, approximately thirty-four hundred pounds a year. Contemporary correspondence, which teems with references to places and offices, gives the impression that, if the scale of this provision was unusually lavish, there was nothing unusual about the method.

Were English landed families, as a whole, affluent? Did they, on balance, save? Some families were notoriously wealthy; Lord Temple, as he himself modestly observed, "had a great deal of money to spare"; William Pulteney left over a million; the second Lord Foley was reputed to have left in 1766 real estate worth twenty-one thousand pounds a year, mines worth seven thousand pounds a year and five hundred thousand pounds in the funds. But others of the same class were heavily in debt; in 1741, for example, the second Lord Weymouth, whose income, excluding jointures and annuities, was twelve thousand pounds per annum, owed one hundred thousand pounds in mortgages and bonds, and had book debts amounting to about thirty thousand pounds. There was immense variation, not only from family to family but within a single family. In the course of a century, the same family might be affluent at one time and heavily indebted at another. A single profligate—and sooner or later one cropped up in most families—might quickly ravage the family fortunes. Even families who escaped this affliction were at the mercy of birth and death rates; in some generations many children survived, in others few; some wives died before their husbands, others long survived them. A bevy of healthy but ineligible daughters, a hardy and well-jointured dowager might do more damage to a family than the gambling table, as witness the wife of the third Duke of Leeds who survived her husband sixty-three years and drew one hundred ninety thousand pounds in jointure from the estate. Conversely, few children and the absence of a dowager might allow a family to accumulate considerable wealth. Apart, too, from these demographic vagaries, there was a natural history of families. The first generation might inherit money as well as land from the founding father, and sometimes, too, economical habits. In succeeding generations the family was apt to acquire the characteristic habits of the class into which it had risen; it exhausted the reserves, accumulated debt, and became increasingly vulnerable to changes in economic climate. This was a tendency only, which might be checked or reversed by a variety of circumstances; vast estates and wide connections gave the great families a certain immunity, but the tendency is clearly visible in the rise and decline of families among the smaller gentry.

We must therefore expect the facts, when they are established, to reveal very great variety of family circumstances. But the best opinion, that of Malthus for example, assumed that landowners were pre-eminently consumers. And this still remains the most reasonable generalization. Certainly, among the typical landed families of midland England, the greater part of the income was absorbed in current expenditure, taxation, interest payments, and in annuities to members of the family, annuities which in their turn were spent primarily on current consumption. Only when the family built or enlarged the great house did capital expenditure absorb a large part of their resources. Expenditure on improvements, important as this expenditure may have been for agriculture, appears in most cases to have been relatively small; and except in the case of recently established families who had not laid out all their original fortune in land, any holdings in government funds were usually modest. Landowners were indeed characteristically the borrowing class, and the greater part of their mortgages in this century were not for productive enterprise, but to provide portions for their daughters or to fund short-term debts incurred in periods of living beyond their income. Though the more affluent members of the class are to be found among the lenders, most of the loans were provided by lawyers, merchants, and by what was known in contemporary parlance as the monied interest.

We must not adopt a middle-class attitude to the debts of landowning families. Mortgages which at first sight seem overwhelming were in fact light in relation to the capital value of the estate, sometimes very much less burdensome than the mortgages which even provident dons incur on their homes. Still less must we assume that shortage of ready money is a sign of imminent disaster. Individual members of a family might temporarily be very short of cash, though their long-term position, still more than of their family as a whole, was entirely secure. No doubt some families were forced to sell a substantial part of their property; and in many cases the burden of debt made rapid adjustment to changes of circumstances extremely difficult. At one time or other in the century the finances of a number of very substantial families fell into confusion. But there was always a possibility that the next generation would be small, and in the last resort these families could, like Sir Walter Elliot of Kellynch Hall, lease the house to Admiral Croft and go off and retrench in Bath.

Did the general economic position of this class improve during the eighteenth century? There is no reasonable doubt that circumstances were more favourable to landed incomes in the century after 1715 than they had been between 1640 and 1715. Under the stimulus of agrarian improvements, particularly those associated with enclosures, of increasing population, of growing trade and industry, there was a substantial rise of rents; there were variations from region to region and even from estate to estate, but the rise was visible in most parts of the country about the middle of the century, became rapid about the 1770s and spectacular during the wars against Revolutionary and Napoleonic France. Moreover, down at least to Pitt's Income Tax, taxation was less severe than in the seventy years before 1715. When Malthus argued that "in the progress of a country towards a higher state of improvement, the positive wealth of the landlord ought . . . gradually to increase," he was as much generalizing from history as deducing from theory.

What we do not know is how far this rise in income was offset by an increase in expenditure. About the 1770s there is a perceptible change in the social climate, of which the most obvious mark is the increase in speculation and gambling. The position of the eldest son—relatively poor while his father lived but certain at his father's death to inherit the estate—was always the point of weakness in the system of family management that rested on the strict settlement; in limiting the power of the owner to damage the estate, the settlement deprived him of the power to discipline his children. But in the 60s and 70s the temptation to "show the spirit of an heir" seems to have grown stronger, and a good deal of wealth wandered as a result. There was a great increase in the sale of annuities for the life of the seller, a method by which a person of little immediate substance could borrow considerable amounts on terms which often proved disastrous. The two elder sons of the third Lord Foley by this means borrowed one hundred thousand pounds to pay their gambling debts, and permanently impaired the fortunes of their family. Moreover, even when we have no evidence of such spectacular gambling debts, the increase in expenditure appears to have been rapid. The household and miscellaneous expenditure of the Duke of Portland rose from four thousand pounds in 1784 to twelve thousand pounds in 1797, twenty-one thousand pounds in 1801, and, after dropping to twelve thousand pounds in 1803, rose to thirty-eight thousand pounds in 1805. Apart from any change in the tastes of landowners, mortgages incurred to provide portions for daughters tended to accumulate. They were charges on the estate, not on the owner for the time being, who therefore lacked an incentive to pay them off out of his current income. Every generation of daughters brought additional mortgages, and, in the course of a century or so, many were raised and few repaid. Within the very organization of a landed family, therefore, there was a mechanism which persistently worked for an increase in the family debt. Finally, on the income side, it might be long before landowners obtained the full advantage of urban and mineral properties which were let on long leases. The nucleus of what became the Dowlais iron-works was let by the Windsor family for 99 years at a rent of thirty-one pounds a year; when the lease expired in 1848, it was renewed at a rent in the neighbourhood of twenty-five thousand pounds a year. For almost a century the enormous increase in the value of the property had accrued not to the landowner but to the industrialists who leased it.

What was the place of this class in the political arrangements of the period? In many continental states, a characteristic problem of the eighteenth century was how to reconcile the nobility to the rise of bureaucratic absolutism, which was sometimes also the problem of how to reconcile the localities to the growth of central power. Such problems did not exist in England. Not only because the landowners were not an order of society, with privileges which could be infringed and had to be defended, but because the English landowners were the governing class of the country. Ministers were drawn usually from the great families, and though the property qualifications imposed by the Act of 1711 were easily evaded, the normal social and political processes ensured that most M.P.s came from landed families. Local government likewise was in the hands, not of a bureaucracy, but of Justices of the Peace, who were generally landowners. The land tax was administered by the same class, and even in those departments which were run by professionals, the more important and dignified posts were often filled from landowning families.

There was, indeed, a traditional opposition between the country gentlemen who prevailed in local administration and the Court and central government, and this opposition was not without political and social importance, but, because landowning families dominated in both spheres, it did not become open conflict over specific rights. The period between the end of active conciliar intervention in the seventeenth century and the revival of central direction in the early nineteenth was pre-eminently a period of local autonomy. The initiative in dealing with new social and economic problems was taken, if taken at all, in the locality, partly by the promotion of private acts to establish turnpikes, build canals, etc., but probably as much in the course of administering the existing law. The great extension of outdoor poor relief at the end of the century, for example, resulted from administrative decisions taken by Justices in Quarter Sessions, who were neither stimulated nor controlled by the central government. The machinery of local government in the eighteenth century had notorious shortcomings, and in the latter part of the period there was a rapid increase in problems which local initiative either could or would not deal with. Nevertheless, to the end of the century the Justices remained the most active organs of adaptation in English society.

In the army, the navy and the church, success depended on anything which would give a man influence—wealth, family, friendships, and abilities of every kind; and no single one of these was overriding. In such a society it was possible for men of low social origins to rise to prominence; and insofar as landed families did in fact predominate in these occupations, it was because of wealth, connection or aptitude, and not because of prescriptive right or birth. The predominance was most marked in the army. The higher officers were usually the younger sons of landowning families, or the sons of younger sons. Among the English generals in the war against the American colonies, for example, Howe and Gage were the second sons of Irish Viscounts, Clinton was the only son of the

second son of an Earl of Lincoln, and Burgoyne the only son of a
younger son of a wealthy baronet family. It was difficult for men of
moderate means to attain high rank since commissions had to be purchased, but the higher ranks were open to anyone with the necessary
money; and if no sons of merchants are to be found among our generals, it is primarily due, not to social exclusiveness, but to the feeling, by no means confined to the landed families or to the eighteenth
century, that by upbringing and aptitude the sons of landed families
were likely to make the best military leaders. The navy was more
democratic, and political influence and considerations of birth,
though certainly not negligible, were curbed by the more exacting
demands of naval service; it was more difficult to handle a ship than
a regiment. The second son into the army, the third into the church:
this was a traditional fate of younger sons. Since landowners owned
the right of presentation to many livings, their connection with the
church was more intimate than with any other profession, and the
rise of the "squarson" suggests that in the eighteenth century it was
becoming closer. Many of the bishops, too, North and Barrington,
for example, came from landed families, though they sat side by side
on the Bishop's Bench with several of humble birth, since a great
man's chaplain might by influence rise as high as a great man's
brother.

The grades of title within the landowning class from Duke
down to plain gentry were primarily social gradings. They probably
corresponded in a very rough and ready way with gradations of
landed wealth, and there was a general notion of the estate appropriate to maintain a given rank. But there was no sharp break in wealth
between the higher ranges of one rank and the lower ranges of the
next, and there was indeed a fringe of impoverished peers and baronets who had inherited the title but not the estate. Even the line of
division between peers and commoners—a line to which, judging by
the efforts made to cross it, contemporaries attached importance—
was not a decisive one. The attempt to make the peerage an exclusive caste, the Peerage Bill of 1719, failed and was in any event a
political manoeuvre rather than a product of class feeling.

Nevertheless, within the peerage itself, there was a group of
great families clearly distinguished in point of wealth and influence
from other landowning families, "the great oaks that shade a coun-

try," as Burke described them. Their origins were miscellaneous, but a high proportion were founded with fortunes made in government service, and many were descended from Tudor "new men," who had acquired monastic property. If the dissolution of the monasteries contributed to the rise of the gentry, it was no less a formative episode in the history of the modern English aristocracy, as one can see from a distribution map of the great eighteenth-century estates. Like the House of Austria, these families extended their estates by fortunate marriages, and in the eighteenth century they owned large properties, often scattered over several counties. A number of them, the Devonshire family, for example, the Rockinghams, Egremonts, Shelburnes, and Hertfords, had also considerable estates in Ireland. Many of these families were linked together by an intricate network of intermarriage, so that sometimes they bore the appearance more of tribes than of families.

Sir Lewis Namier has shown that the electoral influence of the great families has been exaggerated; at the accession of George III, even such a grandee as the Duke of Bedford had only four boroughs at his disposal, the Duke of Devonshire only three and several of the Dukes none at all. In respect of borough patronage there was no line of division between the great families and the rest of the peers, nor between peers and commoners. Nor in the counties did the territorial magnates exert unchallenged dominance, but divided their power with the gentlemen of the county. Moreover, their influence reflected the geographical distribution of the great houses; their characteristic spheres of influence were the north, the northern midlands and some of the eastern counties. The southwest and west were areas of smaller properties, and there the social and political influence of the gentry was relatively greater. But electoral influence does not fully measure the political significance of the great families. A large part of English history has consisted of the relations of Crown, magnates, and gentry. The relations between Crown and magnates have usually involved elements of partnership as well as conflict. And, though the nature of the binding ties has varied, the magnates have usually been the centers of groups and connections bound together by ties of blood, friendship, and obligation. What distinguishes the eighteenth century is that, in their partnership with the Crown, the magnates were more powerful than in previous periods, and that the aristocratic connection was a more integral part of political arrangements. It would be absurd to suppose that these families had a monopoly of political power, if only because the greatest statesmen of the century were not, in fact, drawn from their ranks. Yet, by reason of their great stake in the country, and their long and close association with government, they bore a heavier responsibility for the fame and fortune of the country than did the rest of the political nation. And, as Miss Sutherland has suggested, it was because English politics were dominated by such families, "whose main source of riches remained outside the sphere of politics" and who "in the last resort felt some responsibility for and interest in the maintenance of the king's government," that influence, interest, and connection did not prove incompatible with ordered government.

According to the traditional view, this aristocracy was more intimately linked with other social classes, the bourgeoisie in particular, than were the aristocracies of the Continent; it recruited itself from talent displayed and wealth acquired in the professions, and sent back into the professions the families of its younger sons. Of the broad truth of this view there can be no doubt. In England political power and social standing depended to a greater extent than elsewhere on the ownership of landed property as opposed to lineage or royal favor. Since there were no legal restrictions on the right to acquire land, any man, however humble his origin, who had enough money might purchase an estate, and thereby acquire social consequence. And not only was it easy for wealthy bourgeois to acquire an estate; in relation to the landowners there were more of them than on the Continent. For all these reasons the English landed class was constantly recruiting new members. Because Englishmen who had made fortunes in law, government or trade transformed themselves into country gentlemen, England had no urban aristocracy on the Dutch model. There were wealthy merchants but few mercantile dynasties, and the great London houses were the town houses of the landed nobility. It would indeed be difficult to exaggerate the wider social repercussions of this flow into landownership.

We know very little, however, about the speed of this flow during the eighteenth century, and it is often exaggerated. For lawyers, merchants and other "new men" could buy estates only if established landowners were prepared to sell; established landowners for the most part only sold when they had to; and, it may well be argued, during the eighteenth century the occasions when landowners had to sell were less frequent than in the seventeenth century. It does indeed appear that in the two or three decades after 1715 a large number of estates were sold—an aftermath, perhaps, of high war taxes and sometimes even of Commonwealth impositions—but in the second half of the century, when rents were buoyant, the land tax light and political impositions absent, there were times when would-be purchasers found it very difficult to find the estates they wanted, and it is possible, though it cannot be put any higher, that there was a slackening in the rate at which new families were recruited. Whatever the merits of this suggestion, it is clear that few individuals, except perhaps Paymaster-Generals in time of war, were able to make in a single lifetime enough money to buy an estate as large as those of the greater aristocracy, many of which represented the accumulation of several generations.

Furthermore, while it was easier in England for a man of humble birth and great fortune to acquire considerable landed property and a title, there might be a long time-lag between the acquisition of the property and its recognition by a title. The English peerage in the eighteenth century was not as accessible to mere wealth, even to landed wealth, as one is apt to suppose. It must not be assumed that it was easily accessible merely because it was not a status; the privileges of a nobility, their scope, and the precision with which they are defined, are one question, the ease with which nobility is acquired is quite another. The creation of peers rested with the monarch, who might have prejudices or convictions in the matter. Until the burst of new creations of 1784, the peerage remained a small body, and the new creations were little more than enough to replace peerages which had become extinct. There were 161 temporal peers in 1704 and 182 in 1780, excluding the representative Scottish peers. The number of new creations was indeed larger than this might suggest, for the mortality among noble families in the eighteenth century was high; of the forty-five peerages created by Anne, thirteen had become extinct before 1784. Still, by most standards the number of new creations was small. Anne created thirty new peerages (apart, that is, from promotions within the peerage),

George I twenty-eight and George II thirty-nine; in the first twenty-three years of his reign, George III created forty-seven. George III was jealous of the honour of the peerage. As he wrote to Bute after refusing Egremont's request for a Marquisate, "I looked on our Peerage as the most honourable of any country, and I never would hurt it by putting the juniors of them over the seniors."

But more significant for our present purpose than the number is the character of the new peers. The largest single group consisted of men ennobled for service to the state; statesmen like Walpole and Pitt, politicians of second rank like Speaker Onslow and George Lyttleton, lawyers like Cowper, Harcourt and Macclesfield, soldiers like Cadogan and Cobham, sailors like Hawke and Rodney; of these only the lawyers can properly be said to represent new men. Another group, not entirely exclusive of the first, consisted of the sons of peers, men who had acquired a claim to titles by marrying into the families which had borne them in some previous period, Irish peers and baronets of old landed families. All these were men to whom a peerage was only one step in promotion. The peer of obscure social origin was rare, and there were none who had been actively engaged in trade, nor, until Smith was made Lord Carrington, was there any financier. The great merchants and financiers were rewarded less lavishly, by baronetcies or by Irish peerages. In 1784 an exceptionally large number of new peerages was created, which did radically change the size of the English peerage. But even then it was not, *pace* Disraeli, from "the alleys of Lombard Street and the counting-houses of Cornhill" that the new peers were drawn, but predominantly from among the older and more substantial families of squires.

It is true that even the oldest of the families raised to the peerage in the eighteenth century were recent by continental standards, and indeed that the greater aristocracy themselves were of no great antiquity. Because of the high mortality in the Wars of the Roses and the proscriptions of the Tudors, there were few survivors of the medieval nobility. England was not, of course, alone in this respect. If many of the great English families were established in the sixteenth century, many of the Austrian nobility were not established till the seventeenth. But granted the relatively recent origin of many of our great families, what does it tell us about them? According to one historian, that "the aristocracy of eighteenth-century England was really little more than a wealthier middle class." We must not, having renounced the legend that they were an oligarchy, substitute the much less plausible legend that families like the Fitzwilliams, the Russells, the Leveson-Gowers, the Seymours were a middle class. In their wealth, style of living, social standing, and habits of mind, the great English families were an aristocracy, a separate species, but of the same genus as the greater families of the Continent. The English memory for social origins was, indeed, shorter than was general on the Continent; since few families were very old, newcomers were less conspicuously new. But social origins were not forgotten. On this point the catholicity of English social life is apt to mislead. London society was open to the amusing, the talented, and the able; the visible signs of rank and birth which, in German states for example, inhibited social intercourse were absent here. But the marriages of a class are a better index of its social feelings than the composition of its dinner parties. And few children of the great families married into families far removed from them in rank and general standing. There were, of course, marriages between aristocrats and bourgeois heiresses. No one has yet calculated their frequency, but it is evident from the terms of the settlements on such marriages that considerable material gains were necessary to induce the great families to contract them, and, when the relevant statistics are available, we may perhaps find that actresses were not much less common than bourgeois heiresses. The contemporary attention which mésalliances commanded is proof of their rarity rather than of their frequency; they were sufficiently frequent to provide a plausible theme for novel and play, but sufficiently rare to prove an interesting one. When the daughter of the Duke of Richmond, flouting her parents' wishes, married Henry Fox . . . "I thought," said Carteret, "our fleet or our army were beat, or Mons betrayed into the hands of the French."

The closest links with other social classes were provided not by incoming peers, but by outgoing younger sons. Reservations must be made even here. Voltaire observed that in England a peer's brother did not think trade beneath him, but added, "this custom . . . begins to be laid aside." It was, in fact, extremely rare for a younger son of a peer to go into trade. Most of them went into the army or the church, or were provided with pensions and places. It was only among the gentry with large families that trade was at all a common occupation for a younger son. And though the fact that younger sons contributed their energies and abilities to the professions is immensely important, it may well be argued that their departure from the family hearth was as much a condition of the wealth and superiority of the main line of the family as it was a link with other social groups. The real distinguishing feature of English society was that even had these cadet branches of great families remained aristocratic they would not have been marked off from their fellows by a barrier of privilege. If in England the relations of the aristocracy and the middle classes did not constitute a problem, it was not because the aristocracy were bourgeois—far from it—but because the exclusive rights of the nobility which created the problem on the Continent did not exist in this country. There were divergencies of economic interests, and wide differences in way of life and mental habit, but, except for the game laws, economic and social differences were not accentuated by differences of legal right.

I do not intend to discuss the morals and habits of aristocracy. These are embalmed in Horace Walpole's letters. Wealth and leisure are likely to produce great diversity of character and taste, and among the aristocracy of this period were architects, philosophers, scientists, agricultural improvers, and every type of character from the rake to the puritan. But unless the members of such a class are restrained by religious feeling or strong moral conventions, their lowest common denominator is apt to be dissoluteness of manners. Gout was the occupational disease of the English aristocracy, and mistresses a frequent by-product of their arranged marriages. Dissoluteness did not, however, mean breakdown of character as often as it does among classes subject to more rigorous moral codes, and it by no means implied absence of refined taste and feeling. The eighteenth-century aristocracy were probably more widely cultivated than their seventeenth-century predecessors. The Grand Tour, by the mid-century an established rite, whatever it did for their morals, polished their manners, enlarged their interests, and educated their taste. Vanbrugh and the brothers Adam built their houses; Chippendale and Sheraton designed their furniture; Reynolds and Gainsborough painted their portraits. As Voltaire remarked, and as their libraries suggest, they esteemed learning and literature, in a gentlemanly sort of way; and if in the course of the century the growth of a middle-class reading public diminished the importance of the individual aristocrat as a patron of letters, they continued to set the public taste in the visual arts.

But the most important single fact about the English nobility is that they were, in the locality and at the center, the politically effective class, and therefore felt a responsibility for the way things went. They were prepared to tax themselves, and in the two great wars against France, to tax themselves heavily. The Hammonds conclude a sustained indictment of the activities of the enclosing English landlords with this reluctant tribute: "The other European aristocracies crumbled at once before Napoleon: the English aristocracy amid all its blunders and errors kept its character for endurance and fortitude."

J. H. Plumb, Professor of Modern English History in the University of Cambridge, is the foremost historian currently working in the field of eighteenth-century England. His Ford Lectures at Oxford in 1965 yielded the most important book to appear in the field during the past decade, The Growth of Political Stability in England 1675–1725 (1967), published in the United States as The Origins of Political Stability, England, 1675–1725 (Boston, 1967). It is a book for serious students. Plumb, however, has developed a rare gift for engaging the interest of almost any audience, a gift that is amply evidenced in his long essay on The Italian Renaissance (New York, 1965), his collected essays, chiefly on eighteenth-century England, in Men and Places (1963), and his recent collection, In the Light of History (Boston, 1973). He has published numerous other books and articles, the most widely read being his brief survey, England in the Eighteenth Century (Harmondsworth and Baltimore, 1950).*

The selection printed here is the second chapter of Plumb's Sir Robert Walpole: The Making of a Statesman, the first volume (two have been completed) of a major biographical study. It portrays the anatomy of eighteenth-century political and governmental power—encompassing the counties and towns as well as the nerve center in Whitehall—with clarity, authority, and enlivening detail. Sir Robert Walpole: The Making of a Statesman was first published by the Cresset Press in 1956; this chapter is reprinted with the permission of Professor Plumb and the book's present publishers: Allen Lane, The Penguin Press (Longman Group Ltd.); and Houghton Mifflin Company, Boston.

VI

Robert Walpole's World:
The Structure of Government

BY J. H. PLUMB

Walpole grew up in a world of political instability in which the Revolution of 1689 seemed to his contemporaries to be but a phase, lacking finality, in the struggle which had lasted for generations between Crown and Parliament. Men of property, great or small, squire or merchant, farmer or shopkeeper, longed for a settled government. The vast majority believed without question that the King should rule, for the disasters of the Commonwealth experiment had made republicanism distasteful to most Englishmen. But the authority of kings varied from the absolute authority wielded by Louis XIV to the very limited powers exercised by the Dutch Stadtholder. On the question of which type of kingship was best for them, Englishmen had been very much divided. Neither experience nor tradition was a great help although both were endlessly debated. Both sides appealed to history and as was only to be expected found complete documentary evidence for their opposing views. Dr. Brady, the formidable Master of Caius College, a friend, oddly enough, of Walpole's father, who was to save young Walpole's life when he was sick of smallpox at Cambridge, maintained that all authority was in the King—Parliaments existed only by his grace. This William Petyt flatly denied; Parliaments were as old as the nation, contemporaneous with its King. for *Parlement* was merely the Norman name for the Saxon Witanagemot. To strengthen his case he had Dr. Brady excluded from the Tower records after the Revolution, but posterity has acknowledged Brady's accuracy and scholarship. As with historical scholarship so with political philosophy, though here perhaps the victory was reversed. The authoritarians were convinced by the theocratic arguments of Filmer and Bossuet. The King was the nation's father as Adam was the father of creation. The family was divine in origin and the father's authority over his children absolute and sanctioned by God. This was not an absurd argument but an extremely forceful and cogent one to the thousands of men who believed explicitly in the truth of the Old Testament. Locke recognized its power when he devoted the first treatise of his book on civil government to its refutation. To men imbued with the new learning, who had read Harrington and Wharton or listened to Locke, such theories were nonsense; institutions, including kingship, were devices of men to secure their own happiness; if that happiness were to be threatened then the institutions would have to be changed. The basis of all human happiness was, they argued, the free enjoyment of property which was not merely lands or money, goods or chattels. Property for them had a more mystical significance. Property could exist in a man's status or in the free exercise of his professional privileges. When James II dismissed Dr. Hough, the president of Magdalen, from his office, even that crusted Tory declared that he had lost his freehold.[1] This was no figure of speech; his contemporaries knew exactly what he meant. And many of them regarded these rights as both natural and inalienable. When authority in the state threatened the free enjoyment of such rights then resistance became a duty.

The patriarchal theory of Filmer and Bossuet was held very strongly by Charles II and James II and their courtiers, who believed not only in the divine nature of kingship but also that monarchical authority had achieved the perfection of form in France. Furthermore, a few, particularly James II and his closest friends, sincerely believed that their own religion—Roman Catholicism—not only sanctioned and blessed royal authority but also provided a stronger means for securing social discipline and that proper sense of subordination which was an essential part of their social ethic. But the difficulty of the full royal creed of Charles II and James II for most

Englishmen was twofold. First, it would lead to the destruction of the Church of England which men loved, not perhaps so much for its doctrine, but because it was a symbol of national independence. And secondly, the royal policy was bound to lead to subservience to France, England's most dangerous commercial rival. Yet men were extremely reluctant to believe that this must be so. Shaftesbury thought that he could steer Charles II clear of the tentacles of Louis XIV. He failed. Halifax, frightened by the implications of the Exclusion crisis, thought likewise. He too failed. After him the most conservative statesmen were brought only reluctantly to the same view. And it was with the utmost hesitation that men of great power and wealth, merchants as well as aristocrats, brought themselves to reject the attitude to monarchy which these two Stuart brothers had nourished.

Some men, however, had consistently opposed all attempts to extend royal authority. They had supported Shaftesbury in his attempt to exclude James and to strengthen the authority of Parliament. They wished to see the country ruled as the United Provinces were ruled. These men, though not republicans, held that monarchy should be strictly limited; both royal servants and royal policy were to be controlled by Parliament, the representative assembly of England's propertied interests. They hated France and they hated popery, for both were symbols of arbitrary government. And they saw the gravest danger to the wealth of England in the French leanings of the Stuarts. Many of these men had dabbled in treason; others had gone into discreet exile in Holland; the majority, like Walpole's father, tended their estates and bided their time, waiting for the folly of James to accomplish its own ruin.

They had not long to wait. The acts by which James II brought about his downfall need not be recounted here. There is, however, one aspect of his foolishness which receives too little notice. This was his attack on local government. Charles II had been disturbed by the violence of the House of Commons during the Exclusion crisis and by the utter inability of his ministers to keep it under effective control. He went to the root of the matter. Borough after borough was forced to surrender its town charter and then it was graciously granted a new one. The new charters reserved more often than not the privilege of electing a member of Parliament to the chief officials of the town, and the King himself either appointed these officials or controlled their appointments.[2] By this means the royal control of the composition of Parliament was to be steadily extended. James II pursued the same policy but with more thoroughness; age-old alliances between great local families and the boroughs which they had patronized were broken. Corporations were bullied and cajoled into pledging their support in future elections to men lacking in property or distinction but willing to acquiesce in James's policy. Worse followed. Even after a most thorough remodeling of the parliamentary boroughs James felt far from secure. He was frightened of the unspoken but massive opposition of the country gentry who, as justices of the peace and deputy-lieutenants, ruled their neighborhoods as of natural right. He decided to displace them unless they pledged themselves to support him.[3] Commissioners were dispatched to all counties. Their investigations were thorough and very distasteful to the gentry, who refused as tactfully as they could to acquiesce in James's policy. In county after county men who had been loyal to James hitherto were discovered to be as adamant as their Whig neighbors, but Whig or Tory, they were turned off the bench and cleared from the militia. They were infuriated when they learned that they were being replaced by men of no property, by obscure Catholics and dissenters; sometimes even by bailiffs and servants. Sir John Reresby worshipped the Crown as the symbol of God's authority. His whole life had been spent in unswerving devotion to Charles II and James II. For their sakes he had helped to humble the proud corporation of York by securing the surrender of its ancient charters. For years he never questioned the wisdom of James's measures, but even his eyes were opened in 1688 and he sat down on 14 November with foreboding in his heart to write to the Duke of Newcastle.

> . . . in the afternoon we was all surprized by the clerke of the peace comming to supersede Sir Henry Goodrick, Mr Tankard, Sir John Kaye, Sir Michael Wentworth, Sir Thomas Yarburgh, and above twenty more principall gentlemen of this rideing (the most eminent for quality and estates) from being justices of the peace, bringing at the same time another commission wherein severall new ones are put in, and amongst others John Eyre of Sheffield Parke, Mr Ratcliff, &c. The first can neither write nor read, the second is

a bailiff to the Duchesse Dowagere of Norfolk's rents, and neither of them have one foot off freehould land in England. My Lord, I fear this matter being unseasonably notified at such a time may change the good measures we were upon and divide the country. . . .[4]

A few were not disturbed by these proceedings, but for the majority they violated nature and implied a social revolution which could not be tolerated. Such an attack on the gentry's vested interest made the country almost unanimous in its rejection of James.

The Revolution brought a restoration of the borough charters and new commissions were issued, appointing justices of the peace; the old familiar names, a Knatchbull for Kent, Onslow for Surrey, Rolle for Devon, Walpole for Norfolk, Strangways for Dorset, Stanley for Lancashire, indicated to all that the natural order of society had been restored. Moreover, this restoration came to be regarded as sacrosanct. Generation followed generation and still the Onslows, the Knatchbulls, the Walpoles ruled their neighborhoods as their fathers and grandfathers and great-grandfathers had done before them; and not only ruled, but ruled in the same way, using the same unchanging machinery of local government, no matter how inadequate it was for the problems of a changing society. The Revolution confirmed the right of the gentry to rule by its old traditional methods. In the same way, it confirmed the old corporations. Small, self-electing bodies of men, wielding great wealth, yet divorced from all but the most ancient of social obligations, and frequently even these, they came to be regarded as a part of the divine order of things. From the point of view of the structure of political society, the Revolution had been thoroughly conservative, a rejection of the revolutionary designs of Charles II and James II.

2

It is necessary to understand the structure of local government because it was the basis of all political power in the eighteenth century. The source of Walpole's massive strength was the institutions by which the English countryside was governed. The Lord Lieutenant was the greatest of all local officials. He was the King's representative, particularly in military affairs, and with his deputies he was responsible for the county militia. In times of war and rebellion, the office could be onerous, but more frequently duties were formal if important. Nevertheless it was a key position and eagerly sought after.[5] On the death of the Duke of Norfolk in 1701, Walpole's friends were extremely agitated in case Lord Townshend might fail to succeed him, for they realized that their position in the county would be weakened if they failed to capture this office.

The great importance of the Lord Lieutenancy was that it gave local friends and clients of the Lord Lieutenant a spokesman at Court, at the center of patronage. And he himself was able to keep an eye on all appointments, including those of justice of the peace, sheriff, and the like, which might be to the advantage of his local faction to hold. The vital nature of this office can be seen from the type of men who held it. The Duke of Newcastle was Lord Lieutenant, throughout most of his life, of no less than three counties—Sussex, Nottingham, and Middlesex—the spheres of his greatest influence. The Duke of Bolton held Hampshire, Dorset, and, because his wife was a Vaughan, Carmarthenshire, but the moment he quarreled with the government in 1733 he was dismissed from all three. The government knew the power which the Lord Lieutenant wielded and insisted on reliability. On the accession of Anne, rumors spread through Norfolk that Townshend might lose this office because the Queen was determined to weed out the extreme Whigs. Such news, fortunately untrue, caused great consternation since the loss of a Lord Lieutenancy might be the reversal of fortune for hundreds of lesser men; no longer would they become the cynosure of sycophantic friends at Quarter Sessions or at the convivial evenings when the corporation met in the local tavern. Instead they would know the gnawing envy of those who stand and watch whilst their rivals, self-satisfied and self-important, contentedly savor the sweet delights of power.

It was not wholly a question of influence; the Lord Lieutenant also controlled a few highly desirable and very profitable sinecures.

"The Clerk of the Peace of Oxfordshire is dead," Lady Cowper wrote to Mrs Clayton, the Mistress of the Robes (to the Princess of Wales), "and the place is in the gift of Lord Godolphin (Ld. Lieut. Oxon) who I believe would willingly put my brother Edward in, if Mr Clayton would be so kind as to name him to my

> *Lord Godolphin. It would strengthen the King's and the Wood-*
> *stock interest . . . we are sure he is a zealous Whig.*"[6]

Edward, of course, had no intention of *acting* as Clerk of the
Peace, an office worth about four hundred pounds per annum. A
deputy, a local attorney, and of course an ardent Whig would willingly undertake the work for fifty pounds per annum for there
would be plenty of opportunity to help both himself and his friends
equally zealous for the King and the Cowpers. Just as important as
three hundred and fifty pounds per annum for nothing was the
status. Edward's appointment would demonstrate to the world that
he was "in," a recipient of Court favor. A prosperous marriage became more probable and certainly debts would be far easier to float.
By such means the Lord Lieutenants kept their adherents in devoted
subjection.

3

If the Lord Lieutenancy was the loom upon which the pattern of
local patronage was woven, the justices of the peace were its restless
shuttles. The nature and functions of this peculiar English institution
are as intricate as they are extensive. The justice was expected to
supervise, administer, and judge every aspect of life of his neighborhood. Not only did he deal with petty crime but he controlled the
poor rates, the repairs of highways, the licensing of alehouses; he
fixed wages, apprenticeships, settlements; he made affiliation orders;
disposed of orphans; supervised gaols and workhouses. All persons of
inferior status were in his power, and he had a strong temptation to
become a rural tyrant. Petty offenses could be dealt with in his own
parlor; more serious cases demanded the presence of a neighboring
justice; four times a year all the justices met at quarter sessions when
they settled the major problems of law and administration for the
county.

Any man of great estate could expect to be a justice almost as
of right, whether he supported the government or not. Sometimes
the Lord Lieutenant could secure the exclusion of his rabid opponents, but it was extremely difficult if they belonged to a long-estab-
lished, wealthy family. The control of the bench had to be secured
among the smaller fry; dependable clergymen or stewards gave the

Lord Lieutenant his majority. The fact that the bench always comprised men of opposite factions and attitudes led to considerable excitement and intrigue at quarter sessions when the county expressed its views on current affairs by sending up a loyal address either to the Sovereign or to Parliament. The phrasing of such addresses could lead to bitter wrangling and the final wording was a clear indication to the politically astute of the shifting emphasis of political opinion on the bench. But the sense of the county could also be taken at the Assizes where the Grand Jury, composed as it was of all the leading county figures, had the traditional right to address. In 1706 the Tories in Norfolk were stronger on the Grand Jury than at the sessions, and they resolved to address the Queen separately on the success of her arms at Ramillies. Townshend, infuriated and somewhat alarmed at this maneuvre, wrote agitatedly to Walpole:

By a letter I received from my brother yesterday I find an Address was to be presented to the Queen on Wednesday last; I heartily wish Sir Jacob Astley had signed it. The Grand Jury have resolved to send up theirs by Mr Cook who is to go for London on Monday next. Your uncle was with me yesterday to know whither I would join with them in it, but did not bring me the Address (however I have seen a copy of it), I told him I had sent up the Address which was made at the sessions, which in my opinion was a very good one, that for the Grand Jury to make another was in my opinion very irregular, and tended to create divisions and therefore I would not join in it. It has been the constant practise of the country when ever there has been any occasion for Addressing to draw the Address at the first publick meeting either sessions or assizes and I am sure it would have been thought the deputy lieutenants and justices of peace had shewed very little zeal for the Queen and her Government if, after the wonderfull success of her arms, they had omitted making an Address at the sessions. I suppose the chief reason the Grand Jury had for refusing the session's Address, was, that they might have an opportunity of sending one up by Mr Cook, his party is extremely pleased with these proceedings, and think it will be a great step towards carrying the next election. I have sent you a list of the Grand Jury who signed their Address, I think the session Address has many and as considerable hands to it, and if this method of proceeding is countenanced above, I suppose the next victory we shall have four or five Addresses from the county.[7]

The danger, of course, lay in the loss of face; for a separate, Tory-inspired address to be made to the Queen indicated to all that Townshend's hold on his county was not secure.

The core of a justice's strength lay in his own neighborhood, frequently one of the old county hundreds. There his preserves were jealously guarded.

"That yo are sworne justice of peace," John Wrott wrote to Walpole on February 11, 1702, "I think is very good news. My old master[8] always acted for the hundreds of Galloe, Smythdon and Brother Cross and Coll Browne mett him in Galloe hundred, and Sir Charles Turner sometimes and Mr Dunsgate at Bircham for Smythdon and Brother Cross hundreds. Now there being no other justice of peace in Galloe hundred but yourself, I presume you may take who you will to meet you there and I think that Sir Charles Turner have a better pretence of coming into that hundred then either the Coll. at Holkham[9] or Capt. at Sandringham.[10] And for Bircham if you take Capt. Hoste to meet you there, I thinke you have a good claim for meeting him in his hundred of Free-bridge citra Lynn."[11]

In this way the tentacles of the Walpole's power spread over the whole of this corner of North-West Norfolk. And it was so important to control the life of his neighborhood that Walpole remained a justice of the peace throughout his life and took his place on the bench whenever he was in Norfolk. With his strong political realism he knew well enough that the strength of his party rested on the loyalty of his brother justices. Without their tacit consent no political structure could last for long. They were the most vital part of local government.

4

There was only one other office of any distinction in the county and that was the office of sheriff, but oddly enough political power was measured, in this case, by the ability to guard one's friends from being chosen for it, because the duties of a sheriff were both onerous and expensive and at the same time the office lacked authority and controlled little patronage. It had one further disadvantage; no sheriff could be elected to Parliament. So at times it became necessary, vitally necessary, to prevent the appointment of a friend; yet it might be highly desirable to secure the appointment of an enemy. This could involve risk in an election year for the sheriff controlled the place and time of polling. Consequently, the office was often wished on to young men eager to work their way into the party caucus. During the early years of their alliance Townshend's correspondence with Walpole is filled with alarms and excursions about shrieval appointments. On 6 November 1704, he wrote agitatedly from Raynham to Walpole who was in London.

> I am very heartily concerned to find three of my particular friends named in the list for Sheriff and am in such perplexity that I know not what to do, however I have by this post, I hope, secured my Cosin Windham, as to the two others, I have not done anything, though I must confess I do not think making Sir Edward sheriff is the best way to prevent his standing, for he will think he is made upon that account only, and consequently he and his friends, amongst whom I reckon Mr Harvey, will be very much disobliged, and if there is any division on that side of the country, I believe it will be difficult to propose anything in matters of election with any success. Whereas I believe it will not be very difficult to prevail with him not to stand, especially if he is excused being sheriff by my interest for this year, and you know his name brought into Exchequer the next. As to Hoste you can best judge of the inconveniences that will attend his being made sheriff, I should be glad to hear from you as soon as you can.[12]

Townshend's surmise about Sir Edward Ward was correct. Almost as soon as he had written to Walpole, a servant of Ward's arrived at Raynham with a letter from Sir Edward, complaining that he was put into the sheriff's list to prevent his election to Parliament. Townshend, realizing that such a rumor would badly damage his influence in Norfolk, at once approached the Dukes of Somerset and Newcastle as well as Robert Harley in order to make certain that neither Ward nor Windham would be picked. He was successful, but only at the price of sacrificing Walpole's uncle Hoste of Sandringham. Immediately he heard of his danger, Hoste had ridden over to Raynham to see Townshend in person. It was a saddening interview, for Townshend told him bluntly that he was apprehensive that he would be the sovereign's choice and that he could do nothing to help him as he was engaged to extricate Ward and his own cousin, Ashe Windham of Felbrigg.[13]

Hoste was a choleric man, full of *amour propre*; and he was always overplaying his part as a leader of the county. He irritated Walpole by giving heavy-handed advice. Furthermore their relations were somewhat soured by Walpole's failure to repay a large loan, or even to pay the interest on it. During his first years in London, Walpole had been full of little attentions to the Hostes; supervising the construction and finishing of his uncle's new coach and even buying his wigs for him. But as he became absorbed in affairs, Walpole found Hoste increasingly tedious and no doubt the sense of an obligation which he could not discharge also made Walpole neglectful of him. His failure to help over Hoste's appointment as sheriff made matters worse, but Hoste was even more infuriated when Walpole made a complete hash of his orders for a High Sheriff's livery. For Hoste this was the last straw—the unmistakable display of a total lack of respect in a nephew who thought too much of himself. He became clamorous for his money, spread rumors of Walpole's extravagant living, stirred up strife with the hot-tempered Colonel Horatio Walpole of Beckhall, and intrigued against Walpole in his pocket borough of Castle Rising, not once but at every general election until his death. Even in 1722, at one of the most difficult moments of Walpole's career, he was distracted by Hoste's attempt to seduce his voters.[14]

Hoste, however, suffered for the luxury of his opposition. Turners, Holleys, Allens, Cremers, all enjoyed tidbits of patronage as Walpole rose in the world. Although his benevolence responded quickly to loyalty, his hostility was as quickly aroused by aggressive independence. The Hostes failed to prosper. This was the danger of a world of politics in which personal attitudes were more important than any principle. The total lack of any sort of party organization, local or national, the absence of any but the vaguest political dogmas to which men could subscribe, meant that political alliances were at the mercy of the human temperament in all its vagaries. Such a system gave Townshend and Walpole a heightened sensitivity to personal problems; and it made it necessary for them to assess every action in human terms. The reason why such detailed attention was given to the appointment of local officers was because one man's sense of disappointment might change the delicate political balance of a neighborhood with, perhaps, dangerous consequences for parliamentary representation. The composition of Parliament was, of course, the governing factor of local politics, the end for which all the arts of personal management were designed and the reason why Walpole devoted the most detailed attention not only to Norfolk affairs but also to those of all the counties of the land and of all the boroughs, great or small.

5

In 1726 Thomas Madox published his *Firma Burgi*, a fascinating panorama of the wide variety of communities enjoying special franchises in Hanoverian England. There was extravagant diversity. Beccles in Suffolk was ruled by the owners of its fen; Newport in Northumberland by the owners of its quay. Haverfordwest, a tiny hamlet, was the only town to enjoy the same privileges as the City of London, proudly boasting a Lord Lieutenant and Custos Rotulorum of its own. Or there was Durham where the Bishop exercised privileges more akin to those of a Prince-Bishop of the Holy Roman Empire than those of an English prelate. Franchises had nothing to do with the size of urban communities.[15] Birmingham and Manchester, both large and growing towns, were administratively speaking, only parishes. Fortunately for Walpole in this bewildering variety there was a dominant type in which significant changes were taking place which were to make for the ease of his government. Corporations, whose privileges were based on royal charters, had developed, and were developing, in similar ways. They were governed by a mayor, aldermen, and common-councilmen; the latter were frequently elected by the freemen of the borough, that is those who by birth, by marriage, by servitude of apprenticeship, or admission by the corporation were free to exercise their trade within the corporation's jurisdiction without the payment of a fine.

Theoretically, a qualified democracy, in practice, except in London, it was nothing of the sort. During the seventeenth century certain changes had taken place which brought about a concentration of power into the hands of oligarchies as narrow as those which dominated rural society. No one very much cared. Most human beings are prepared to be ruled; their energies are absorbed by their pursuit of wealth and by humanity's deepest needs—daily bread and family life. Only bodies of politically active and politically astute freemen could have preserved their privileges against the steady and insidious attack of the aldermen. To these men who aspired to dominate their communities the freemen were a hindrance, so their power was curtailed in a variety of ways. At Boston, the fine for admission was raised from five pounds to fifty pounds between 1689 and 1719, thus effectively reducing their number to a manageable proportion. The Corporation of Retford ceased to admit any freemen at all, so did Plympton. At Hastings two were admitted yearly, friends always of the Duke of Newcastle, more often than not men of great substance, who paid for the honor by providing the Corporation with a sumptuous banquet and then never troubled it again—except to appear and vote for the Duke's parliamentary candidates. Other corporations failed to summon their freemen except for formal and unimportant business meetings, which most freemen were too bored to attend.

It was not long before the common-council went the way of the freemen; instead of an organ of government it became a sort of antechamber where friends and relations of the aldermen who became the real rulers of the towns waited for them to die and make a place. The aldermen were, by virtue of their position, justices of the peace, which armed them with the authority of law. They had at their disposal great wealth, accumulated by the corporation during the centuries of its existence. They controlled important charitable trusts. Yet it was exceedingly rare for any of this wealth to be ploughed back into social services[16]; usually it was spent on feasts and plate, frittered away into each other's pockets in a thousand and one forms of petty corruption. Only the children and dependants of their sycophants found their way into the schools and almshouses. These aldermen were the tradesmen and merchants of the town, long practiced in the amiable art of feathering each other's nests. Naturally they married into each other's families, creating neat conglomerations of wealth and interest until a few self-perpetuating families controlled the life of a town for a century.

This concentration of power into the hands of a small number of men was to be advantageous to Walpole in many ways. The fewer the men, the easier it was for him to have a sound working knowledge of the pattern of personality and influence in all boroughs that were politically important. The patronage and honors which he controlled were limited, so the fewer pockets to fill the better—a point quickly appreciated by the recipients.

There was, however, a more subtle aspect of this change. Oligarchs quickly learn to know their place. They saw no value likely to accrue to them from sending up two merchants of the town to represent them in Parliament as their fathers had so often done. A member of a great landed family in Walpole's world would prove far more influential; the son of a peer or a well-established placeman would be better still and a much stronger link in the great chain of patronage.

This is exactly what had happened at King's Lynn. For most of the seventeenth century Lynn had been represented by merchants who dwelt and traded in the town, but in the early eighteenth century both Walpole and Sir Charles Turner belonged to the neighboring gentry, Sir Charles being the first of the Turners to leave trade and lead the life of a gentleman. And this was true of many towns like Lynn. Hence the astonishing homogeneity of the House of Commons in which the vast majority of members were country gentlemen, although technically speaking most of them were there as burgesses. Of course, not all the town oligarchies favored Walpole. Often they took the color of their politics from the neighboring gentry or aristocracy. Sometimes there were special interests, as at Bristol and Liverpool, which dominated; and there were also a few towns where this slide into oligarchy was not taking place. The greatest of these was London.

6

The constitution of London was a complex qualified democracy. There were so many advantages associated with the freedom of the City of London that it was always keenly sought after even when the admission fine was abruptly raised from 2 pounds 6s. 8d. to twenty-five pounds. The freemen participated in the administration of their wards; they elected both the aldermen and the common-councilmen who represented their ward in the government of the City. About half of these freemen belonged to the livery of the great City Companies, membership of which had brought them their freedom. Those who were of the livery took part in the yearly election of sheriff, an office of considerable importance in the judicial and administrative life of the City. The vital components of the City's government were the twenty-six aldermen and the two hundred and thirty-four common-councilmen. During the Commonwealth the Common Council had improved its position in relation to the aldermen. The point at issue was the right of the aldermen to veto the acts of the Common Council. The remodeled charter of Charles II had restored to the aldermen what was probably their ancient right, but the Revolution had witnessed a new confirmation of the independence of the Common Council.[17] This was far more than a constitutional issue, for the Common Council was more radical in its approach to political problems than the aldermanic bench, which was full of directors of the Bank and the great chartered companies who naturally tended to favor the government. But Walpole was to find that he could not be certain of controlling the aldermanic bench, for aldermen were elected and Tories or critics of his administration were frequently to be chosen. By tradition the office of Lord Mayor rotated in strict seniority. An unhappy consequence of this for Walpole was that during the most critical years of his life he was faced with a Tory Lord Mayor. London was the one great institution in which the arts of management were hamstrung. There was a vociferous and literate public opinion, well catered for by newspaper, pamphlet, and ballad, an opinion which could in a limited way make its voice heard in the deliberations of the nation either by using its ancient right to petition the King or by creating such uneasiness in commercial and financial circles that the ministry was forced to take notice. But its independence was aided by its institutions which no minister, not even Walpole, much as he hated the City, dared bring into final subjection. The key to a great deal of the politics of Walpole's day and of the rest of the century lies in the City's continued independence.

7

In the interplay of local government, the decisive factor was the effect any action might have on parliamentary elections, for final assessment of any man's power lay in his ability to influence voters. Also, from the time of the Revolution, the desire to get into Parliament became more intense and a tremendous battle for power flared up, which lasted well into the eighteenth century. Before 1689 the existence of Parliaments had depended on the King's will. They might last two months or seventeen years; at times men doubted whether Parliaments would be called again. This factor of uncertainty made many men reluctant to invest their time, energy, and money in pursuit of the doubtful privilege of sitting at Westminster. Also the lack of frequent elections presented parliamentary candidates with completely changed conditions in their constituencies; and, in order to flourish, influence and patronage need constant use. But after 1689 men realized that Parliament was to be a perpetual feature of constitutional life, that it would meet every year. In 1694 the Triennial Bill made a general election certain once in three years, unless the sovereign thought fit to dissolve Parliament earlier. The Revolution Settlement had, however, ignored the need of parliamentary reform, so strongly stressed by Shaftesbury. A few pious platitudes were written into the Bill of Rights on the need for freedom and purity of elections.[18] Subsequently one or two Acts were passed, half-hearted attempts to stop the racketeering which the parliamentary franchise invited; they had no effect. Frequent elections, a feverish desire to get into Parliament or to control elections, the extraordinary franchise—these conditions caused a violent struggle for political power in the parliamentary constituencies, which in its turn influenced the whole structure of politics in the early eighteenth century. Fully to understand the significance of these changes, something must be said of the nature of parliamentary franchise.

Before the union with Scotland, the House of Commons was composed of 513 members. There were twenty-four Welsh members; eighty Knights of the Shire for English counties; four University members; the rest, the overwhelming majority, were returned by boroughs. The distribution of parliamentary seats was remarkbly uneven. At the time of Elizabeth and the early Stuarts a considerable increase in parliamentary boroughs had taken place, particularly in the southwest.[19] The upshot was that 25 percent of all members came from the five southwestern counties, Cornwall, Devon, Dorset, Somerset, and Wiltshire, which between them returned 142 members, Cornwall leading with forty-four. Such a distribution bore little relation either to population or wealth, but it was not so outrageous, judged by these yardsticks, as it was to become by the early nineteenth century. The bulk of the population lived south of the Trent, and there, too, was to be found most of the nation's wealth, industry, and commerce. Even so there was no rhyme or reason about representation. East and West Looe, two halves of a tiny Cornish fishing village, returned as many members as the City of London. Old Sarum had long ceased to have any inhabitants except the sheep which grazed its iron-age ramparts, yet its representation equaled Bristol's, the second city of the land. The accidents of history had brought these boroughs into being; and their diversity of franchise was due to the same cause. The right to vote differed from borough to borough, but the variety can be reduced to five main types.

There was a small group in which there was universal male suffrage; three groups, much larger, in which the right to vote was confined either to the corporation, or to those who paid the poor rates, or to the owners of specific pieces of property, usually houses.[20] Finally, there was the largest group, of about eighty boroughs, where the right to vote was enjoyed by the freemen of the town. None of these franchises gives an accurate idea of the size of the electorate, except in the roughest fashion. All male inhabitants of Gatton in Surrey had the right to vote, but with a population of less than a dozen such a generous suffrage meant little. Nor did it necessarily follow that the fewer the number of voters, the easier the borough was to control. It was generally true but not always so. Nottingham and Bedford docilely obeyed the dictates of the Dukes of Newcastle and Bedford, although they each possessed over a thousand voters, whereas the obdurate independence of the thirty-two electors of Bath was notorious. They would brook no patron and scorned influence. If allowance is made for the vagaries of human nature, then it is generally true that the fewer the voters, the easier the borough was to control. On the other hand absolute ownership of a borough was very rare. The most complete control was achieved in burgage boroughs where the vote was attached to property. Patrons purchased the houses, temporarily conveying the ownership to a relative or a menial servant. But even in burgage boroughs there were rivalries and difficulties, and it was quite rare in the early eighteenth century for a family to have absolute control.

Castle Rising was a burgage borough where most of the property was owned by the Duke of Norfolk. After the Revolution, in

1695, he sold most of his property there to his relative Thomas
Howard of Ashtead in Surrey. The Duke's ownership of the burgages, however, had never been quite complete; a few belonged to
the Walpoles, some to merchants in Lynn; Hoste of Sandringham
also possessed a few, so that the Howards thought it politic to allow
Walpole's father to sit for one of the seats.[21] Colonel Walpole, realizing the insecurity of his position, rallied his forces, the Turners and
Hostes who had just married into his family and the Hamonds of
Wootton who were also close friends. They were persuaded to split
their burgages, thus bringing dependable extra voters into being.[22]
His brother Horatio of Beckhall purchased a few cottages and did
likewise. The Howards recognized the threat to their hold on the
borough and fought back; the price of a burgage cottage soared from
thirty pounds to three hundred pounds. The election of the mayor
of the borough was a vital factor in the control of its parliamentary
elections. In 1695, Colonel Walpole took advantage of the recent
change of ownership between the Duke of Norfolk and Thomas
Howard, using all his influence to get his nominee appointed. Bailiffs
moved in on the parson, a strong Howard supporter, who hid from
them in the church steeple, a cunning ruse as the mayor was elected
in church. Other voters were conveniently arrested for debt and the
tiny town was in an uproar. Peace was saved by the arrival of a
letter from the Howards accepting Walpole's right to a seat and to
the privilege, implicitly rather than explicitly stated, of appointing
his nominee to be mayor in alternate years. Colonel Walpole was
overjoyed by this recognition of his influence in the borough on
equal terms, although he possessed less of the property than the
Howards. The latter, however, acknowledged that his proximity to,
and their distance from, the borough canceled that advantage. Secure
in his triumph he graciously allowed the parson to leave his steeple
and not only take part in the election of Howard's candidate as
mayor but also in the great feast which Colonel Walpole ordered
afterward. He "sent in 4 stone of beef and 2 dozen double bottles of
his hogan to the Mayors, and after invited us to the Mayor Elect and
treated us with several bottles of wine there. He was very generous
and brisk." But several of Colonel Walpole's party were less happy
at the compromise, particularly his brother Horatio, who had spent
considerably. He had hoped to occupy the second seat, if the How-

ards had been ejected, and it was said that he "could not recover himself of his dump all day."[23] For the rest of his life, this affair of Castle Rising rankled; in politics he was Tory, which made his family reluctant to see him represent the family borough. But the compromise with the Howards proved very uneasy. Colonel Walpole was deeply disturbed in 1696 on his return from London where he had been for the parliamentary session. He was told in Rising "that noe Burgher that was a freind of mine should rent any of your [i.e. Howard] lands as they have constantly done." And to make matters worse Howard expressed displeasure with Walpole's favorite mayor. An uneasy truce was patched up. Grave difficulties recurred in 1699, which were only resolved by a visit of the Howards to Houghton.[24] When Walpole succeeded his father, the affairs at Rising continued to tax his ingenuity.

The expense of Rising was not confined to the purchase of the burgages. When the cottagers were assembled they had to be royally entertained. In 1701, the voters dined at three tables, according to their social status, and their fare varied accordingly; the first table had such luxuries as dried ham with pigeons, green geese, and the forequarters of house-fed lamb; the second table had to be content with a buttock of beef and a shoulder of mutton, while the third was given but a large leg of pork and the hind quarters of lamb; but drink was common to all tables, and the amount was prodigious, about thirty gallons of port being drunk by the forty-seven voters; this in addition to "beer and cyder in plenty." And expense did not stop with election feasts. There were a few independent burgage owners at Rising and they had to be treated with extravagant generosity.[25]

And yet by any standards, the Walpoles were very secure at Rising, far securer than the majority of patrons who possessed nothing so concrete as a piece of property which carried a vote, and naturally such patrons were forced into greater expense with far less certainty of success. As general election followed general election after 1689 the owner of a vote became adept at trading it. Costs of election rocketed as families fought to secure control of boroughs with small electorates. It cost Samuel Pepys just over eight pounds to lose his election at Harwich in 1689; in 1727 the same number of electors, thirty-two, drew nearly one thousand pounds from the Earl of Egmont's pocket.[26] A contest at Weobley cost a candidate seventy pounds in 1690; in 1717 he laid out seven hundred twenty-two pounds.[27] The costs of entertainment were frequently prodigious. At Clitheroe Guicciardini Wentworth intended to spend two hundred to three hundred pounds on a tiny electorate.[28] Nor did costs stop at elections, for the insecure loyalty of voters demanded constant attention. Lawrence Carter provided Leicester with a piped water supply. Sir Cloudesley Shovel and Sir Joseph Williamson built Rochester a town hall, and Sir Joseph threw in a grammar school for good measure.[29] And there were other costs; the clerk of the poll, the carpenters who built the booths; the town-criers and bell-ringers; the scores of officials who sprouted like mushrooms on election day, all these had to be paid for by the candidate. It was rare, too, for an election to be finally decided at the poll. There were always votes of doubtful legality, and frequently actions more dubious—bribery, kidnapping of voters, polling of dead men; no candidate ever lacked grounds to petition Parliament against the return of his rival though he might, like Sir Pury Cust, lack the money to do so. In 1690, Robert Harley had to transport witnesses from Radnorshire to London, which could only be done by hiring a coach at Oxford for the purpose. He supported them in London at his own expense, paid their wages, and of course made it worth their while to be his witnesses. It is not surprising that when his brother heard of the success of the petition he fell on his knees and offered his humble thanks to God.[30]

Only the wealthy could stand such a vast expense; many families beggared themselves trying to maintain an old family interest which had cost their forefathers little more than a glass of beer and a side of beef. The small squires and merchants tended to be forced out of electioneering, and by and large, the electorates did not want them, for they quickly learned that there was more to a good patron than mere money. Influence was even more valuable, as Walpole was quickly to learn:

"The bearer hereof," wrote Charles Turner to Walpole on February 21, 1704, "Mr Benjamin Holly is the nephew of Mr Alderman Holly of our Towne, and haveing through excess and the follys of youth reduced his estate would gladly if possible assume a career in the forces now to be raised. His unckle will advance forty

guyneys but if noe such imployment cann be gotten then that you would please to procure him to be admitted a Midshippman in one of the Majesties shipps of warr."[31]

Alderman Holley, a power in Lynn, had been reluctant to accept Walpole as burgess, but his reluctance had been overcome. Now the price was to be paid. Walpole lost no time and secured for him the post of ensign in Wightman's Regiment of Foot.[32] Another wastrel, Daniel Goodwyn, had to be found a place in the Customs. Lynn's bankrupt teacher of arithmetic was "forced from the theory to the practick part of navigation," so Walpole got him a berth on the *Cumberland*, bound for Smyrna. It was this capacity to please all and sundry which endeared a member to his constituents, and made constituents seek men who were well placed to dispense patronage.[33]

The growing cost of elections, the need to dispose of influence, made a place in the government or an alliance with a minister of state exceptionally desirable to many members of Parliament; and so places and pensions came to be as eagerly sought as seats in Parliament. Administrations were quite eager to provide them in return for loyalty, expressed by regular attendance in the Commons and an appearance in the government lobby at critical divisions. Governments, whether Whig or Tory, desired security and an easy passage for the annual budget; without any strong party discipline, a majority tied by self-interest to the administration was the soundest form of government. Hume saw with exceptional clarity that the exclusion of pensioners and placemen would lead to administrative anarchy, just as he also realized that the deliberate exploitation of places and pensions must lead to the weakening of political principle. But, like most of his contemporaries, he could see no way out of this dilemma; to him as to them a reform of Parliament could not be contemplated; yet without a reform of the franchise, the growth of patronage, influence, and oligarchy was inescapable, which was bound to lead to a destruction of political parties or inhibit their growth.[34]

In Walpole's early years, the party names, Whig and Tory, were still something more than labels; so to describe a man was the conventional method by which men defined their political attitudes. On the very broadest issues there was a clear distinction between Whigs and Tories. A man who detested the war against France, who would brook no toleration of dissenters, such a man was clearly a Tory; just as an out-and-out supporter of the war and of religious toleration could with justice be called a Whig. In parliamentary politics, these attitudes came into conflict in boroughs with large electorates, whereas in towns with few voters a candidate's political opinions were not of much moment. It was in the counties, however, that party strife became most intense, because Whig and Tory were names about which factions could crystallize their natural hatred for each other, a hatred which had in some cases lasted for centuries. In Leicestershire, long before the Wars of the Roses, the Hastingses and the Greys had hated each other; one family became Lancastrian, the other Yorkist; the Hastingses supported Mary Tudor against the Greys' own pretensions; in the Civil War the Hastingses ruined themselves in the King's service, the Greys fought for Parliament. After the Restoration the Hastingses were Tory, the Greys Whig. From time out of mind the lesser gentry had linked their destiny with one of these families; the strife of these factions was timeless although the names under which they fought each other changed with the centuries.[35] The same is true of Norfolk. The animosity between the Pastons and the Townshends was deep and bitter before the Exclusion crisis enabled them to hurl the epithet of Whig and Tory at each other. Elsewhere party strife was due to age-old conflicts between the north and south or east and west of counties. But the fact that such terms as Whig and Tory existed gave a focus to factional strife and a justification for its continuance. And in the immediate post-Revolution period added force was given to this division by a very real fissure in society; the smaller gentry found the land tax a crippling burden; and this gave an added bite to their Toryism.

But all the facts of political life were destructive of party warfare. Contest followed contest in county after county from 1689 to 1714; Essex, for example, went to the poll no fewer than eleven times, as rival factions tried to secure control of its political life. The excessive expense of county elections in the end forced men to adopt a variety of compromises; once the compromise was achieved, the party conflict withered through lack of use.[36] Party labels, however, must quickly lose their meaning in the heart of politics. Although Godolphin and Marlborough passed as Tories, they were Walpole's close friends and patrons, and so was Orford who called himself a Whig. Newcastle and Somerset, both Whigs, threw in their lot with Harley in 1710, because they thought he was more likely to follow a middle course rather than with the Junto Whigs with whom they had previously associated. Tory groups split as easily as Whig. Harley deserted Nottingham over the Tack; Rochester was at loggerheads with Nottingham; Bolingbroke worked for the ruin of Harley. This created a bewildering world of intrigue where party attitudes could suddenly acquire importance and then cease to have meaning just as quickly. They were picked up or laid aside according to the politician's need as he fought for power or clung to office. As the years passed men recognized the danger of excess in political life. Too much money, too much time and energy were consumed in getting into Parliament for men to wish to see their capital dissipated. Patrons of boroughs naturally preferred long-continuing, stable administrations with which the complicated process of influence could be evolved in a mutual security. Party fervor became a menace to all governments, although it remained the wine of life to oppositions—a lesson Walpole was quick to learn from Harley.

A further twist was given to the complications of party by the resentments which arose from the increasing cost of elections and by the blatant exploitation of patronage which, more and more, was becoming the decisive factor in political life. These things did not pass unnoticed.

> *"I believe Sir Pury Cust," Peregrine Bertie wrote to his brother, the Earl of Lindsey, "will not be very willing to enter into battle with so great a family (i.e. the Berties) for I told him he must expect, if he stood, to spend £500 or £600."*[37]

Naturally, such an attitude caused envy to flare up, stimulating men to take counsel as to how best to protect their interests. They put their faith in strange cures—frequent Parliaments, preferably annual; the total exclusion of all office-holders from the Commons; a high qualification in land for all members; the prevention of aristocratic influence in elections; severe penalties against bribery; entertainment to be stopped once the writ has been received. Bills on such topics were perennial; some became law; others were modified until they were meaningless; standing orders were framed against the interference of the peerage. Yet none of these things had the least effect. All that they achieved was the creation of a few traditional war-cries which could always be relied upon to rouse that corner in the Commons where the knights of the shire and a few independent members clustered together. For a time in the reigns of William and of Anne, the attempt to stop the glissade into corruption was a vital concern of many members, sufficiently vital for it to be worth Harley's while to adopt many of these measures as his own and to incorporate them into the official Tory program although they sprang from the resentments and jealousies of that self-same country party which had been one of the strongest allies of Shaftesbury. Harley's solicitude for the purity of elections needs little explanation; the country gentlemen who supported such a measure numbered nearly two hundred. The spread of corruption and the growth of oligarchy steadily diminished this number until it reached about one hundred, a figure at which it remained for the rest of the eighteenth century. But for the early years of Walpole's career these independent country-gentlemen remained a vital factor in politics. Their existence forced politicians to clothe their actions in the respectable garb of party principle and to justify themselves in the same terms. Their presence greatly complicates the politics of the period and makes the Augustan age one of the most difficult in English history. The nature of Parliament, the needs of government, the instinct of politicians were all opposed to any system of party politics. But a complex web of patronage could not be spun in a decade. The parliamentary franchise being what it was there could only be one end—oligarchy; events being what they were, the oligarchy had to be Whig. But until the battle for power had been fought out in the counties and little boroughs and until Harley and Bolingbroke had proved their folly, party slogans and party issues had their role in politics.[38]

8

The clergy as well as the laity were under no misapprehensions about the political role of the Church. In spite of infinite provocation the Church had followed the Stuarts with unswerving loyalty and it was not until the bishops were clearly faced with the probable destruction of the Church's privileged position that they could bring themselves to a protest. The Revolution endangered the Church only momentarily. Few of the bishops and fewer of the clergy had any difficulty in repudiating their belief in the divine hereditary right of Kings or the doctrine of passive obedience. The minority who followed Sancroft were ineffective and the non-jurors remained a small eccentric sect of no political importance. Indeed their greatest value was to empty a number of bishoprics which William proceeded to fill, naturally enough, with men like Gilbert Burnet—a sound Whig and a low churchman, who believed in toleration for dissenters. Whenever opportunity offered, William strengthened the bench of bishops with men of similar views; during his reign the ladder of preferment was closed to all passionate high-churchmen. The accession of Anne called a halt to this process. There were many men in the Church who had found it possible to square their consciences in order to take the oath of loyalty to William and Mary but, once done, they shut their eyes to the logical consequences of their act and maintained the same stiff-necked high Anglican principles which had dominated the Church since the Restoration.

The major point of contention arose from the problem of toleration. In order to avoid toleration the High Church party under the Earl of Nottingham had tried to bring in a measure of comprehension: they were prepared to make a few meaningless modifications in the liturgy in order to draw off the right wing presbyterians, so that they could happily deny toleration to the rest. This project failed and toleration of a sort was granted in 1689. The dissenters, however, were still denied full civic rights, which they failed to obtain for another century. Many of them got around their legal difficulties by taking communion in their parish church once a year, a practice which infuriated the high-churchmen, who were so shocked by such a cynical treatment of the Sacrament that they demanded the suppression of occasional conformity. They harbored another grievance for they strongly disapproved of the rapid growth of dissenting academies after the Revolution. These schools were so excellent both in what was taught and in how it was taught that they were patronized not only by dissenters but also by Anglicans. Naturally, the high-churchmen wished to close these schools; they were a danger to the Church's monopoly of education and an insidious threat to Anglican doctrine.

Some high-churchmen felt also a prick of conscience about

the future succession. They argued that Mary and Anne were both true Stuarts whereas the Hanoverians represented a complete break with the sacred line of direct inheritance. So they dreamed of a Jacobite future and this helped to soothe their resentment toward a world which was rapidly becoming alien to them. In their hearts they probably knew that the tide of life was setting against them. But for the twelve years of Anne's reign these crypto-Jacobites prospered; the Queen was moved by their profound veneration for the Stuarts and her dislike of dissenters was as ardent as their own. For better or for worse, it was impossible to remove a bishop, which limited the opportunities of these high-churchmen for advancement. Also for many years, Anne's advisers were moderate men who hated religious fanatics of any variety. Nevertheless the High Church party obtained sufficient places of importance for them to become a formidable force in politics. Bishops had seats in the House of Lords and perhaps more important—votes. They could strongly influence the attitude of their chapter which, as in York, Winchester, Salisbury, Durham and elsewhere, played a vital part in the local parliamentary elections. Many of the higher clergy were gifted writers with a natural love of polemics, so that much political propaganda came to be written by the clergy. Perhaps the deepest divisions of opinion in Anne's reign were caused by the struggle within the Church between erastians and high-churchmen, but the accession of the Hanoverians soon put an end to it, for a determined government could very easily secure a complacent Church; the system of preferment made it a relatively easy task.

Bishoprics varied in value; some, such as Winchester, Salisbury, London, Durham, and of course Canterbury and York, were exceedingly valuable, possessing incomes of five to seven thousand pounds a year, a princely salary for the early eighteenth century, enabling these prelates to live in the greatest magnificence. Other dioceses carried only a moderate salary; some, mainly the Welsh, were quite poor, bringing the bishop but a moderate stipend of three or four hundred pounds a year. But bishops could climb; they were never doomed to Welsh obscurity if they studied to please, for a bishop could be translated—at the sovereign's pleasure.

The career of Bishop Hoadly is a perfect illustration of method. All that Hoadly had to recommend him was wit, force of character, bold ambition and a tireless pen. He was severely handicapped in more than one way, for he was so badly deformed, he could only preach on his knees and as the son of a Norwich schoolmaster, he lacked all aristocratic influence. He adopted the Low Church attitude and until the Hanoverian succession slowly struggled up the ladder of preferment. After 1714, he never looked back. His support of the government was undeviating. He could be relied on in the House of Lords, even for the most disagreeable of tasks such as denouncing Place Bills. His pen was always at Walpole's service not only on ecclesiastical matters but also for foreign affairs and general ministerial propaganda. His political tasks were so onerous that he was unable to visit his diocese during his six years as Bishop of Bangor. But a man like Hoadly did not remain a Welsh bishop for long; the fruits of his loyalty were large and juicy. He was translated first to Hereford, then to Salisbury, and afterward to Winchester—the fourth richest bishopric, worth five thousand pounds a year. Naturally the High Church party did not relish this rise to greatness; but there was nothing they could do about it except vent their rage on Hoadly with biblical fury, denouncing him as a "Deist Egyptian! A rebel against the Church! A vile republican! An apostate of his own order! The scorn and ridicule of the whole kingdom!" But it was Hoadly's world.[39]

Gibson, Bishop of London and for sixteen years Walpole's lieutenant for Church affairs, was determined that promotion should be given only to men who were absolutely devoted to the administration. Every bishop's appointment was so closely scrutinized that Walpole could rely on twenty-four of the twenty-six bishops' votes in the House of Lords, usually sufficient to ensure him a majority; wherever possible the same discipline was imposed on the lower clergy. A number of fat benefices attached to cathedrals and collegiate churches could be used to reward the faithful. The Rev. James Baker acted as an election agent for the Duke of Newcastle in Sussex. An active man, he rushed round the county from horse races at Steyning to a cricket match at Lewes, proselytizing the reluctant Tories. Indeed, he so irritated the spectators at Lewes that he was nearly mobbed for his pains. A part of his ardor may have been due to the fact that already, through the Duke's influence, he enjoyed the comforts of plurality. But his rewards more than outweighed the danger of a martyrdom, for his political loyalty secured him the Archdeaconry of Chichester, and afterward a most lucrative prebend's stall at St. Paul's. Thoroughly and systematically the patronage of the Church was used to reward clergymen or their relatives for services rendered to the State.[40]

Townshend and Walpole learned to weigh the appointments of all Norfolk clergymen with the same care and attention that they were to devote to the selection of justices of the peace. On 23 September 1706 Townshend wrote urgently to Walpole: "Mr Crispe, Minister of Ellingham being either dead or dying, I must beg assistance on behalf of one Mr Baron who is a very honest man and a near neighbour of Sir Charles Turner. Ellingham lyes not far from Kirby and the living is worth between sixty pounds and seventy pounds p.an. It is in my Lord Walden's gift. If you could either yourself or by any friend prevail with my Lord to give Mr Baron this living it would be of very good service to our interest in that part of the country. Pray take all the care you can in this matter and above all things be sure to loose no time, that my Lord may not be engaged before you apply to him."[41]

Sir Charles Turner wrote by the same post and he was more urgent and more specific:

> I should not have troubled you again so soon but on a matter of very great consequence which in short is this. Mr Crispe a notorious Jacobite parson in my neighbourhood of Kirby is a-dyeing if not dead. . . .[42] This is the first opportunity I have had towards enabling myself to be a checkmate to my loving friend and neighbour, Sir Edmund Baron.[43] There are ten or twelve freeholders in Ellingham and as it joins to Kirby so as to be almost the same town (being generally wrote Kirby-cum-Ellingham) could I but get an honest parson in I should not much question but with his assistance to strike a good stroke towards bringing these poor deluded people to their senses again . . . therefore beg of you for the sake of the publick more than upon my own account that you would leave no stone unturned to obtain it and set about it the moment you have read my letter. . . . For God's sake do not neglect this affair.[44]

Townshend's and Turner's agitations were in vain. The living of Ellingham was in the hands of Lord Suffolk who was unsympathetic to the Whig cause and Sir Charles had to wait for another opportunity before he could deliver his neighbor a checkmate.

There were of course patrons who were largely indifferent to politics, and who refused to be dragooned by the politically minded into making a political appointment. Many parsons lived out their lives unconcerned with either great men or great affairs. For the most part they were steady commonplace men, inclined to Toryism, strongly distrustful of all change or innovation, unmoved by the deeper problems of religious faith, who nevertheless tended their flocks with care and with charity. Often they acted as physician and lawyer as well as parson, for it was natural that their parishioners should bring to them all problems which required skill in book-learning. About most of their lives there was a steady, self-indulgent benevolence which comes to men locked in a narrow world of easy circumstances.[45] But for the ambitious clergyman there was but one way of advancement: a well-placed patron and unwavering devotion to politics.

9

Local government, Parliament, the Church were the three bases upon which the pyramid of government rested. Their management and control absorbed most of the time and a great deal of the energy of all the ministers of state, yet without the forceful backing of the Crown, their time and energy would have been wasted. The position of the Crown in the late Stuart and early Hanoverian times has been constantly misunderstood. Anne could on occasion be overborne, particularly by the resourceful and vigorous Duchess of Marlborough, but she could be extremely obstinate and her views on policy as well as on appointments had to be respected. Nor were the Georges mere cyphers. George I possessed more than a smattering of English, and all his ministers, including Walpole, had a fair or fluent knowledge of French, the language used naturally by the King.[46] Both George I and his mistresses had a keen interest in domestic politics, while George II's and Caroline's was avid; no promotion was too small to escape their attention and they insisted on listening to lengthy and detailed reports of the debates in Parliament. Lord Hervey's *Memoirs* would make this clear enough even if we did not possess many of Walpole's memoranda, listing matters which he wished to discuss with the King, ranging from ambassadorial appointments to the rules of the college which Bishop Butler wished to establish in Bermuda. The Court was the heart of political life and without the entire and loyal support of George I or George II Walpole could not have lasted a month; it was as vital to his power as was his majority in the Commons, indeed more so, because had he not possessed the royal good-will his majority in the Commons would not have been secured. It is necessary to look more closely at the machinery of government to appreciate the power of the Court in eighteenth-century politics. Parliamentary sessions were short and mainly concerned with the passage of financial bills. Legislation as we know it was quite rare, with the consequence that the actions of the executive became the main target of criticism in debates; foreign affairs and the cost of the armed forces took up most of Parliament's time. The King's ministers were not, however, usually troubled with Parliament for more than four or five months of the year and for the rest they could devote themselves to diplomacy, patronage and administration, of which patronage and diplomacy were the most important.

The King controlled an immense field of patronage. Every civil servant was the King's *own* servant, appointed by him and paid out of the royal pocket. The entire administration of the country was carried out by the Royal Household, which, like the constitution, had grown up haphazardly over the centuries; when new problems had arisen they had been met either by increasing the duties of a minor official or by the creation of a new office. Old ones were never abolished. Many offices became sinecures with no duties; if the office had duties, more often than not (unless they were great offices of State) they could be easily discharged by a deputy, so that the Household became the haven for the needy place-hunter. Walpole's strength as a minister arose from the fact that nine times out of ten the King accepted his advice on appointments. Naturally Walpole used this power to secure himself in the Commons, and all places great or small were made to pay political dividends. This was a wasteful policy financially, for the abolition of such offices as the Taster of the King's Wines in Dublin, useless and absurd as it was, could never be entertained; its bestowal on a member of Parliament or his relatives would keep him in dependence on the Court. So the resources of the Household came to be ruthlessly exploited by place-seekers and politicians, with the result that historians have come to overstress the corruption of eighteenth-century politics. Sinecures might be without duties, but they were rarely without obligations and often entailed hard work.

In 1726, the Board of the Green Cloth had become an archaic survival of the Middle Ages. Its function was to settle disputes arising amongst the King's servants. By 1726 it had long ceased to have much business, yet there were four clerks—Richard Sutton, Sir Robert Corbet, Gyles Earle, Robert Bristow—all drawing five hundred pounds per annum.[47] Naturally they were to be found in the government lobby in all critical divisions. They could be mistaken for typical place-holders selling their vote for the sake of a sinecure. This, however, is a distortion, for these men played the part of junior ministers. They attended debates with great assiduity, served on countless committees, and helped with energetic skill to pilot government measures through the Commons. Although they lacked administrative responsibility in a narrow sense, in all other ways they may be regarded as hard-working members of the government, fully deserving their five hundred pounds per annum. Many sinecures were so filled, and a great deal of the jockeying and intrigue which went on to obtain a place at Court was as much for the sake of cutting a figure in government as for the money it brought. These places possessed one other attraction; they conferred distinction. The whole of London's social life revolved around the Court; its gaiety, wit and malice were inbred; it was a closed yet glittering world which dazzled all who did not belong to it by birth. This mixture of luxury and power intoxicated the ambitious, and its compulsive quality only weakened as the monarch aged. Then, as his hold on the future loosened, the young and the discontented drew closer about his heir and spent happy days sharing the spoils of future office as they awaited the King's death. At such times cautious men found in an independent attitude the way of virtue and profit, and ministries encountered difficulties in securing their majorities. For many years of Walpole's ministry both he and the King were in the prime of life, and age and death did not cast their disturbing shadows across the political scene.

Naturally there were gradations of power within the Court. The great officers of State were of two kinds, those with and those without departmental duties. As Chancellor of the Exchequer and First Lord of the Treasury, Walpole was to be burdened with exceptionally heavy day-to-day business, whereas the Duke of Montagu, as Master of the Great Wardrobe, had nothing more than a few traditional duties to perform for the King personally. These offices of great honor and small duties were usually bestowed on loyal noblemen of great wealth and territorial power—the Dorsets, Graftons, Richmonds and their like, whereas the offices with administrative duties went to the active politicians, the men who ran the Lords and Commons on behalf of the Crown.

Traditionally both types of official were the King's advisers on questions of policy; and there were times when they all met together as a cabinet. But these large cabinets were not loved by the politicians. Walpole came to distrust them and avoided them when he could, for in such a large body it was easy for disagreement on points of policy to fester and to create factions competing for the King's approval.[48] Also there was a great deal of business, particularly foreign affairs, where detailed knowledge was essential and could only be acquired by close application to ambassadorial reports.

Naturally the politicians preferred to decide such questions in close conclave. In time of war, the need for secrecy became more critical, and as carelessness was more likely to arise from a large cabinet, so smaller ones were favored. And lastly, there was the undeniable fact that many holders of great household offices were not clever men, and their opinions were more likely to befog than clarify business. These factors resulted in the early development of a small inner cabinet which met frequently and consisted almost entirely of the political officers of the Household—the Lord President, the Privy Seal, the Chancellor of the Exchequer, the two Secretaries, and the Lord Chancellor—the men who bore the burden of government. They met informally wherever it suited them best, sometimes at the Cockpit, which housed the Treasury and the Secretaries, but frequently in their own homes; sometimes one of the Secretaries jotted down their decisions or made a few notes, but many meetings have gone unrecorded.[49] Once this inner ring, or "efficient cabinet" as it is called, had determined its policy, it had little difficult in imposing its views on the large cabinet which from time to time was required to meet to give a more formal sanction to certain acts of State. This system did not develop during the early years of Walpole's career when the formal cabinet with the Sovereign present discharged a great deal of business, but under the Georges the formal cabinet suffered an eclipse. George II maintained that no good ever came from it, an opinion which Walpole encouraged. When the King was in Hanover the meeting of a more formal body could not be avoided, and then policy was considered by the Lords Justices, a body which was almost identical with the large cabinet, but not, of course, before the vital decisions had been decided by the efficient cabinet.

We have a very clear picture of how this system worked from the diary of Lord King who was Lord Chancellor from 1725 to 1733.[50] Walpole, naturally, took the initiative. Technically he was often invading territory which by right belonged to others. Foreign affairs, strictly speaking, were the concern of the Secretary of State and none of his business. He had to find the money for subsidies or to pay for war, if war ensued, and this was sufficient excuse, if excuse were needed, for his interference. When a treaty or a negotiation was on foot, Walpole would dine with each of the chief ministers or spend a night with them in their country houses. In the benevolent and easy atmosphere induced by good food and better wines, Walpole would air his views, counter criticism, and plant his suggestions. The ground prepared, the efficient cabinet meeting would be called. Unanimity, in the heyday of his power, did not take long to achieve. Once the inner ring was certain of its line, the Lords Justices or the formal cabinet would be summoned and, with alacrity and little discussion, formalized the decisions previously taken. Then, of course, came the struggle to persuade the King to accept the proffered advice. The Hanoverians were deeply interested in foreign affairs and often held to their views with great obstinacy. The Secretaries did not present the King with a decision but with an advice, and it is essential to remember this, for it explains why Walpole, Townshend or Newcastle were forced to spend so long at Court cajoling and persuading the monarch to go the way they wanted him to go; why it was necessary for them to have Court spies, such as Hervey, who could report at once the purveyors of counter-advice, men who were hunted remorselessly by Walpole until he secured their destruction.[51] And, of course, the jealousies and envies of those who were excluded from this inner ring were always at work. Because the King was head of the executive, policy-making demanded extreme care and dexterity; and a fluid, semi-formalized system was much easier to manage than a rigid constitution.

But policy was largely a matter of foreign affairs. A great deal which nowadays would demand the attention of the cabinet was settled out of hand by Walpole himself. In 1731 the Earl of Egmont wanted to secure an easing of the trading conditions between Ireland, Great Britain and the Colonies. To strengthen his case he secured the support of most of the Irish peers and members of the Commons with Irish interests, who held formal meetings at the Thatched House Club and passed resolutions in favor of his policy. A situation of great complexity arose which entailed decisions involving relations with Ireland and America. On this matter Walpole consulted no one but his brother Horace, whose office as Cofferer of the Household lacked the remotest connection with Ireland; yet he was present at meetings called by Egmont in order to put forward his brother's views. When at last Egmont brought the matter before the House he was dexterously outmaneuvred by Walpole, who from start to finish seems not to have consulted any other minister, so that Egmont wrote bitterly and with a certain justice in his diary:[52] "Thus we see how the welfare of that poor Kingdom (Ireland) lies in the breath of one Minister's nostrils." Rarely has a minister wielded such independent authority.

There is one further point about the central government at this time that needs to be stressed. There was less, infinitely less, administration. There was only one really large department and that was the Treasury. A series of reorganizations undertaken at the end of the seventeenth century had greatly increased the number of its employees, both in London and the provinces, for it controlled both the Customs and Excise. But even here methods were primitive by modern standards and business was small. Other departments were tiny. Matters which required the attention of the secretaries of State were extremely varied—all foreign dispatches, which involved ciphering and deciphering, passed through their office; at the same time they were responsible for law and order, for the Colonies, for Scotland; all final decisions about the Army and Navy were their concern. In fact, all that touched the King's affairs, except finance, had to be dealt with by them. Even when a child was eaten by a tiger, they needed to be consulted. Was the tiger forfeit to the King? If so, could it be destroyed? Only a Secretary could decide.[53] But such oddities seldom strayed into the Secretaries' office, for the people at large ignored the official world and made their own decisions. The Secretaries' minute staff—twenty-six including the caretaker—devoted themselves mostly to ambassadorial dispatches and agents' reports, leaving the country to govern itself as well as it could. Without protection, the poor, the weak and the sick went under; the rich and the strong prospered. But few cared, and any increase in the government's power, any extension of its activity, was bitterly resented.

This was to be Walpole's world—a small prosperous nation which had thrown off the shackles of monarchial despotism and created the undefined compromise of a parliamentary monarchy. So long as the King remained head of the executive, the Court was bound to be the focus of political power and this in turn weakened the party basis of politics. Patronage, in all its complexity, became the dominant theme in political life. At such a time force of personality and skill in human relations were more than ever desirable in a statesman. Walpole had both in good measure.

NOTES

VI. *Robert Walpole's World: The Structure of Government*

[1] F. C. Turner, *James II*, p. 344. The idea that a man's office was a freehold had a long history and was no innovation; it was stated more emphatically at this time.

[2] The King's own keen interest in the process is illustrated by A. Browning, ed., *The Memoirs of Sir John Reresby*, p. 321. There are some very peremptory letters from the Earl of Dover to the Mayor of Bury St. Edmunds about the King's wishes and the composition of the corporation in the *West Suffolk Records* at Bury.

[3] James's investigations into the loyalty of the gentry are to be found in Sir G. Ducket, *Penal Laws and Test Act*.

[4] A. Browning, ed., *Memoirs of Sir John Reresby*, p. 584.

[5] Spencer Compton urged the Earl of Dorset, only sixteen, to apply at once for the Lord Lieutenancy of Sussex in 1706, on the death of his father. Charles J. Phillips, *History of the Sackville Family*, II, p. 3.

[6] A. T. Thomson, *Memoirs of Viscountess Sundon*, I, pp. 329–330. The letter is undated, but *c.* 1717.

[7] C(H) MSS, Townshend, August 1706.

[8] Walpole's father.

[9] Walpole's uncle, Horatio, a difficult volcanic character and a Tory.

[10] The captain was James Hoste, an uncle of Walpole's by marriage. He was to prove very unreliable.

[11] C(H) MSS, John Wrott, 11 February 1702.

[12] C(H) MSS, Townshend, 6 November 1704.

[13] *Ibid.*, Townshend, 6 November 1704; 8 November 1704. As a further illustration of the importance of the sheriff's appointment, Townshend recommended a Mr. Rogers as sheriff in 1707 "because I thought it might be of service to have one of our friends sheriff next year upon the account of the election," *ibid.*, 8 November 1707.

[14] C(H) MSS, various letters of Hoste; also references to him particularly in the letters of John and Charles Turner. The intrigues of Hoste in 1722 are in a letter of Jonas Rolfe, 19 August 1721. Further correspondence of Hoste is to be found in the *Chicago (Walpole) MSS*.

[15] For boroughs and borough franchises, see S. and B. Webb, *English Local Government*, II.

16 Liverpool was a notable exception, cf. Webb, *op. cit.*, II, pt. 2, pp. 481–491. An excellent study of an eighteenth-century corporation is by R. W. Greaves, *The Corporation of Leicester, 1689–1832*.

17 For a more detailed description of the City constitution, cf. Webb, *op. cit.* II, pt. 2, 574–581.

18 For Shaftesbury cf. D. Ogg, *England in the Reign of Charles II*, II, 482–483. *Report of the Deputy Keeper of the Public Records*, XXXIII, 229–230; also Locke, *Two Treatises on Civil Government* (Everyman ed.), p. 197.

19 Cf. J. E. Neale, *The Elizabethan House of Commons* in which he demonstrates that the extension was due not to a desire to increase royal authority but to a demand on the part of her privy councillors who desired clients. For this section in general cf. A. E. Porritt, *The Unreformed House of Commons*, and Sir Lewis Namier, *The Structure of Politics at the Accession of George III*.

20 At Droitwich the franchise belonged to those who possessed shares in the salt mine.

21 Thomas Howard was the son of Sir Robert Howard, KB, MP, the dramatist who was a great-grandson of the Duke of Norfolk and a grandson of the Earl of Suffolk. Thomas's only daughter and heiress, Diana, married the Hon. William Feilding, son of the Earl of Denbigh, a staunch Tory family. Feilding sat for Castle Rising in his wife's right. [Ed. note: The Duke of Norfolk did not reside in the county.]

22 This practice was stopped in 1697 by Act of Parliament.

23 Bradfer-Lawrence, "Castle Rising and the Walpoles," *Supplement to Blomefield*, ed. C. Ingleby.

24 *Howard MSS*, Castle Rising. Colonel Walpole to Thomas Howard, [Aug.?] 1696; 11 September 1696; 15 September 1699.

25 For Castle Rising cf. Bradfer-Lawrence, *op. cit.*, and a great deal of correspondence in *C(H) MSS*.

26 Bodleian, *Rawlinson MSS*, A. 174, fo. 177; HMC, *Egmont Diary*, I, p. 293.

27 BM, *Add MSS*, 34,518, fo. 57.

28 HMC, *Kenyon MSS*, p. 275.

29 HMC, *Bath MSS*, II, p. 176.

30 *Ibid.*, *Portland MSS*, III, p. 451.

31 *C(H) MSS*, Charles Turner, 21 February 1704.

32 C. Dalton, *English Army Lists*, VI, pp. 92, 274. Holley had risen to be a lieutenant by 1710.

33 *C(H) MSS*, John Turner, 3 October 1705.

34 Hume, *Essays Moral, Political, Literary* (1742), especially "of

Parties in General" and "of the Coalition of Parties." Also, Sir Lewis
Namier, *Monarchy and the Party System* (Romanes Lecture, 1952).

[35] For the influence of the Hastings-Grey struggle on Leicestershire politics cf. J. H. Plumb, "Political History of Leicestershire," *VCH
Leicestershire*, II, pp. 102–121.

[36] In 1715 it cost Walpole £110 13s. 7d. to take his freeholders
with a county vote to Norwich for the election; one wagon load consumed four gallons of brandy on the journey. *C(H) MSS*, "Account of
the Disbursements of Mr. John Turner, Jnr, for the County Election, 1
February 1715." His father on 2 February 1679 spent £1 8s. 6d. "att the
election att Norwich." *C(H) MSS*, Account Books, 15(1).

[37] HMC, *Ancaster MSS*, 250. Lady Elizabeth Cust, *The Records
of the Cust Family*, 250–251. The income of Sir Pury Cust at this time
amounted to £656 per annum, derived from rents, but he was over five
thousand pounds in debt; the Berties were immensely rich.

[38] Cf. R. R. Walcott, "English Party Politics (1688–1714)" in
Essays in Modern History in Honor of W. C. Abbott (Harvard, 1941).
Although I am in substantial agreement with Professor Walcott, I think
that he allows too little significance to conceptions of party, particularly
among the Whigs.

[39] For Hoadly, cf. *DNB* and N. Sykes, *Church and State in the
Eighteenth Century*; Hervey, *Memoirs*.

[40] Sykes, *op. cit.*, p. 81 *et seq.*

[41] *C(H) MSS*, Townshend, 23 September [1706].

[42] Samuel Crispe was presented to Ellingham by James, Earl of
Suffolk, in 1670, Blomefield, *Norfolk* (ed. 1775), IV, p. 233.

[43] Sir Charles Turner had married for a second time, Mary,
daughter of Sir William Blois and widow of Sir Nevil Catelyn of Kirby
Cane, GEC, *Barts.* V, p. 66.

[44] *C(H) MSS*. Sir Charles Turner, 23 September 1706.

[45] An excellent illustration of a typical eighteenth-century parson's
life is to be found in C. D. Linnell, ed., *The Diary of the Rev. Samuel
Rogers*. Bedfordshire Historical Society, XXX (1950).

[46] The myth that Walpole could only converse with the King in
dog Latin is based on a legend started by Horace Walpole in his reminiscences, written in advanced old-age for the Misses Berry. Cf. Paget Toynbee, ed., *The Reminiscences Written by Horace Walpole in 1788*, pp.
14–15. All foreign dispatches were duplicated in French for the King's
benefit. Cf. Townshend's diplomatic correspondence at Raynham and
Horatio Walpole's at Wolterton Hall. Walpole when Secretary at War
had the French gazettes sent over to him.

[47] Chamberlayne, *Magnae Britanniae Notitia* (ed. 1726), Pt. II, Bk. III, p. 106.

[48] Professor A. Aspinall in his Raleigh Lecture, *The Cabinet Council, 1783–1835*, quotes a number of remarkable instances of cabinet quarrels. Although of a much later date, they reflect a situation which was common in Walpole's day.

[49] The cabinet notes of Harley, Sunderland, Townshend, and Dartmouth survive. Harley's notes are among the documents deposited by the present Duke of Portland in the British Museum; the Sunderland notes are at Blenheim, the Townshend notes at Raynham, and the Dartmouth notes at the William Salt Library, Stafford.

[50] Lord King's diary is printed in volume two of King, *Life and Correspondence of Locke* (ed. 1830). I have compared this with the original in the possession of the Earl of Lovelace; the transcript is accurate. Cf. also Hervey, *Memoirs*, I, pp. 121–131.

[51] At Raynham there is a large file of Townshend's correspondence with George II. Each letter was carefully annotated by the King, no matter how trivial. Coxe printed some of his correspondence, *op. cit.*, II, pp. 520–543.

[52] HMC, *Egmont Diary*, I, pp. 173–175.

[53] Mark Thomson, *Secretaries of State, 1681–1782*, p. 111.

*S*tudents *of eighteenth-century English politics have learned, largely from the work of Sir Lewis Namier, to pay attention to the role of aristocratic connection and the problem of the independent country gentleman—and with good reason. But a student who engages the subject at close quarters is certain to notice the sound and fury of eighteenth-century politics and to wonder perhaps where it came from and how to explain it. Mostly it came from London. For it must not be overlooked that the English Parliament, the executive, and normally the court, were all situated in London; not, of course, within the boundaries of the old city, but that was of small consequence. London was therefore the center of political discourse, and nearly all foreigners who visited the City during the eighteenth century were struck by its highly charged political atmosphere, the pervading influence of which accounted for much of what was for sale in the bookshops and even infected the lower orders of society. When M.P.'s spoke of politics "out of doors" they generally meant public opinion in the metropolis. In this essay Dame Lucy Sutherland examines the ingredients of London politics and shows, among other things, why the London electorate, for all its immersion in shopkeeping and commerce, tended to side with the Tory opposition. She is the pre-eminent historian of London politics in the eighteenth century. Among her works,* A London Merchant, 1695-1774 (Oxford, 1933) *and her Creighton Lecture,* The City of London and the Opposition to Government 1768–1774 *(1959), may be mentioned in this connection; but above all, her most important contribution is her major study of* The East India Company in Eighteenth-Century Politics *(Oxford, 1952). Dame Sutherland was Principal of Lady Margaret Hall, Oxford, from 1945 to 1971. The essay here is reprinted from* Essays Presented to Sir Lewis Namier, *edited by Richard Pares and A. J. P. Taylor (London and New York, 1956), with the permission of Dame Sutherland and Macmillan, London and Basingstoke.*

VII

The City of London in Eighteenth-Century Politics

BY DAME LUCY SUTHERLAND

A study of the part which the City of London played in the politics
of the eighteenth century involves the examination of two distinct
but interrelated topics. The first is limited and specific: the nature
and influence of the City in what was then a comparatively new
sense, that of its "monied interest." The second is wider and more
nebulous: the nature of the political opinion and political influence
of the City of London in its older sense of a civic entity.[1] Though
the borderline between the two is necessarily often more than a little
blurred, they involve two very different issues: the study of the first
is a matter of the mechanics of government; that of the second is, in
general, a study of the organization and inspiration of opposition.
Though the first will be touched on in this article, its chief purpose
is to indicate, however tentatively, the main considerations affecting
the second.

    The "City" in the modern use of the term, the "monied inter-
est," was composed throughout this period of a small but growing
number of persons closely and habitually concerned with that machinery for creating and mobilizing credit which had been taking
shape since the late seventeenth century. Its organization was developing throughout the eighteenth century, particularly in time of
war. Its institutional center was to an increasing extent the Bank of

England, assisted to a lesser degree by the other members of what contemporaries called the "three great monied companies," the East India Company (with its own issue of short-term securities) and the South Sea Company, since its recovery from the crash of 1720 almost wholly a financial as distinct from a commercial organization.[2] With these were associated to some extent the two insurance companies formed in 1720, the Royal Exchange Assurance Corporation and the London Assurance Corporation.[3] Around this institutional center there clustered the individual operators working on embryonic markets in stocks and shares, in insurance, and in dealings in certain raw materials, a nexus of activities already foreshadowing the organization of a future when London was to become the money market of the world,[4] and already the opportunities it opened up to enterprising individuals were so promising as to lead the most vigorous and successful of the London merchants away from purely commercial activities toward those which were primarily financial. The purposes for which capital and credit were mobilized were much more restricted then than now, and were more limited than they had been before the Bubble Act of 1720.[5] They were, at least till the last quarter of the century, almost entirely restricted to the needs of overseas trade and public finance, and the second, particularly in time of war, bulked very large. Indeed the fortunes of the richest of the monied men would seem at this time to have been largely made by satisfying the credit needs of the State; in subscriptions to government loans, in government remittances, and in financing government contracts. It was this fact that gave the monied interest its significance in politics.[6]

Though the rise of an embryonic money market was making it possible for the State to mobilize to its own use the resources of the monied individual, there was as yet none of the impersonality of the modern public subscription. The method of raising loans was still so undeveloped and the number of credit-worthy lenders so small that—although shares in government loans passed freely from hand to hand and market prices were regularly quoted—the actual subscription to loans was normally undertaken as the result of personal negotiations between the more important of the monied men and the directors of the monied companies on the one hand and the Treasury on the other. Thus each Treasury in turn took pains to forge its personal links with the monied interest in the City, and the relations between them became very close. Moreover, in the intricate game of eighteenth-century political management the Treasury would often make it clear not only that they would tend to confine financial advantages to their friends in the City, but that they would give preference to those friends who were also members of Parliament and could thus provide a vote on the government's side in the House of Commons. In consequence, the chief monied men in the City, unless they were disqualified by religion[7] or nationality,[8] found it worthwhile to buy expensive borough seats (they might, of course, have done so in any case if they were seeking to use their wealth to move into the ranks of the landed gentry) to qualify for the reception of financial favors from the government. And the men who made up the nucleus of the monied interest, both within and outside the House, remained throughout the century in close alliance with the government of the day.

The influence of such men on the governments with which they were in alliance was considerable, both in purely financial matters[9] and on other issues related to them. The combined opposition of the monied interest prevented the reduction of the interest on the national debt, though Walpole was known to favor it, in 1737,[10] and Pelham only succeeded in carrying out his conversion operation of 1749–50 after making liberal compensations to the main institutions involved.[11] Not only were the terms of government loans bargained for in advance between the Treasury and their leaders,[12] but their advice on the finance of war was taken on occasion in connection with peace negotiations,[13] and those of them who sat in the House were often employed as experts on a variety of commercial issues. Their importance as a political force can, however, easily be over emphasized. Eighteenth-century politicians sometimes gave credence to a myth not unlike that of the "bankers' ramp" of the twentieth century, and maintained that ministries could be overthrown or rendered impotent by the "loss of the City" engineered by political opponents. But their only illustration of a ministry "losing the City" to opponents (and this a confused and inconclusive one) dated back to 1710–11.[14] Though it was sometimes claimed that the attempt to oust the Pelhams in 1746 was defeated by the determination of the monied interest to refuse supplies to an alternative administration,[15] this does not seem to be supported by facts; the difficulties which the Devonshire-Pitt administration found in raising supplies in 1757[16] were not due to political causes; and the hopes of the Duke of Newcastle, when dismissed from office in 1762, that his successors would be unable to obtain credit, were disappointed.[17] In fact, the City, in the sense of its monied interest, was throughout the period a broken reed for the purposes of party politics, for the good reasons that the prosperity of all its members depended on their being on terms with the government of the day, and that, even if it might have paid them to hold out for a short time, they were much too competitive among themselves to do so. As early as 1711 Daniel Defoe had argued that it was not the maxim "They that have the Money must have the Management" which was true, but "They that have the Management will have the Money."[18]

So much for the City in the modern sense of the word. In its older sense the City was a great urban center, by far the greatest in the British Isles, with a population within its ancient boundaries of about 150,000, and a dependent population of about 700,000.[19] It had a proud and ancient corporation from which many of its residents were excluded but which nevertheless comprised some 12,000–15,000 freemen by birth, apprenticeship, or redemption[20] (some 8000 of whom were also liverymen of the City companies) and a vigorous corporate spirit which expressed the attitude of its "middling men," as contemporaries called them, the class of small merchants, tradesmen, and master craftsmen. It was they who dominated its Common Council, elected its four members of Parliament, and, both in the Common Hall and Common Council, played a great part in the election of City officers, from the mayor downward.[21] And if the richest men in the City, its "monied interest," were supporters of the governments of the day, the City in this wider sense was almost always in opposition to them. If the state of City opinion be examined for the sixty-two years between the rise of Walpole in 1720 and the fall of Lord North in 1782, in the records of the Common Council,[22] in the utterances of the City members, in pamphlet and press and the comments of contemporaries, it becomes clear that the City abandoned its anti-ministerialism only on occasions when there was some special explanation of the fact, and that the occasions were comparatively few. Such exceptions were the years 1747–54, when Henry Pelham had set himself to placate the City, as he was placating all the opponents of his Broad-bottomed Administration;[23] the years 1756–61, when William Pitt was carrying on his two war ministries on principles with which the City was deeply concerned; to them may perhaps be added the first months of the Chatham administration, when the name of the late Great Commoner still exercised its spell.[24] But these years are, at the most, no more than eleven out of a total of sixty-two. For the rest of the time there was suspicion and antagonism, flaring from time to time, in the excitements of political life, into violent hostility.

The question arises, what was the reason for this remarkable consistency in opposition, a consistency which survived changes of kings and administrations and bore so little relation to the ruling persons or forces of the day? There are several possible explanations. Two of them are at bottom based on economic considerations. The first possible explanation is that the attitude was the outcome of friction and conflict within the City itself. In eighteenth-century London there was, partly as a heritage of seventeenth-century strife and even earlier traditions, and partly as a result of contemporary tendencies, a good deal of that latent hostility between the richest citizens and the lesser men which is familiar (as the struggle between "Magnati" and "Popolani") to students of the independent communes of Europe. The antagonism was social, economic, and political in its origin and showed itself in friction within the City constitution (for instance, in disputes between the Court of Aldermen and the Court of Common Council)[25] and a tendency to seek emancipation from oligarchic leadership and control (for instance, in the choice of the four City members of Parliament and sometimes of the chief City officers).[26] The fact that many of these rich citizens were supporters of the government was in itself likely to lead the lesser men to array themselves with the opposition,[27] and there were two special reasons which strengthened this trend. Firstly, in 1725, in his London Election Act, Walpole had ranged the government on the side of the oligarchic faction in the City by giving the sanction of law to the traditional power of "Aldermanic Veto" over the Common Council, and though Pelham repealed the relevant clause of the act twenty-one years later, much bitterness had been engendered in the meantime.[28] Secondly, those outside the "monied interest" were bitterly jealous of the advantages made available to the monied men by the method of taking up subscriptions to government loans already referred to, and they clamored loudly for an "open" subscription in which they could all join, a demand which the Treasury seldom thought it prudent to satisfy.[29] Thus it felt of most ministers, as was said of Walpole (however unjustly), that "he is hated by the City of London, because he never did anything for the trading part of it, nor aimed at any interest of theirs, but a corrupt influence over the directors and governors of the great monied companies."[30] But this internal friction, though no doubt an important contributory factor to the City's attitude in national politics, does not seem of itself sufficient to explain the vigor of its anti-ministerialism. Nor does it explain why this anti-ministerialism was abandoned in special circumstances.

A second economic explanation might lie in the interest of the City in maritime and colonial war. The commercial classes of the eighteenth century were exceedingly bellicose in their sentiments, provided that the wars they were fighting were sea-wars and the aim of them was the retention or gain of colonial territory, for in such wars they saw prospects of private commercial gain as well as hopes of national glory.[31] Indeed, there is some truth in Burke's bitter description of the merchants in 1775 as beginning "to snuff the cadaverous *haut goût* of lucrative war."[32] They were also, however, the first to be struck in their pockets as well as their pride when such wars went badly, so that the events of the period in time of war, or in the years leading up to war, or (in the reign of George III) the years of conflict with the American colonies, gave ample opportunity for friction between the governments and the body of commercial and trading opinion finding expression in the City. But this explanation, too, though it may account for the timing of most of the biggest outbursts of anti-ministerialism, is insufficient in itself to explain the whole movement and fails to make clear why it was maintained in years of peace. Nor do either of these economic explanations account for the forms in which this feeling found expression.

If these two explanations are dropped the conclusion remains that the key to this tendency in the City must be sought in causes less obvious but perhaps even deeper-seated. These causes are best elucidated by considering the relations of the City with the other opposition interests in national politics, bearing in mind at the same time the stamp set on the activities of the City by its own traditions and experience. If the parliamentary oppositions of the eighteenth century are examined, the first thing that becomes clear is that (oddly enough, at first sight, in an age when ministries made majorities and not majorities ministries) they always sought to bolster themselves up and embarrass their enemies in power by attracting the support of bodies of opinion outside the House. As Burke, one of the most experienced opposition leaders of the century, remarked, "we know that all opposition is absolutely crippled if it can obtain no kind of support without doors."[33] They sought this support in general from two classes, the country gentry, who influenced and were influenced by those independent country gentlemen in the House whose role Sir Lewis Namier has so brilliantly analyzed in his Romanes Lecture,[34] and in the body of organized commercial and trading opinion in the City of London. And, when they were successful in gaining this support, they did so by calling to their aid political assumptions and prejudices which were accepted by gentry and merchants alike without question—and which were indeed accepted by everyone except the small ring of persons directly concerned with the day-to-day questions of political power—the seventeenth-century suspicion of the Executive and the desire to limit the scope of its activities. For some forty-five years after the Hanoverian Succession every opposition, whatever its nature and its real end, pinned its faith on rallying the support of these two powerful extra-parliamentary forces by "out-Whigging the Whigs." They produced a program which expressed an archaic, academic Whiggism, by incorporating the demand for a Place or Pensions Bill, the return to triennial parliaments, and the reduction of the standing army.[35] And even in the reign of George III when opposition found new and sometimes more realistic war-cries, the old ones had not lost their charm.

Moreover, though everyone with inside knowledge of politics knew that no group or party intended to implement these doubtful political principles, the fact that they were so widely accepted made them embarrassing to governments. These even went so far on occasion (particularly just before a general election) as to let measures incorporating them through the House of Commons, to be quashed in the safety of the Lords, knowing, as it was said in 1731, that to vote against such measures "would put a great many gentlemen under difficulties" so that they "must have left them or have hurt their own interest very much in the places they serve for"[36]—an argument which also throws some light on the passing of Dunning's famous Resolution of 1780.[37]

The counties and the City filled somewhat different roles in the system of opposition parties. Opinion expressed in the counties was intended to impress the country gentlemen in the House and was dispersed and loosely organized. That stirred up in the City was much easier to organize and mobilize. City leaders were expert, from long experience of organizing commercial agitation affecting both London and the "outports," in the art of bringing pressure to bear on authority from without. Petitions, instructions from the Common Council to the City representatives, pamphlets, and press campaigns were rapidly planned there, while whenever political excitement ran high the London crowd could be relied on to emerge and give the added support of their clamor to the opposition cause.

Both these extra-parliamentary allies presented opposition leaders with some problems, but they were different ones. The country gentry might get out of hand, as from the point of view of the opposition parties they did at the time of the County Associations. The Duke of Newcastle warned his colleagues in opposition in 1767, "I know the nature and the pulse of our country gentlemen. They are now as well and as quiet as possible; set them in motion and nobody can tell what may arise."[38] But this problem was only an extension of the general one of handling the independent gentry in the Commons. But the City, though it could be rallied to the opposition cause, always had to be handled as a separate entity, following (as the country gentry never did) some specifically City leader who was thought of as one of themselves, and it was a force which approached politics in a manner from outside. It was, indeed, this sense of separatism, of standing outside the dominant social and political system of the time, that gave the City in opposition its peculiar flavor, and it was this sentiment (which lay at the root of the attitude which the nineteenth century was to call Radicalism) which really explains the persistency of the City's tendency to political opposition. Socially the attitude expressed itself in some resentment against and suspicion of the aristocracy and landed classes, with their easy arrogance and assumption of superiority, and in a somewhat self-conscious and self-righteous pride in their bourgeois virtues and bourgeois traditions—this finds its echo in literature and in drama intended largely for their consumption.[39] Politically, there is evidence of a feeling that they and their interests lay outside the framework of a political system dominated by and organized for the interests of the aristocracy and landed classes, and an irritation because they, with their stake in the prosperity of the country and their contribution to it, were apt to be in the position of outsiders having to bring pressure to bear on the political machine.

It is true that arguments have been adduced which would seem to run counter to such an explanation. It is pointed out that there was an easy and constant transit from the merchant classes into those of the landed gentry, and that, not only were commercial questions one of the major concerns of eighteenth-century Parliaments, but also that a very considerable number of merchants sat in the House of Commons.[40] But it is important to bear in mind the cleavage between the rich merchant and financial classes and the lesser men. Most of the latter lived lives entirely circumscribed by their urban traditions; a seat in Parliament was quite outside their ambitions, and they neither considered that their richer fellow citizens who obtained seats in the House represented them nor that they represented the commercial interests with which they were concerned. The author of *The Remembrancer*, for instance, in 1748 complains bitterly of the prominent citizens who are to be seen cringing at levées and seeking seats in the House of Commons "and instead of assisting as they ought to preserve and enlarge the traffic of the kingdom, assisting to traffic it away for the sake of a lucrative share in some contract, some remittance or some other dirty consideration of a like nature;" and he urges that a line should be drawn "between the m[inisteria]l posse of stock-jobbers, contractors, remitters . . . etc., and the fair and upright exporter" and that one should "confine the reputable title of *merchant* to the latter and admit of his verdict only in commercial matters."[41]

This combination of participation in the general political assumptions and activities of the nation and of peculiar local separatism and self-consciousness can be traced throughout the history of the City's political activities during the century. It is possible also to trace the way in which the City's self-consciousness became stronger and more articulate under the pressure of events and with the passing of time; and as it grew, so too did the scope and effectiveness of City influence in and over the parliamentary oppositions with which they were in alliance. A brief (and necessarily imperfect) analysis of those stages in the City opposition, corresponding also to stages in the history of eighteenth-century parliamentary opposition, will illustrate this development. The same three periods correspond roughly with those of the personal predominance of three of that curious succession of leaders on which the City's political influence so strikingly depended.

The first period runs roughly from 1720 to 1754, that in which united parliamentary oppositions, composed of combinations of discontented Whigs and broken Tories (grouping themselves for some years around the Prince of Wales), fought what was 'on the whole a losing battle against the great Whig governing connection built up by Robert Walpole and continued by Henry Pelham—a losing battle, though Walpole himself was overthrown during its course. At this time the City's leader was a stout, high-principled merchant and ship-insurer of no more than moderate wealth, Sir John Barnard,[42] who represented the City in Parliament for nearly forty years. During his prime he was a constant and effective speaker, hardly ever missed a debate,[43] and never compromised a principle. He was an inveterate enemy of the financial interests,[44] was responsible for the act for preventing "the infamous practice of stock-jobbing,"[45] which, if it had been effective, would have prevented the rise of the Stock Exchange altogether, and though he never compromised his independence, he seems to have believed implicitly that the purpose of the opposition which hounded Walpole from power was to carry out those Whiggish measures to which it paid lip service. Under this leader the commercial interests of the City were kept well to the fore, and one of the biggest of the opposition drives, that against the Excise Bill of 1733, arose on a question primarily of commercial importance, but the remoteness of the City from the day-to-day realities of politics and its political naïveté made it little more than an adjunct to any opposition leader who chose to play on its academic "Whiggism" and its sense of grievance and isolation. The oratory of William Pulteney,[46] for instance, greatly attracted City support and, on the fall of Walpole in 1742, it was widely believed that sweeping constitutional changes would follow. A contemporary describes the ferment of excitement on this occasion, in which the City warmly joined.

Among those who thought themselves most moderate, no two men agreed upon what was necessary;—some thinking that all security lay in a good place bill . . . some in a pension bill. Some in triennial parliaments . . . some [were] for annual parliaments . . . some for a reduction of the Civil List . . . some for the sale of all employments . . . some for taking the disposition of them out of the Crown . . . some for allowing them to subsist but to be given only to those who were not in Parliament, that is, among themselves . . . some for making the army independent; others for no regular troops at all.[47]

When it became apparent that, in fact, nothing was to be done, the disillusionment in the City knew no bounds. For years Pulteney appears in City oratory as the great betrayer, whose example must be a warning to those who put their trust in politicians.[48]

During this time, though their detachment from the day-to-day preoccupations of politics was marked, there was still little overt expression of their political and social sense of separateness. There is, however, a good deal of indirect evidence of social and political malaise quite apart from their response to the demands of oppositions upon them. It is usually disguised, in contemporary references, under the title of City Jacobitism; but the more this alleged Jacobitism is examined, the more it appears to be nothing other than a vague and unorganized dislike of the authorities. Horace Walpole said of the "popular" Alderman Blakiston that he had "risen to be an alderman of London on the merit of that succedaneum to money, Jacobitism."[49] But the sober Lord Waldegrave was nearer the mark when he told George II in 1758 "that as to Jacobitism, it was indeed at a low ebb; but there was a mutinous spirit in the lower class of people. . . ."[50]

The next period, however, brought some major changes. This

second period may be taken to cover that strange interlude in English political history when, in the war years between 1756 and 1761, William Pitt, the Great Commoner, broke through the chains of government by connection and forced himself, on equal terms, on the group who had been ruling the country for the last forty years. He maintained himself in this precarious position by the general recognition of his essentiality to win the war and by his popularity not only with the country gentry in Parliament but with public opinion outside the House. It has sometimes been claimed for the Great Commoner that he was the first eighteenth-century politician to realize the value of the support of public opinion. This is not true, but he was the first to try to continue using in power the support of outside forces hitherto thought to be available only to opposition.[51] In consequence, in this period the City suddenly found itself in alliance with government instead of opposing it, and though, after Pitt's coalition with Newcastle in 1757, the City leaders continued as suspicious of his allies as ever—at one time Newcastle accused Pitt of "letting the mob loose" on them[52]—they adopted with enthusiasm the role of representatives of the nation supporting the actions of a great national leader. The means by which this support was applied to administration were the same as those by which it had been given to leaders of the opposition. It was, as before, under the guidance of a City leader, no longer Sir John Barnard, who was not only nearing the end of his career, but had lost some of his popularity by coming to terms with the Pelham Administration, but a new man, Alderman William Beckford,[53] a rich Jamaica sugar-planter. The new leader was very different from the old: Barnard was first and foremost a merchant and citizen; Beckford had some interests in and connections with the City,[54] but also much in common with the landed classes, had sat for Shaftesbury before he became member for London, and he began to foster his interest in the City (taking up his freedom in 1752 and becoming an alderman in the same year) only two years before offering himself as a parliamentary candidate. Active for some time in opposition politics,[55] he obviously saw the chance of strengthening his political position by having the support of the City behind him, and after he had become the devoted supporter of Pitt he made no secret of the fact that he meant to use his power in the City to further the cause of his patron in national politics.

The propaganda and leadership of Beckford and the personal magnetism of Pitt produced, paradoxically, two conflicting results in the City during these years. In the first place, the City gained greatly in its sense of importance and the articulateness of its traditions and outlook. A speech by Beckford in the House in 1761 expresses the attitude of those he was leading. Having referred to the "sense of the people," he proceeded to define it.

> *The sense of the people, Sir, is a great matter. I don't mean the mob; neither the top nor the bottom, the scum is perhaps as mean as the dregs, and as to your nobility, about 1200 men of quality, what are they to the body of the nation? Why, Sir, they are subalterns, I say, Sir, . . . they receive more from the public than they pay to it. If you were to cast up all their accounts and fairly state the ballance, they would turn out debtors to the public for more than a third of their income. When I talk of the sense of the people I mean the middling people of England, the manufacturer, the yeoman, the merchant, the country gentleman, they who bear all the heat of the day. . . . They have a right, Sir, to interfere in the condition and conduct of the nation which makes them easy or uneasy who feel most of it, and, Sir, the people of England, taken in this limitation are a good-natured, well-intentioned and very sensible people who know better perhaps than any other nation under the sun whether they are well governed or not.*[56]

Odd though these words must have sounded in the mouth of a wealthy slave-owner, they reflect accurately the social and political outlook of his followers, views middle-class, commercial, anti-aristocratic, and clearly likely to prove difficult for opposition groups trying to use them for their own purposes in the game of politics.

But if the strengthening of this feeling was one result of the experience of these years, there was another that was rather different. As a result of the example set by Beckford and soon followed by others, the City was brought more closely into day-to-day politics, since the leaders it trusted were themselves, as John Barnard had never been, the agents of political groups.

Both these effects were to become increasingly apparent in the third period under consideration, which was not slow in coming, for Pitt's position was essentially temporary, the product of war and crisis, and with his resignation and the return of peace this curious interlude was over. But it left behind it a City opinion more self-conscious, more closely engaged in national politics, in a state of frustration at the loss of its recent importance; and this at a time when postwar dislocation, bad harvests, political instability, and the impact of a variety of national problems were to exacerbate all social and political problems. It is not surprising that the City was so deeply affected by the excitements surrounding the case of John Wilkes and General Warrants, nor that in 1763 a popular pamphlet-eer claimed that the constitution represented interests once predomi-nant but now so no longer and that the merchant classes should enjoy a greater share in representation.[57]

The period 1762 to 1782 is that of the climax both of the eighteenth-century development of City self-consciousness and of its influence on national politics. The years which saw the rise of the Whig opposition *par excellence*, the years in which the Whig inter-pretation of history was born, were those in which extra-parliamen-tary pressure on politics became open and organized, first in the City and then later, and for a limited period but with great effect, in the counties. In these years the parliamentary opposition groups were forced to trim their sails and adjust their courses to meet the demands made on them by supporters whom they had hitherto been able to control and had been apt to have to stimulate, but whom less than ever they could afford to lose.

After the first confused eight years of George III's reign, two main opposition groups emerged, that which followed Chatham, and of which Lord Shelburne and, later, Pitt the younger were the out-standing figures, and that which was built up round the person of the Marquess of Rockingham, of whom Burke and, later, Charles Fox were the most active members. They were at one in their violent opposition to the King and his ministers, but united in nothing else. They were in active competition with each other in their attempts to capture the support of the extra-parliamentary forces on which opposition traditionally depended. During the later years of the American War, they competed for the support of the counties, where the gentry were driven to unparalleled independence and activity by the expense and misfortunes of the war. Between 1768 and 1772,[58] and more sporadically up to 1775,[59] competition for influence in the City played a considerable part in their plans.

This competition would in itself have been likely to increase the concern of the City with the day-to-day business of politics but to detract from its position as a semi-independent political force, for the aim was to employ the machinery of City government for the needs of one or other of the groups active in national politics. The Chatham-Shelburne group had the initial advantage of the support in the City of William Beckford, who still had the most crowded years of his City career before him (he died in 1770, having completed a highly popular second term of office as Lord Mayor). Later, they had the support of certain close followers of Lord Shelburne in the City, Alderman James Townsend[60] and Alderman Richard Oliver.[61] The Rockingham group, however, tried to build themselves up a rival force, using as their chief City supporter Alderman Barlow Trecothick, member for the City and in 1770 Lord Mayor (who had been their agent in organizing the commercial agitation for the repeal of the Stamp Act in 1766).[62] They also had some hopes of using in the same way William Baker, son of Sir William Baker who had in his time been a prominent City supporter of the Duke of Newcastle.[63] These tactics of opposition led, as was inevitable, to comparable activity by the government, who were able to give indirect assistance in the traditional way to the declining oligarchic influences in the City. Hence in the election of members for the City in 1768 and in elections for City offices for the next few years there was an obscure triangular struggle in process between groups who hoped to use the City as a political weapon or at least to prevent their opponents from doing so.

This struggle was, however, interrupted almost before it began and suddenly cut across by a startling revival of City independence in the political field. There emerged in 1768 the strangest of all the City leaders of the century, John Wilkes.[64] With his meteoric rise to power the City appeared once more as a powerful but external force in politics, as independent as in Sir John Barnard's day, but much more formidable and incalculable.

The sudden appearance of this cynical and able demagogue, whose cause had been fostered by opposition leaders in the past, but who had not occurred to them as a possible rival for the control of the City, struck contemporaries, as it does posterity, with astonishment. Benjamin Franklin, who was in London in 1768, thought it inexplicable.

> 'Tis a really extraordinary event to see an outlaw and exile of bad personal character, not worth a farthing, come over from France, set himself up for candidate for the capital of the Kingdom, miss his election only by being too late in his application and immediately carrying it for the principal county. The mob, spirited up by numbers of different ballads sung or roared in every street, requiring gentlemen and ladies of all ranks as they passed in their carriages to shout for "Wilkes and Liberty," marking the same words on all their coaches with chalk, and No. 45 on every door; which extends a vast way along the roads into the country. I went last week to Winchester, and observed that for fifteen miles out of town there was scarce a door or window-shutter next the road unmarked.[65]

Posterity has found it no easier to explain. It has sometimes been assumed that his power rested essentially on his influence over the London mob. He certainly had remarkable success in whipping them up at a time when there were various causes for unrest—a fact which in the end contributed considerably to the collapse of the movement with which his name was associated. But examination of the stages of his career in the City suggests that his real political strength lay elsewhere. It lay in just those classes of lesser merchants and tradesmen on whose support oppositions always depended, and he was thus directly competitive with the City leaders who were working to obtain the support of this class for the rival parliamentary opposition groups. He was indeed assisted in his rise by their jealousy of each other. Though Beckford at first opposed him secretly,[66] he soon decided it was wiser to appear to back him; but when, in 1771, after Beckford's death, his successors Townsend and Oliver quarreled with Wilkes, Rockingham and Burke thought on the whole they would rather see Wilkes victorious than their political rivals. Rockingham thought Wilkes might be "perhaps not so dangerous as the others would be . . . and probably Wilkes single would be easier to manage than a whole pandaemonium."[67] It was an inept judgment, for it soon became apparent that Wilkes, in the strength of his popularity, could break through the webs of connection which they were weaving, and, though his personal popularity depended on his remaining in active opposition to government,[68] he could deal on equal terms with the parliamentary opposition groups.

There seems to be no explanation of the phenomenon of his rise and the hold he gained on this type of follower but the fact that he appealed powerfully to forces in the City which resented subordination to opposition as well as to government, that he voiced their hostility to the aristocracy as well as to the Crown and the Executive, and (a strong point in view of the personal nature of his power) that he appealed to them in his own person as the victim of the forces which they resented. Perhaps the best example of the attitude of his main City supporters—men of some substance and education—is the rich but misfit and plebeian parson Horne Tooke,[69] who played so big a part in his rise and was so bitterly disillusioned by its results.

Wilkes, strong in this support and backed by the funds of the Bill of Rights Society which his City friends founded, was soon not only driving the rival opposition groups out of the City[70] but putting them at a grave disadvantage in national politics by forcing on them constitutional programs which they had no desire to embrace. These programs were not revolutionary, for his supporters were not revolutionaries; they clung to the idea of shorter Parliaments and of traditional methods of controlling the power of the Crown, but they added two new demands: an attack on the rotten boroughs as the center of aristocratic as well as of royal power, and the proposal to bind their representatives to carry out their wishes by enforcing pledges on them at the time of their election, a proposal very unwelcome to all parliamentary parties.[71] How successful they were is shown by the fact that they forced Chatham to subscribe to triennial Parliaments after he had explicitly expressed his disapproval of them;[72] and that they drove Burke not only to try to distract attention from those parts of their program he thought most dangerous by developing other parts which his friends found less unattractive, but also to lay down as a maxim for preserving the "true country interest" that they should not support candidates nominated by "a mere club of Tradesmen."[73] And most opposition members would probably have agreed with his indignation at the "infinite mischief" done "by the violence, rashness and often wickedness" of that "rotten subdivision of a faction amongst ourselves . . . the Bill of Rights people."[74]

These years mark the climax of the influence of London on the political life of the country during the century, and its traces are to be found in the programs of parliamentary opposition and in the attitude of the country gentry when, during the American War, they followed the City's example and set up their own short-lived but spectacular extra-parliamentary organizations.[75] But it must be admitted that the climax was a short-lived one and that in the City, as in the counties, both the organization and the zeal for exerting pressure on politics disappeared as rapidly as they arose, leaving little obvious trace behind them. In both cases the explanation seems to lie in the limited nature of the aspirations of those supporting the movement, the dependence of these aspirations on the circumstances of the moment, and the unwillingness or inability of most men to realize that the issues they were raising had far wider implications. When something of the nature of what Burke was to call "the portentous comet of the Rights of Man" appeared to them, the merchant and tradesman of the City, like the country gentleman, stopped abashed.

The check in the City came earlier than in the country as a whole, though even there it did not long outlive the exasperation of the American War. The withering away of the turmoils of the years of Wilkes's City dominance was partly due, no doubt, to the fact that Wilkes himself (never, as he said, a Wilkite) made his peace after 1779 with vested interests and retired to sedate ease in the most lucrative position the City had to offer, that of its chamberlain. But even before he did so the support he could count on was beginning to decline: he lost his following in the Common Council and his supporters became progressively limited to what George III had called "a small though desperate part of the Livery."[76] And when, in 1780, the London mob burst its bounds in the Gordon Riots, and this without any stimulation from those who normally expected to exploit it, Joseph Brasbridge spoke for many when he said: "from that moment, though previously contaminated with the mania infected by Wilkes, the political mountebank of the day, I shut my ears against the voice of popular clamour."[77]

But, though the City's fervor was thus summarily checked,

the forces underlying it were not changed. In the turmoils which surrounded the political activities of Sir Francis Burdett[78] at the turn of the century, their continued vitality can be traced. And, when the great Reform agitation of the 1830s came on, one can see, in the organization and activities of the radical London master-tailor Francis Place,[79] the unmistakable mark of eighteenth-century City experience and traditions, with its long history of cooperation with parliamentary oppositions but also its characteristics of isolation and separatism.

NOTES

VII. *The City of London in Eighteenth-Century Politics*

[1] The phrase "the City" was used in both senses by contemporaries throughout the century, and the context alone can indicate which is meant.

[2] For this, see J. Clapham, *The Bank of England: a History* (Cambridge, 1944), Vol. i; L. S. Sutherland, *The East India Company in Eighteenth Century Politics* (Oxford, 1952), chap. ii; and "Samson Gideon and the Reduction of Interest, 1749–50," *Economic History Review*, 1946, pp. 15–29.

[3] The two Assurance Corporations were included, though in a lesser degree, with the three greater companies in arrangements for subscriptions to government loans. The most able financier of the first half of the century, Samson Gideon, addressing the Treasury on the means of raising the loan in 1757, speaks of the importance of "securing the five Companies" (Chatsworth MSS. 512.3).

[4] The history of the origins of the Stock Exchange is still an uncharted field. On the growth of marine insurance, see C. Wright and C. E. Fayle, *A History of Lloyd's* (1928).

[5] 6 Geo. I, c. 18. See A. B. DuBois, *The English Business Company after the Bubble Act 1720–1800* (New York, 1938), pp. 1–41.

[6] Sir Lewis Namier first analyzed this situation in *The Structure of Politics at the Accession of George III* (1929), i, pp. 56 *seq.*

[7] As was Samson Gideon, the great Jewish financier.

[8] As was Sir Joshua Vanneck, of Dutch birth. See L. B. Namier, *op. cit.*, i, p. 70.

[9] Namier, *op. cit.*, p. 56 *seq.*, and L. S. Sutherland, "Samson Gideon: Eighteenth Century Jewish Financier," *Transactions of the Jewish Historical Society of England*, xvii, p. 79 *seq.*

[10] The best contemporary evidence for this abortive attempt is the diary of the first Earl of Egmont, *Historical Manuscripts Commission, Diary of the first Earl of Egmont*, ii, p. 380 *seq.*, and correspondence in the *Carlisle MSS., Hist. MSS. Comm.*, p. 182 *seq.*

[11] L. S. Sutherland, "Samson Gideon and the Reduction of Interest," *loc. cit.*

[12] This is shown by L. B. Namier, *op. cit.*, i, p. 68 *seq.*, for 1759, and L. S. Sutherland for other occasions in the two articles quoted above.

¹³ For instance, W. Coxe, *Memoirs of the Administration of the Rt. Hon. Henry Pelham* (1829), ii, p. 318, H. Pelham to Newcastle, 23 Sept.–4 Oct. 1748. "I have made the best inquiry I can, amongst all the men of business in the city, and I can assure you, they are all of opinion, that peace is absolutely necessary." On 1 Oct. 1762 the Duke of Cumberland consulted Newcastle, recently out of office, on the financial prospects if the peace negotiations fell through. Newcastle consulted a City friend, Thomas Walpole, son-in-law and partner of Sir Joshua Vanneck, who replied that, given a Minister they trusted, "he thought the money might be had, taking advantage of the present general dislike to the terms of Peace" (Brit. Mus., Add. MSS. 32944, f. 36).

¹⁴ The part played by the monied interest led by the Bank in the fall of Godolphin in 1710 (see J. Clapham, *The Bank of England: a History*, i, p. 73 *seq.*, and C. Buck and G. Davies, "Letters on Godolphin's Dismissal in 1710," *Huntington Library Quarterly*, 1940, pp. 225 *seq.*) and the financial difficulties in Harley's Ministry (see "Memoirs of the Harley Family, especially of Robert Harley, first Earl of Oxford, by Edward Harley, Auditor of the Exchequer," *Hist. MSS. Comm., Report on Portland MSS.*, v, p. 650 *seq.*) remains an obscure incident. Eighteenth-century politicians bore it in mind. In 1762 Newcastle deplored the threat of the governor of the Bank of England to retire in disgust at the Bute Ministry. "Besides his successor would probably not be so good a friend as he is, and the Bank might fall into bad hands as it did when Sir G. Heathcote was overpowered by Sir James Bateman and John Ward in my Lord Oxford's time" (Add. MSS. 32940, f. 373, Newcastle to Hardwicke, 16 July 1762).

¹⁵ H. Fox to Ilchester, 13 Feb. 1746, quoted in Ilchester, *Henry Fox, First Lord Holland* (1920), i, p. 125. But see W. Coxe, *op. cit.*, i, p. 289.

¹⁶ Add MSS. 32870, ff. 437 *seq.*

¹⁷ *Ibid.* 32944, ff. 22 *seq.* (Substance of a conversation with the Duke of Cumberland, Oct. 1762), and Add MSS. 32940, ff. 302b-3 (Newcastle to J. West, 9 July 1762).

¹⁸ *Eleven opinions about Mr. H[arle]y; with Observations*, 1711, p. 43.

¹⁹ For the problem of the population of London, see M. D. George, *London Life in the Eighteenth Century* (1930), pp. 21–29.

²⁰ S. and B. Webb, *English Local Government . . . The Manor and the Borough* (1908), ii, p. 574 *seq.*

²¹ *Ibid.*

²² The Journals preserved in the Guildhall Records Office. See also Vol. 8 of the Common Hall Books. 1751–88.

[23] Sutherland, "Samson Gideon and the Reduction of Interest," *loc. cit.*

[24] The first Rockingham Administration, despite its active support of certain trading interests (Sutherland, "Edmund Burke and the First Rockingham Ministry," *English Historical Review*, xlvii, p. 40 *seq.*), never succeeded in winning a good press in the City, even the repeal of the Stamp Act being generally attributed to Pitt (*e.g.*, *Public Advertiser*, 1765, *passim*).

[25] The internal friction in the City and its connection with national politics has been carefully analyzed by A. J. Henderson, *London and the National Government, 1721–42* (Duke University Press, 1945).

[26] Instances of the latter are the election of Deputy James Hodges as Clerk of the City in 1757 (for the controversy surrounding this, see *The Test*, 23 April 1757, pp. 134 *seq.*, and *The Contest*, 28 May 1757, pp. 165 *seq.*).

[27] The aldermen, though popularly elected, were elected by wards, the characters of which varied considerably; they held office for life and it was widely held that a fortune of not less than £30,000 was a necessary qualification. In consequence, though there were always some "popular" aldermen among them, the majority tended to express the views of the monied interest, though few of them at any one time played a prominent or active part in this interest. When feeling ran very strong in the City, as in the later years of Walpole, or during Wilkes's predominance in the City, they tended to bow to it in the long run, but only after a considerable time-lag and always with a strong minority holding out.

[28] Henderson, *op. cit.*, pp. 74 *seq.*

[29] Sutherland, "Samson Gideon and the Reduction of Interest," *loc. cit.*

[30] *Some Materials towards Memoirs of the Reign of King George II by John Lord Hervey*, ed., R. Sedgwick (1931), i, p. 138.

[31] R. Pares, *War and Trade in the West Indies, 1739–1763* (Oxford, 1936), pp. 56–64.

[32] FitzWilliam and R. Bourke, *The Correspondence of the Rt. Hon. Edmund Burke* (1844), ii, p. 50.

[33] *Ibid.* ii, pp. 51–52.

[34] L. B. Namier, *Monarchy and the Party System* (Oxford, 1952). See also his "Country Gentlemen in Parliament 1750–1785," *History Today*, Oct. 1954, pp. 676–688. Both are reprinted in *Personalities and Powers* (1955).

35 Extremists sometimes demanded annual Parliaments and the total abolition of the standing army, but in the first half of the century they were rare and somewhat eccentric.

36 *Hist. MSS. Comm., Carlisle MSS.*, p. 82. Hon. C. Howard to [Lord Carlisle]. The Pensions Bills of 1730, 1731, and 1732 were handled in this way. The Place Bills of 1734 and 1739 were thrown out by the House of Commons only by small majorities, the first by 39 and the second by 16 votes. The ministers tried to avoid speaking on them.

37 "That the influence of the Crown has increased, is increasing and ought to be diminished." 6 April 1780 (*Parliamentary Register*, xvii, p. 453). It was passed by a majority of 18 votes in a full House against the Ministry, despite the fact that the North Administration was normally strong in the House at this time; but it had no consequences. The general election which took place later in the year had not yet been decided on, but it was clear it could not be long delayed. Lord Shelburne told the Common Council of London in reply to a congratulatory letter on the Resolution: "It is universally acknowledged that the approaching Election has a considerable influence on the members who now support the petitions of the people," and added that the county members "are understood to have voted for the most part uniformly on the same side." Guildhall Records Office. Journal of the Common Council, 68, f. 49.

38 Add. MSS. 32980, f. 355, Newcastle to Richmond, 20 March 1767. The occasion was a suggestion by Richmond that the Grand Jury of Sussex should thank the county members for their vote on the reduction of the Land Tax in which the government was defeated. He remarked, ". . . I am not for opening a correspondence between the Grand Jury and their members. Every man may start a disagreeable thing in a Grand Jury, who can do no hurt in the County. It may put it in the head of some lively geniuses to give instructions, or, at any time, to observe upon the votes and behaviour of their members, which would not be pleasant." *Ibid.* f. 354.

39 The writings of Daniel Defoe are early expressions of this attitude. The so-called "bourgeois" drama of the period shows its influence very strongly.

40 For the merchants in the House, see Namier, *Structure of Politics*, i, p. 56 seq.

41 *The Remembrancer*, 3–10 Sept. 1748, quoted in the *Gentleman's Magazine* (1748), pp. 411–412.

42 1685–1764, *b.* Reading, son of a wine-merchant, M.P. for London 1722–61, knighted 1732, sheriff 1735, Lord Mayor 1737: *Memoirs*

of the late Sir John Barnard, Knight (1776); *Reasons offered to the Consideration of the worthy citizens of London for continuing the present Lord Mayor . . . for another year,* 1738.

⁴³ *Reasons offered to the Consideration of the worthy citizens of London for continuing the present Lord Mayor . . . for another year,* 1738.

⁴⁴ See Sutherland, "Samson Gideon and the Reduction of Interest," *loc. cit.*

⁴⁵ 7 Geo. II, c. 8.

⁴⁶ William Pulteney, Earl of Bath, 1684–1764.

⁴⁷ *Faction Detected by the Evidence of Facts* [Lord Perceval, later Earl of Egmont] (1743), pp. 69–70.

⁴⁸ *E.g.* [Richard Glover] *Memoirs of a Celebrated Literary and Political Character* (1813), pp. 1–7.

⁴⁹ Horace Walpole, *Memoirs of the Last Ten Years of the Reign of George II* (1822), i, p. 31.

⁵⁰ James, Earl Waldegrave, *Memoirs from 1754 to 1758* (1821), p. 130.

⁵¹ In December 1761 the *Gentleman's Magazine*, p. 579, giving extracts from *Charges against the Late Minister with remarks extracted from a variety of Letters*, including the statement "An opposition to government will always please and gain the people of England, who are great levellers," adds the note that this has not been true for the last four years.

⁵² Newcastle to Hardwicke, 27 March 1758, quoted in P. C. Yorke, *Life and Correspondence of Philip Yorke Earl of Hardwicke* (Cambridge 1913), iii, p. 44.

⁵³ 1709–70, born in Jamaica, where his family had great estates and his father was governor; M.P. for Shaftesbury 1747–54, London 1754–70; Lord Mayor 1761 and 1769. A statue was erected to him in Guildhall for his speech when delivering a petition to the King in 1770.

⁵⁴ He was described as a West-India merchant, but his trading interests seem to have been restricted to handling the produce of his own estates. In *The Gazetteer and London Daily Advertiser,* 25 April 1754, "A Liveryman" asks "if one of your candidates is not Member of a Club of Planters, where merchants are judged unworthy of admittance?" Beckford claimed that his "family were citizens, and some of them had borne the highest offices for a century past." (Speech when elected Lord Mayor in 1762, *Public Advertiser,* 30 Sept. 1762.)

⁵⁵ See, *e.g., The Diary of the late George Bubb Dodington* (ed., H. P. Wyndham, 1784), p. 100, and pp. 235–236; Namier, "Country Gentlemen in Parliament," *loc. cit.*, pp. 683 *seq.*

56 Add. MSS. 38334, ff. 29 *seq.* [13 Nov. 1761].

57 *Political Disquisitions, proper for Public Consideration in the Present State of Affairs in a Letter to a Noble Duke* (1763).

58 Evidence of this activity is to be found in the *Burke Correspondence*, i, p. 228 *seq.*, and the Burke and Rockingham MSS., Sheffield; Portland MSS., Nottingham University; *The Correspondence of William Pitt, Earl of Chatham*, ed., W. S. Taylor and J. H. Pringle (1839); and the Lansdowne MSS. at Bowood. At the general election of 1768 Barlow Trecothick, a successful candidate, was called in a City squib (*City Races* [1768]) "Lord Rockingham's wall-eyed horse Mercator."

59 *Burke Correspondence*, ii, p. 55. E. Burke to Rockingham, 23 Aug. 1775. "Lord John [Cavendish] has given your lordship an account of the scheme we talked over, for reviving the importance of the City of London, by separating the sound from the rotten contract-hunting part of the mercantile interest, uniting it with the corporation, and joining both to your lordship."

60 1737–87. Son of Chauncy Townsend, a prominent London merchant; M.P. West Looe 1767–74, Calne 1782–87. Took up freedom of City by patrimony in 1769, alderman 1769, Lord Mayor 1772. In close touch with Shelburne at least from 1760. (W. P. Courtney, "James Townsend, M.P.," *Notes and Queries*, 11th Series, v, pp. 2–4.)

61 1734?–84. Born Antigua, brought up in London by his uncle, a West-India merchant; M.P. for the City 1770–80, alderman from 1770; committed to Tower by the House of Commons 1771. (*Notes and Queries*, 8th Series, iv, p. 217.)

62 For him, see Namier, *ibid.*, p. 270, and L. S. Sutherland, "Edmund Burke and the First Rockingham Ministry," *loc. cit.*; W. P. Courtney, "Barlow Trecothick," *Notes and Queries*, 11th Series, iii, pp. 330–332.

63 Namier, *England in the Age of the American Revolution* (1930), pp. 280–281.

64 H. Bleackley, *Life of John Wilkes* (1917).

65 *Memoirs*, quoted in W. P. Treloar, *Wilkes and the City* (1917), p. 56.

66 Camden to Beckford, 28 March 1768. "I give you joy of your success in London and hope Middlesex will follow the example of your City and send Wilkes to Jewry (?) which they say is to be his next excursion. If he fails there, I presume he will retreat into that strong fortress the King's Bench Prison" (Hamilton MSS., National Library of Scotland. I am indebted to Miss H. Allen for a transcript of this letter).

67 Rockingham to Burke [Jan. or Feb. 1771], Fitzwilliam MSS., Sheffield.

[68] This remained true even after the days of his great popularity were over. As late as 1784, John Robinson said: "Mr. Wilkes's support of any government is very uncertain, because the safety of his situation depends on his watching as he calls it all administrations and having no apparent connexion with any, but taking the side of all popular questions." *Parliamentary Papers of John Robinson, 1774–1784*, ed., W. T. Laprade (1922), p. 68.

[69] A. Stephens, *Memoirs of John Horne Tooke* (1813).

[70] Burke, *Correspondence*, ii, p. 3. "It was but a few months after Lord Shelburne had told me, gratis (for nothing led to it), that the people (always meaning the common people of London) were never in the wrong, that he and all his friends were driven with scorn out of that city."

[71] Burke dated the driving from the City of "all the honest part of the opposition" to "all this professing, promising and testing." (Burke, *Correspondence*, ii, p. 110).

[72] On 1 June 1770 he had refuesd to agree to the Common Council's demand that he should support triennial Parliaments (Chatham, *Correspondence*, iii, p. 464), but by 1 May 1771, with much uncertainty and disquiet, he announced in the Lords his conversion.

[73] E. Burke to Portland [28 April 1770], Portland MSS., Nottingham University.

[74] E. Burke to R. Shackleton, 15 Aug. 1770, Burke, *Correspondence*, i, p. 229.

[75] The best account of these Associations is G. S. Veitch, *Genesis of Parliamentary Reform* (1913). The primacy of the City movement is shown by H. Butterfield, *George III, Lord North and the People, 1779–80* (1949).

[76] *Correspondence of George III*, ii, p. 256. The King to North, 26 June 1771. The King antedated the development.

[77] Quoted by J. P. de Castro, *The Gordon Riots* (1926), p. 147.

[78] M. W. Patterson, *Sir Francis Burdett and his Times, 1770–1844* (1931).

[79] Graham Wallas, *Life of Francis Place, 1771–1854* (1918).

*O*ne of the best ways to understand the aristocracy's place in society, to assess its command of patronage as well as society's sense of status, is to look at the professions. This essay illustrates in brief compass the nature of professional opportunity and ambition in eighteenth-century England. Specialized studies of particular professions during the century exist, but no historian has been better equipped to take an overall view than Edward Hughes (1899–1965), for twenty-six years professor of history at the University of Durham. Through life-long archival research he came to know eighteenth-century England at firsthand and developed an unusually keen sense of the hopes and fears of society's middle and upper ranks. His solid work on the revenue departments and their officials, Studies in Administration and Finance, 1558–1825 (Manchester, 1934), is a mine for scholars. Anyone with a taste for social history would enjoy his two volumes on North Country Life in the Eighteenth Century (1952, 1965). The essay here was originally published in The Durham University Journal, *Vol. XLIV, No. 2 (March 1952)* and is reprinted with the permission of the editor.

VIII

The Professions in the Eighteenth Century[1]

BY EDWARD HUGHES

Already by the beginning of the eighteenth century the word "profession" had acquired its modern meaning. Addison spoke of the three great professions of Divinity, Law, and Physic: Dr. Johnson in his dictionary defines the term as "a calling, vocation (or) known employment." So far so good. It is when we come to the finer distinctions that difficulties arise. For example, it is not possible as yet to distinguish sharply between a profession and a trade. Throughout the century, entry to both was by the time-honored system of apprenticeship and, as we shall see, the officials in the Stamp Office made no distinction between them. Garth in his poem *The Dispensary* (1699)[2] laments—

> How sick'ning Physic hangs her pensive head
> And what was once a Science, now's a Trade.

Students of Boswell may recall how a certain Mr. Memis of Aberdeen sued the corporation for alleged defamation, having described him as a "doctor of medicine" when in fact he was a physician.[3] Dr. Johnson discussed the matter with the president of the Royal College of Physicians in London and we learn that in common usage—in England at any rate—the two words were virtually synonymous and they quickly became so, Sir D'Arcy Power suggests,[4] as increasing numbers of Scots graduates took the road that opened up "the noblest prospects."

For almost exactly a century, 1710–1808, the premiums paid by apprentices on their indentures were subject to a stamp duty. The returns, giving the names and trade of both master and apprentice, together with the amount of premium paid, have survived in the records of the Stamp Office; they are bound up in enormous vellum volumes—seventy-nine of them in all—any one of which, in sheer bulk, is bigger than Doomsday Book.[5] Indeed, they constitute a veritable Doomsday Book of the professions, telling us of recruitment not only to the guilds and city companies but of attorneys, "writers," scriveners, goldsmiths, barber-surgeons, schoolmasters, music and dancing masters down to milliners and the lesser crafts. We shall have occasion later to note the sharp rise in the amount of premium paid—sums of six hundred pounds and upward were common by the end of the century—but we may note here that the highest recorded figure, one thousand two hundred and sixty pounds paid to a London merchant in 1802, was considerably higher than that paid in the leading professions, law and surgery. (The eighteenth century had a realistic sense of values.) Unfortunately, the records of the Stamp Office do not furnish a complete guide to the professions or our present task would be comparatively simple. The sums paid for army commissions, for instance, were not strictly speaking premiums; they were untaxed and unrecorded. And diligent though the eighteenth-century tax official often was in the ceaseless war against evasion, he did not quite keep pace with developments in society. By the end of the century, new professions begin to make their appearance in the returns—a fair number of chemists, half a dozen London architects, brokers, a musician in Oxford Street, land surveyors, a veterinary surgeon in Shropshire, though the official was at a loss how to describe him and he is entered as "a Cutter of colts and pigs and Destroyer of Nature therein." Significant as these examples are of incipient professions they are in no sense exhaustive. Take, for instance, the notable developments in banking which took place in the second half of the century. Sir John Clapham has shown that there were over seven hundred licensed note-issuing banks by 1808,[6] but so far I have found only one case in the returns of a banker's apprentice, and that significantly enough from Lancashire (I do not of course claim to have combed all the seventy-nine massive volumes and I know from other sources of two County Durham boys, educated at Eton, whose parents paid six hundred pounds plus sixty pounds stamp duty each to apprentice them to a London banker in 1755). Again, there were certain posts of such exceptional responsibility or demanding unusual qualities and skill that appointments to them had always been made by personal selection. For instance, eighteenth-century agrarian economy, canvassing in county elections, and much else hinged on the steward or estate agent[7]—but he was recruited by personal selection not by apprenticeship. In the coal mining areas, below the "agent," though strictly subordinate to him, was the "colliery viewer"—the expert who knew where to sink a shaft, what seams to expect to find at a given depth, the line of the dip, the state of the roof and thill, the probable weight of water, and the correct methods of working. "The viewer," says Dr. Raistrick, "was the equivalent of, but something more than, our present Mining Engineer."[8] The great expansion in the mining industry could not have taken place without their accumulated skill and experience, and when we know more about them we may well decide that they deserve to rank among the makers of modern England. The same is true, in shipbuilding, of the "surveyor," the prototype of the naval architect. Now both estate agents and colliery viewers existed in the seventeenth century and were in full bloom in the eighteenth, though they were not organized in professional associations until the end of the nineteenth or the beginning of the present century. Here, if I may be so bold as to say so, is a major defect of Sir Alexander Carr-Saunders and Mr. Wilson's standard book on the professions—these authors, as it seems to me, mistake the shell for the living organism, and, not being historians, are occasionally guilty of postdating the evolution of a particular profession by a century or more. Most professions, I venture to submit, had a long history before ever they were organized in professional associations.

"I entirely agree with you in your resolution of breeding up all your sons to some profession or other," wrote Lord Chesterfield to a friend in 1756, and he went on to suggest certain "general rules by which I would point out to them the professions which I should severally wish them to apply to: I would recommend the Army, or the Navy, to a boy of warm constitution, strong animal spirits, and a cold genius; to one of quick, lively, and distinguishing parts—the law; to a good, dull, and decent boy—the Church, and Trade to an acute, thinking, and laborious one."[9] By that date, a shrewd and well-placed observer, John Baker, a director of the Royal Exchange Assurance Company in London, recognized what some parents already knew only too well,—that it was no easy matter to find openings for young men, particularly the younger sons of gentle families, especially if their inclinations did not run along the conventional lines of the army, the law, or the Church. In short, any study of the professions in the eighteenth century must take account of social pressure from below, and perhaps one should add, from above—the gentry. It was not simply the growth in population, though that is important, or the fact that society and government became much more complex as the century wore on. For instance, such was the bewildering complexity of the tariff system that many merchants did not feel equal to the task of calculating the amount of customs duty payable on a normal consignment of imports: they had recourse to an expert in the Long Room at the Custom House, a Saxby or a Baldwin, just as modern firms make use of chartered accountants to prepare their income tax returns.[10] (Incidentally I have found no case of an accountant in the returns of the Stamp Office.) In particular, we have to take account of what was happening to the gentry and small landed families in the early years of the century. My own great teacher, George Unwin, was coming to realize that a basic social revolution occurred in this country between the Restoration and the accession of George III.[11] Had he lived and worked in the Northeast, his brilliant intuition would have been abundantly confirmed. Certainly in Northumberland and Durham that period saw the liquidation, in varying degree, of scores of ancient families, lesser gentry and freeholders, and the rise out of the ashes of vast new agglomerations of landed estates. So that for many a gentle family in reduced and often parlous financial circumstances, a place under government, a living in the church, or a commission in the services became a pressing necessity. This elemental fact colored the whole complexion of politics from the Restoration onward. The problem of finding professional "pasture for the beasts that must feed"—to adapt Chesterfield's famous phrase—has to be set against this larger social background.

To come now to my immediate task. In this paper I propose to discuss four leading professions—the legal and medical professions, the fighting services, and the civil service. You will note that I deliberately exclude for lack of time a most important profession—the 10,000 or so beneficed clergy—nor will time permit me to discuss the interesting problem of educational maladjustment, very marked in the public schools, which is self-evident in the survival of the apprenticeship system. (Robert Ellison of Gateshead who had been five years at Eton, on being apprenticed to a London banker, had to go to Mr. Footer's Academy to learn arithmetic, geography, and modern languages.)

* * *

If we exclude from consideration the greatest of all eighteenth-century professions—the profession of a country gentleman—pride of place clearly belongs to the lawyers using that term in its widest sense. When Charles Yorke, Lord Chancellor Hardwicke's son, thought of abandoning his studies for the bar, his father reminded him that "the law was the most independent and advantageous profession a man could enter."[12] Lord Chesterfield—in the letter which I have already cited—continued:

> I wish that my godson may take a liking to the Law for that is the truly independent profession. People will only trust their property to the care of the ablest lawyer, be he Whig or Tory, well or ill at Court.

Burke went even better.[13] In a letter to a friend whose son had just embarked on legal studies, he spoke of the legal profession "which is so leading in this country and which has this peculiar advantage—that even a failure in it stands as a sort of qualification for other things." To attempt an explanation of the age-old attraction for law in this country is no part of our present task—its roots strike deep into English and American soil. In 1718 Charles Saunderson of the Inner Temple, who had so large a practice that his friends complained they could only see him for half an hour on Sundays, was asked by one of them for an estimate of the probable cost of maintaining a student at the Middle Temple. He gave a figure of two hundred pounds a year—which was about four times the contemporary cost of sending a boy to Eton and about three times an undergraduate's bills at Cambridge. Even so, Saunderson had no lack of students. At least half a dozen north country youths read in his chambers between 1712 and 1727. And here I cannot resist the temptation to remark on the legal eminence of Northumbrians in this century. Lord Chancellor Talbot was the son of a bishop of Durham; his successor, Hardwicke, read in Serjeant Salkeld's chambers—Salkeld and Saunderson were both north country men:[14] John Ord, attorney of Newcastle, became Chief Baron of the Scottish Exchequer in 1755 and, to complete Orion's belt, there are the Scott brothers, Eldon and Stowell, sons of a Newcastle coal factor. Eldon's income from fees alone in 1810 reached twenty-two thousand seven hundred and thirty pounds.[15] This northern galaxy, I submit, was no legal comet. Thanks to coal and its attendant problems—thanks also, possibly, to the survival of Palatinate jurisdiction at Durham—the region had long presented unique opportunities to lawyers.[16]

The question may well be asked, "What business kept so many lawyers busy?" Let me try to answer it with particular reference to the Northeast. Surprising as it may seem there was no firm legal ruling as to what a colliery was until 1693, and a generation later it was said that this ruling applied mainly to County Durham. The number of suits in Chancery connected with mining and its attendant problems—enclosure, wagon-ways, mining leases—is legion and much history still lies buried in them. The future Eldon first won his spurs when he was asked to lead in an Exchequer case to be tried at Durham "of very great importance to coal owners"; "perhaps," he surmised, "they thought that I had an advantage over them in having been born and bred in a coal country."[17] Or consider the legal business which the act of 1715 entailed. This act required Roman Catholics to register their estates (in duplicate) at Quarter Sessions. The task of preparing the detailed schedules of properties together with the rents and services due from tenants fell to the local attorneys. Legal fortunes were not made on modest half-guinea "opinions" or even from the occasional windfall which came from clearing up the estate of a great peer like the Duke of

Somerset in 1752, nor from the delicate and often protracted business of negotiating a marriage settlement and probing into titles, but from deals in real estate. The new rising gentry lost no opportunity of adding field to field and in addition to what we may term the free market in land, great estates were sold from time to time, like bankrupt stock, by order of Chancery, as, for example, the rich coal-bearing manors of Gateshead and Whickham in 1711, the estates of Lord Grey of Wark in 1732, or Baron Hilton's Durham estate in 1753. The opportunities thus presented to a well-placed lawyer of pulling off a really great bargain were enormous. And in this business a local attorney often had a prospective buyer in mind or was merely acting on instructions from one. Indeed, such was an attorney's anxiety to accommodate a powerful client that he would sometimes dangle an anonymous bait for years before a harassed yeoman or freeholder, and much land changed hands without ever coming into the market at all. It was no accident, then, that the eighteenth century was the great age of conveyancing or that Roman Catholics, excluded from practice at the bar by the Test Acts, took up this lucrative branch of business while others turned to medicine or estate management.

The lawyers were the first to organize themselves in a professional association: "the Society of Gentlemen Practisers in the Courts of Law and Equity," the parent of the Law Society, dates from Walpole's day.[18] The circumstances which led to the emergence of this association merit some attention. Ever since Queen Elizabeth's reign there had been continuous complaints of the excessive number of attorneys and of their excessive fees, but so far all attempts to set limits to them had failed. True the principal of registration of attorneys had long existed—only those who were on the roll of the High Court could practice in the courts—and furthermore attorneys, since the Revolution, were required to pay a stamp duty of six pounds for their licenses. It was stated in 1728 that there were some 420 registered attorneys though many more were actually in business for they contrived by partnerships and other devices pretty successfully to evade the stamp duty. In that year the Justices of the Peace of the three Ridings of Yorkshire at Quarter Sessions complained to Parliament of the growing inconveniences occasioned by nonqualified persons acting in legal matters.[19] Their petitions and a subsequent one from Wiltshire were referred to a committee on fees that was presided over by a Yorkshireman, Sir William Strickland, M.P. for Scarborough and a lord of the Treasury. Several witnesses before this committee gave examples of excessive, not to say outrageous, fees charged by attorneys, particularly in actions for trespass and for the recovery of small debts (extents)—fees of sixteen pounds to thirty pounds where the sum involved amounted to only a few shillings, with the result, it was said, that suits tended to be settled out of court, over a bottle, through the good offices of a farmer, a schoolmaster, sailor, or other person. Now in the woolen districts of Yorkshire and Wiltshire, there were frequent complaints of theft and purloining of yarn or cloth under the "putting-out" system and considerable litigation, often for quite trifling sums, resulted. Indeed, in 1778, the worsted manufacturers of the West Riding set up an executive committee of their own, with a paid inspectorate, in an attempt to check such frauds. The important acts of 1729 and 1731, which required law proceedings to be in English and which swept away the distinction between an attorney and a solicitor and reiterated the principle—it was not new—of a five-year apprenticeship for all articled clerks, have to be related to the Yorkshire petitions.[20] Nor is that all. During the committee's proceedings Stamp officials were in attendance, anxious to discover some additional security against tax evasion. Thus attorneys, whether licensed or not, who had now lost the protection afforded by an occult tongue, were in some danger of finding themselves between the nether and upper millstones of popular denunciation and a vigilant department. Complaints of excessive fees continued, however, and in 1737 the government set up a powerful commission, which included the two archbishops, to inquire into them.[21] Faced with this double threat to their profession, "the Gentlemen Practisers in the Courts of Law and Equity" saw fit to grow a protective shell. True, there continued to be a species of snail without shells: in 1763 the magistrates of Bristol and the four Western Counties complained that schoolmasters, and no better, frequently drew up conveyances proper only, since men's properties were involved, to be done by duly qualified solicitors.[22] If the purpose of the 1729 act had been to canalize proceedings in the courts—and one suspects that the clerks of the peace were behind the justices' petitions—the purpose of this latest move was to direct non-court business, namely conveyancing, into the same professional channel. In short, continuing nonprofessional competition forced the lawyers to organize themselves against the layman interloper and in this they ultimately achieved considerable success. Toward the end of the century they petitioned unsuccessfully for a royal charter of incorporation. The Incorporated Law Society, which is responsible among other things for the registration of solicitors and controls the conditions of entry and the standards of professional conduct, dates, appropriately enough, from Peel's great ministry.

Next to the legal constellation in brilliance were the fighting services. In the years of peace after Utrecht the army and naval establishments were small, and it was correspondingly difficult to get on to them; but the wars of the second half of the century saw a rapid expansion of both. Admiral Sir Herbert Richmond has shown that the number of lieutenants in the navy went up from 367 in 1739 to 1,349 in 1783.[23] From the Army List of 1759 I calculate that there were then over 4,000 commissioned officers in the army, excluding the artillery, the engineers, and the companies of invalids. Moreover, we tend to forget that there were 35 garrison towns in Great Britain, some with considerable establishments, besides Gibraltar, Port Mahon, and nine other overseas garrisons. The governorships of these places carried very attractive salaries, while at many the duties can only have been nominal.[24] Plymouth and four others were worth one thousand pounds a year or over, equal to the coveted commissionerships of the major revenue departments; Berwick and Hull at six hundred pounds, the Lord Warden of the Cinque Ports at five hundred pounds (one of Wellington's perquisites later), even Fort William or Fort Augustus at three hundred pounds, notwithstanding the inconveniences of service in Scotland where one was liable to get the itch, were not to be despised. The growth of a recognized and well nigh universal system of purchase of army commissions by the middle of the century and the fact that the official tariff rates for such had from time to time to be scaled upward are sufficient testimony to the pressure from without.[25] Nineteenth-century reformers argued that the system of purchase militated against the development of a professional esprit—but this seems doubtful. I need hardly remind you that commissions in the Guards were most sought after and of course cost more as being more genteely officered, better paid, and capable of being combined with society life in London—Boswell was clearly on the right tack in 1762—whereas the Dragoons and still more the Foot regiments could normally expect to spend a good deal of their service in Scotland or in outlandish places in Ireland or worse still at some foreign garrison—after 1746 Louisburg was the worst spot. The statement of Sir John Fortescue that "the War Office had yet no idea of an organized system of reliefs" for overseas garrisons needs some qualification. After the Austrian Succession War an experiment was tried but it cost the Treasury eighty thousand pounds and there were limits to what could be done in that direction.

One thing is abundantly clear: commissions and promotions in the army involved exceptional and persistent application on the part of political patrons—even the regimental chaplaincies were usurped by government in Newcastle's day. "I must tell you, with great truth," Lord Chesterfield told a friend, "that I could as soon procure you a Bishopric as a company of foot." What an individual peer or M.P. could hope to do in such matters—and equally what an electoral friend or dependant, being a gentleman, might reasonably expect—were liable to misconstruction. Brigadier Kirke gruffly reminded George Liddell, M.P. for Berwick in Walpole's day, that he did not want his regiment filled up with men from Berwick and "was prodigiously surly," noted Liddell. And despite the powerful patronage of the Duke of Queensbury, Lady Northumberland and others at the highest level, Boswell did not succeed in getting his commission in 1762–3. "But I find that it really is a very difficult matter," he noted in his London Journal.[26] Nor were considerations of military efficiency ever completely lost sight of, as Horace Walpole's letter to Mason in 1783 sufficiently demonstrates.[27]

By the middle of the century knowledgeable fathers who designed their sons for the army began to send them at sixteen or thereabouts to the famous military academy at Caen; Mr. Carr of Cocken, near Durham, a friend of Lord Holdernesse, did this in 1749. Moreover, although he was powerfully connected politically, he was advised, when the real business of hunting for a commission began, to employ a commission agent or broker, as likely to produce the desired result more quickly than a personal approach to colonels of regiments. There was reason in this. The famous army agent, Mr. Calcraft of Channel Row, Westminister, the friend of Henry Fox, was agent for no fewer than thirty-six regiments in 1759, practically half the army.[28] We know, too, that Mr. Cox of Albemarle Street was already in the business. It seems reasonable to suppose that the regimental agent was much more than a paymaster, banker, and contractor; he was a commission broker as well. In any case, Calcraft's agency represents an important stage in the breaking down of an ill-assorted congeries of independent units and the development of a unified and professional body.

Just before the outbreak of the French revolutionary war a further step was taken in this direction:

> *His Majesty thinking it highly expedient and necessary for the benefit of his service at large, that one uniform system of Field Exercise and Movement founded on just and true principles, should be established and invariably practised throughout his whole Army is therefore pleased to direct that the Rules and Regulations approved of . . . for this important purpose and now detailed and published herewith shall be strictly followed and adhered to without any deviation whatsoever therefrom . . .[29]*

Accordingly, in 1792, the Adjutant General issued, by H.M. Command, "Rules and Regulations for the Formations, Field Exercises and Movements of all His Majesty's Forces." It ran into six editions before the close of the century; a companion volume for the cavalry regiments appeared in 1797. Previously, officers had to rely on private publications such as Le Blond's *Treatise on Artillery*[30] or Bennett Cuthbertson's *System for the Complete Interior Management or Œconomy of a Battalion of Infantry*.[31] Conformity to a uniform standard of proficiency is an important element in the development of professionalism.

The senior service from its very nature had always been more of a profession than the army, and it was never contaminated by purchase. A sound core of efficiency in conformity with the fifty-five instructions issued to captains and a system of promotion by merit existed in the first half of the century. But politics began to creep into the navy. Admiral Richmond considers that jobbery in the Navy Office got worse with the rapid expansion of the service later in the century, an opinion which Admiral Collingwood would have endorsed. Captains were free to take with them a limited number of boys as "middies," usually recommended by a friend and on a personal basis, but not all proved suitable or came up to the high standards set by a conscientious officer like Collingwood and not all succeeded in passing the examination for a commission. And even if they were successful they might have to wait many years, wholly dependent on their families, before they were appointed to a ship. Collingwood who joined in 1761 did not get his first ship until 1775, and like many others he was without a ship in the years of peace before 1793.

It is significant of the low esteem in which one branch of the medical profession, the surgeons, was held that the normal salary of a surgeon at a military garrison was only forty-five pounds 12s. 6d.; many regimental chaplains got more.[32] In the navy a surgeon's pay was five pounds a month, a pound less than the most junior lieutenant; they were in fact warrant, not commissioned, officers. During the Austrian Succession War the French and Spaniards treated captured surgeons as ordinary seamen, claiming that they were mere barbers. On the other hand, a clause in the Militia Bill of 1746 proposed to exempt physicians, surgeons, and apothecaries from compulsory military service—the latter were already excused jury service and service as parish officers under an act of 1717. What is so puzzling to us is the curious trinity in the eighteenth-century medical profession. A patient might well find himself in the hands of three "dismal visitors" at one and the same time—the physician who diagnosed and prescribed; the apothecary who prepared and administered the "dope," and the surgeon-barber and chiropodist, the latter until their emancipation from the barbers' company in 1745 being regarded as an inferior order of manual operators, while the male-accoucheur, the man midwife, was lower still. As for nurses, smallpox, the dreaded scourge of the century, was thought "too nice a point to be trusted to women . . . too many love to have a province of their own to govern in how little so ever they are qualified to command," declared a writer in the *Gentleman's Magazine*.[33] The first half of the century was the heyday of the apothecary: in 1703 the London Society of Apothecaries won a notable legal victory over the College of Physicians—on appeal to the House of Lords— and secured control over the supply and administration of drugs and medicines. The dispute with the physicians called forth Samuel Garth's poem *The Dispensary*, which ran into ten editions by 1741, and a scheme of free medicines for the poor of London.[34] Readers of Jane Austen's *Emma* and persons well versed in the old regulations of the medical school of London University will recall that the apothecaries were often held in high esteem and enjoyed a favored position though they were not graduates in medicine. The popularity of the "poticary" and the prevalence of quacks was due, in part, to the shortage of qualified physicians—in Bedfordshire a person might have to go fifty miles to find one—and, in particular, to the exclusive character of the Royal College of Physicians. In 1745 there were only fifty-two fellows, three candidates and some twenty-three licentiates.[35] Under the charter of Henry VIII no person could practice physic in London or within a seven-mile radius who had not been first admitted by the president and the college, nor in the rest of the country "without letters testimonial of their approving and examination" except graduates in medicine of Oxford and Cambridge. Dudley Ryder records in his diary the opinion "that the business of a physician required the least time to be perfect in of any profession;" and D. A. Winstanley remarked of the medical school at Cambridge in this period "that it was held indeed in justified contempt."[36]

From time to time the monopoly of the Royal College of Physicians came in for outspoken criticism "for we see they were at all times an impudent, audacious sort of men and almost incorrigible," declared a writer in the *Gentleman's Magazine*. In 1750 they had a dispute with the universities which was settled in the latter's favor.[37] Had their monopoly been less exclusive, the physicians may well have fared better in suppressing the apothecaries and the quacks. On the other hand, the immediate future lay with the surgeons as the high premiums paid to them by the close of the century —two and three times the amount paid by an apothecary's apprentice—sufficiently testify. Moreover, early in the 1720s there grew up a tradition of making payments to them out of Secret Service Monies.[38] Thus Dr. Charles Maitland received one thousand pounds as a special "gift or reward" for inoculating Prince Frederick—the princesses were done in 1723. Maitland had previously experimented on six Newgate convicts and Lady Mary Wortley's elder son. At the same time, Dr. Thomas Rentone received five thousand pounds from the same fund "for making known his art, skill and mystery in cutting ruptures," and Dr. James Douglas, who discovered the "Douglas pouch" in the peritoneum, five hundred pounds "for his performance and publishing his Anatomical Observations." Douglas was subsequently appointed Queen's Physician and is immortalized by Pope:

> There all the learn'd shall at the labour stand
> And Douglas lend his soft obstetric hand.

Early in George III's reign the Duke of Bedford was operated on for cataract; Caesar Hawkins made a fortune and acquired a baronetcy from phlebotomy, and in 1769 Sir John Pringle and Dr. Layard, Court physicians, were instructed to collaborate with Dr. Petrus Camper, professor of anatomy of Gröningen, "who makes the distemper among horned cattle his particular study," in an attempt to find a specific for cattle plague.[39] Time will not permit to relate the fate of two eighteenth-century schemes for "free medicines" for human cattle—one at a famous Tyneside works—nor to discuss William Keenlyside's interesting letter of application in 1760 to succeed Mr. Hallowell as surgeon at the Newcastle Infirmary.[40]

* * *

I come now to what was already the largest of the professions —the civil service, though it was not so called and did not conceive of itself as a single profession until the middle of the nineteenth century. What impresses one about the central departments of government is not the size of their staffs, but that they managed with so few. In 1745 the whole establishment of the Treasury, including the two secretaries but excluding the housekeeper, doorkeepers, and messengers, was twenty-three: at the Secretaries of State's Office the corresponding figure is twenty-six plus a decipherer (Dr. Edward Willes, Bishop of Bath and Wells) and an embellisher. There were only thirteen clerks at the War Office, ten at the Board of Trade, and eight at the Admiralty—on the eve of winning an empire.[41] Even at the close of the Napoleonic Wars when all establishments were inflated, the entire clerical staff at the Treasury (including the Commissariat branch) was eighty-six; at the Home Office nineteen, at the Foreign Office twenty-three.[42] The vast majority of placemen, perhaps 20,000 in all by the end of the century, were officials in the revenue departments, scattered up and down the country, but with particular concentrations in London and at the principal ports. We shall have occasion to remark on the significance of this when we consider the question of patronage.

As an example of the role of the civil servants let me quote again from Lord Chesterfield: he is commenting on the budget for 1759, the *annus mirabilis*.

> *Near £12 millions have been granted this year, not only* nemine contradicente, *but* nemine quicquid dicente. *The proper officers bring in the Estimates; it is taken for granted that they are necessary and frugal; the Members [of Parliament] go to dinner and leave Mr. West and Mr. Martin [the two secretaries of the Treasury] to do the rest.*[43]

This silent tribute to the unobtrusive efficiency of the Treasury officials is the more remarkable when we remember the widespread distrust of placemen earlier in the century.

And here let me say a few words about patronage:—

(i) It is very important to discover just who had the disposal of patronage in any particular case and not to assume vaguely that it belonged to the Treasury or to the government in general. Sir Robert Peel and his Patronage Secretary, Sir Thomas Fremantle, later adopted the sound maxim of first discovering whose the skin was before attempting to dispose of it. The major revenue departments, the Excise and, to a less extent, the Customs, effectively controlled the appointments and promotions of their "inferior officers," and although there was increased Treasury encroachment under Walpole and Lord North, a solid core of efficiency was never completely eroded away. It is true that the most used volume in Lord North's papers at Oxford is a Customs' Book (North *MSS* c.78) which contains, on one side, the applications of powerful local patrons to fill vacancies, actual or impending, and on the other, a note of "promises" and of actual appointments; but I need hardly remind you that there is no obvious correlation between applications and appointments and that the inverse ratio is invariably small.

(ii) Again, it is erroneous to assume that conditions affecting patronage remained static throughout the century: that what was true, say, of the exceptional years 1710–15 is characteristic of more settled times. Jobbery increased as the century advanced, owing largely to the increased political needs and pretensions of the Treasury.

(iii) Finally, the struggle to control appointments turned in the last resort on the delicate question of local prestige, a point on which patrons, whether peers or gentry, were inordinately sensitive. What these men wanted were clear demonstrations of successful influence in their own localities though the process involved application and constant reminders at the center. The fact that there were so many revenue officers in the provinces and that comparatively they were so well paid made these posts the coveted objects of the place hunter.

After all, the outstanding fact about the eighteenth-century civil service is its permanence. This principle is writ large in all the major departments. One example, the family of Brooksbank, must suffice. Stamp Brooksbank, the elder, was a director of the Bank of England from 1728 until Henry Pelham attracted him to the Treasury twenty years later. In the '50s he was sent to Edinburgh as secretary to the commission on Forfeited Jacobite Estates, but he did not much relish exile in the northern capital and in due course he returned to London first as secretary (1763) and later (1775) as Commissioner on the Board of Excise.[44] He was the first of a notable dynasty of civil servants. Stamp Brooksbank II was one of the four Chief Clerks at the Treasury in 1817 and his son(?) Thomas C. Brooksbank was also a senior clerk there.[45] The latter, the recognized expert on government loans, became, in turn, the indispensable kingpin at the Treasury until he retired, worn out in the service, in 1849. Ministers may come and ministers may go, but the Brooksbanks ran on for a century.

Two words in conclusion. The civil service, like the Church, did not demand high premiums of its entrants, a circumstance which may well explain the exceptional pressure to get into them. We have seen that by the middle of the century London merchant houses were asking as much as six hundred to seven hundred pounds of apprentices and the richer professions, law and surgery, followed suit. Sums of this order, or even the four hundred to five hundred pounds demanded in the provinces, must have effectively restricted entry to the sons of rich merchants and the gentry and thus served to consolidate those classes. Finally, the high standards and traditions of professional conduct—in the law, the fighting services, medicine, and the civil service—derive from the eighteenth-century conception of gentility. The "welfare state" is living at present on this accumulated capital.

NOTES

VIII. *The Professions in the Eighteenth Century*

[1] A paper read to the Anglo-American Conference of Historians in London, July 1951.

[2] 1709 *ed.*, p. 53.

[3] Boswell, *Johnson* (*ed.* Croker), pp. 428, 430, 454, *passim.*

[4] *Johnson's England*, II, p. 273.

[5] P.R.O. *Inl.* I, *passim.* Until 1752 the names of the parents are given as well. The Genealogical Society has made a biographical index of the actual indentures.

[6] *History of the Bank of England*, II, pp. 1–2.

[7] See my essay on "The Eighteenth-Century Estate Agent" in *Essays in Honour of J. E. Todd* (*ed.* Cronne and Moody).

[8] *Transactions of the Newcomen Society*, XVII, p. 162.

[9] Chesterfield, *Letters* (*ed.* Bradshaw), III, pp. 1151–1152.

[10] Additional MSS. (British Museum), 32864 § 387.

[11] See his Introduction to Richard Baxter's *The Poor Husbandman's Advocate to Rich Racking Landlords* (the last thing Unwin wrote) in *Studies in Economic History* (*ed.* Tawney), pp. 345–351.

[12] Yorke, *Life of Lord Chancellor Hardwicke*, II, p. 527; III, p. 416.

[13] Burke, *Correspondence (ed.* 1844), p. 395.

[14] Yorke, *Life of Hardwicke*, I, p. 53. Cf. Lord Lovat's sarcastic remark à propos of Murray, later Lord Mansfield: "I wish that his being born in the North may not hinder him from the preferment that his merit and learning deserve."

[15] Twiss, *Life of Eldon*, I, p. 319.

[16] For contemporary criticisms of lawyers, *Gentleman's Magazine*, X, p. 388.

[17] Twiss, *Life of Eldon*, I, p. 127.

[18] Carr Saunders and Wilson, *The Professions*, pp. 44–45.

[19] *Commons' Journal*, XXI, pp. 266, 274, 891.

[20] 2 George II, c. 23 and 4 George II, c. 26.

[21] *Gentleman's Magazine*, VII, p. 699.

[22] *Commons' Journal*, XXIX, p. 445.

[23] *Johnson's England* I, p. 59.

[24] George III called them "governments" and considered that he was entitled to deprive the holders of them who sided with the parliamentary opposition, though not of their army commissions. R. Pares, "George III and the Politicians" in *Trans. Royal Historical Society* (1951), p. 131.

[25] Mr. Eric Robson's article on "Purchase and Promotion in the British Army in the Eighteenth Century" has appeared since the present article was written. *History*, June 1951.

[26] *London Journal*, pp. 132, 223, *passim*. Boswell was of the opinion that colonels of regiments got the profits on sales of commissions.

[27] *Letters* (*ed.* Toynbee), XIII, p. 1.

[28] The number had increased by 1760.

[29] The paragraph headed "Music and Drums" reads:—"The use of musick or Drums to regulate the March is absolutely forbid, as incompatible with the just and combined movements of any considerable body and giving a false aid to the very smallest. They never persevere in the ordered time, or in any other, are constantly changing measure, create noise, derange the equality of step and counteract the very end they are supposed to promote. The ordered and cadenced March can be acquired and preserved from the eye and habit alone and troops must by great practice be so steadied as to be able to maintain it, even though drums, musick or circumstances should be offering a different marked time. On occasions of parade and show and when troops are halted they [i.e. music and drums] are properly used and when circumstances do not forbid it may be sometimes permitted as inspiriting in column of march where unity of step is not so critically required. But in all movements of manoeuvre, whatever and at any time directing the cadence of the step or in the instruction of the recruit, officer, or battalion, they must not be heard."

[30] Translated from French, 1746.

[31] Printed at Dublin, 1768.

[32] *Army Lists* (1759), p. 153. Chamberlayne, *Present State* (1745), p. 117. The basic rate of pay for a regimental surgeon was 6 shillings a day.

[33] XXII, pp. 402–405.

[34] *The Dispensary, loc. cit.*

[35] Chamberlayne, *Present State*, p. 192.

[36] Ryder's *Diary* (*ed.* Matthews), p. 276. Winstanley, *Unreformed Cambridge*, p. 77.

[37] *Gentleman's Magazine*, V, p. 240; XX, p. 473.

[38] Add. MSS. 40843.

[39] *Calendar of Home Office Papers* (1770), § 95.

40 See *North Country Life in the Eighteenth Century*, [I, 94, 103].

41 Chamberlayne, *loc. cit.*

42 *The Royal Kalendar* (1817), p. 254 *seq.*

43 *Letters*, III, p. 1248.

44 Newcastle Papers, *passim.* Correspondence of the Board of Excise and the Treasury [London Custom House].

45 *Royal Kalendar, loc. cit.*

*I*n 1929 Sir Lewis Namier (1888–1960) published The Structure of Politics at the Accession of George III 2nd ed. *(1957), and in the following year* England in the Age of the American Revolution 2nd ed. *(1961). These books transformed the study of eighteenth-century English political history. They are in a sense fragments of a much larger work that was never completed, and, although written with care and craftsmanship, their quality is not easily appreciated by non-specialists. Nevertheless, the importance of these books was instantly recognized in the field, and their reputation has influenced over the years the shape of historical studies in a wide range of fields. An authoritative assessment of Namier's contribution, by John Brooke, entitled "Namier and Namierism," appeared in Vol. III, No. 3 of* History and Theory *(1964). It is enough to say here that, while Namier's investigations were essentially microscopic, his perceptions were broad and sensitive. These qualities are richly displayed in the essay reprinted here on "The Social Foundations" of English politics, which contains a sympathetic and penetrating assessment of the aristocracy's role in government and society. Its purview is mainly the epoch from 1750 to 1780.*

Namier was born into a family of Polonized Jews possessing the right of land ownership. He was educated at Oxford and taught there in the '20s. He wrote not only on eighteenth-century England, but also on nineteenth-century Europe. From 1929 to 1931 he served as political secretary of the Jewish Agency for Palestine, and from 1931 to 1951 he was professor of modern history at the University of Manchester. He was knighted in 1952. In the last decade of his life he saw himself, as he said, "under a heavy mortgage" to a great project on the History of Parliament *during the later eighteenth century; those labors were assisted and brought to completion by John Brooke in 1964. A collection of Namier's shorter pieces,* Cross-roads of Power: Essays on England in the Eighteenth Century, *was posthumously published in 1962. Interested readers may wish to turn to the biography written by his wife: Julia Namier,* Lewis Namier: A Biography *(1971). The essay reprinted here is the introductory chapter of* England in the Age of the American Revolution. *It is reprinted with the permission of Lady Namier; Macmillan, London and Basingstoke; and the St. Martin's Press, New York.*

IX

The Social Foundations

BY SIR LEWIS NAMIER

The Unreformed House of Commons

The social history of England could be written in terms of membership of the House of Commons, that peculiar club, election to which has at all times required some expression of consent on the part of the public. At no time was the House truly unrepresentative, for with us the result of elections does not primarily depend on constituencies of electorates. Live forces break through forms and shape results to suit requirements. Were it decided that the 615 heaviest men in the country should constitute the House of Commons, the various interests and parties could be trusted to obtain their proportionate weight in it. But the idea of representation and the nature of the body politic vary from age to age, and with them varies the social structure of the House of Commons.

In its origin the House of Commons was akin to the jury, and the representative character and functions of the two were in a way cognate; from an intimate knowledge of conditions, the House declared the sense of the commonalty on questions which most patently and directly concerned them, but did not pronounce sentence and did not meddle with matters of government or "mysteries of State." Attendance at it was truly a service. But as the position and prestige of Parliament increased, and seats in the House of Commons began to be prized, it came to represent, not so much the sense of the community, as the distribution of power within it—the two developments being necessarily and inevitably correlated. The leading territorial families, and even the gentry of lesser rank, now invaded the borough representation; and the Crown attempted to secure seats in the House of Commons for its servants and dependants—if a true equation of forces was to be attained, the executive, centering in the King and as yet extraneous to the Commons, had to receive its own representation in the House. As make-weight in favor of stable government, the royal influence in elections continued to be worked after the Revolution of 1688. When the struggle commenced between George III and his grandfather's political "undertakers," an outcry was raised against "prerogative"—the term was still current by force of ideological and linguistic survival, for ideas outlive the conditions which gave them birth and words outlast ideas. In reality, George III never left the safe ground of parliamentary government and merely acted the *primus inter pares*, the first among the borough-mongering, electioneering gentlemen of England. While the Stuarts tried to browbeat the House and circumscribe the range of its action, George III fully accepted its constitution and recognized its powers and merely tried to work it in accordance with the customs of the time.

The demoralizing influence of the eighteenth-century electoral system is obvious, and its nonsensical features are only too patent; its deeper sense and its usefulness are less apparent. The rotten boroughs were a necessary part of the eighteenth-century organization of the British Government, while corruption in populous boroughs was the effect of citizen status in an electorate not fully awake to national interests; even so, it was a mark of English freedom and independence, for no one bribes where he can bully. Without those boroughs the House of Commons in 1761 would practically have represented one class only, the landed interest, and in the first place those independent country gentlemen who in fact supplied most of the knights of the shires; this might possibly have sufficed for a self-centered nation, never for an Empire. A careful student of parliamentary history gives the following description of the fifteen knights of the shire who represented Devonshire between 1688 and 1761, and ten of whom belonged to three families: "Of nearly every one we might say: he belonged to a well-known Devon family; while in Parliament he made no speeches, held no office, and achieved no distinction of any sort; but whenever he is known to have recorded a vote, it was given against the government then in office."[1] The most respectable constituencies in Great Britain returned the dullest members; they did not supply the architects and craftsmen of government and administration. The boroughs under government management, or acquired by the government at the time of the election, opened the gates of the House to budding statesmen and to hardworking civil servants, the permanent secretaries of government departments (who were not as yet disqualified from sitting in it), to various law officers of the Crown, to admirals and pro-consuls; in short, to the men who had the widest and most varied experience of administrative work; while the promising young men and the "men of business" of the opposition were similarly provided for by its borough patrons. Since 1832 the party organizations have tried to fill the place of patrons or the government in providing for men who are required in the House but are not of sufficient fame, wealth, or popularity to secure them seats. These endeavors have not been altogether successful—in 1873 Lord Lytton wrote in a novel about a rising politician: "In the old time, before the first Reform Bill, his reputation would have secured him at once a seat in Parliament; but the ancient nurseries of statesmen are gone, and their place is not supplied."[2] Even now the safest, richest, and therefore most independent Conservative constituencies elect mainly local worthies, while able young men have to be sent by headquarters to doubtful constituencies, dependent on financial support from the party organization, and succumb at a landslide.

Yet another function was discharged by the corrupt and the rotten boroughs: through them the *nouveaux-riches* in every generation were able to enter the House of Commons; and this occurred with such regularity that by tracing the history of these new men one could follow the rise and fall of various branches of commerce, the development of modern finance, and the advance of capitalist organization in industry, and measure the relative importance of the West and East Indies. Thus even a good deal of the economic and colonial history of England could be written in terms of membership of the House of Commons.

The Social Structure

The fact that in England money was allowed to play a great part in the selection of the governing body (much greater than in Scotland and Wales) was the result and expression of the peculiar character of English society, civilian and plutocratic, though imbued with feudal habits and traditions.

England knows not democracy as a doctrine, but has always practiced it as a fine art. Since the Middle Ages, no one was ever barred on grounds of class from entering the House of Commons, and in the House all members have always sat on equal terms; as between freemen, England never knew a rigid distinction of classes. Still, there has been throughout an element of heredity in the membership of the House, largely connected with property in land, but at no time resulting in the formation of close castes; England's social structure to this day retains more traces of feudalism than that of any other country, but it has never been hierarchical. Trade was never despised, and English society has always shown respect for property and wealth. The financial expert, usually a "moneyed" man, was valued in the House, and the Treasury has for centuries held a pre-eminent position in the government. St. Matthew vi: 21 was quoted by the English medieval author of the *Dialogus de Scaccario* to prove by the authority of Christ that the King's heart was, where his treasure was, in the Exchequer; and there the heart of the nation has been ever since—which accounts for the paramount importance of budget nights and for the excellence of British public finance.

The social history of nations is largely molded by the forms and development of their armed forces, the primary aim of national organization being common defense. The historical development of England is based on the fact that her frontiers against Europe are drawn by Nature and cannot be the subject of dispute; that she is a unit sufficiently small for coherent government to have been established and maintained even under very primitive conditions; that since 1066 she has never suffered serious invasion; that no big modern armies have succeeded her feudal levies; and that her senior service is the navy, with which foreign trade is closely connected. In short, a great deal of what is peculiar in English history is due to the obvious fact that Great Britain is an island.

Encroachments on frontier provinces were never possible in the case of England (the Scottish and Welsh borders may be here left out of account); a conquest had to be complete or could not endure. Frontier encroachments are apt to produce chaos, whereas complete conquests tend to establish strong governments. In anarchical conditions those who bear arms obtain an ascendancy over the other classes, and usually form themselves into a close, dominant caste; while a strong central government, such as was established in England after 1066, was in itself a check on class privileges. Where armies serve as "expeditionary forces" militarism has little chance to permeate the life of the nation; and there is more of the knight-errant in a merchant-adventurer than in an officer of the militia.

Feudalism was a system of social organization whereby both army service and administrative functions were bound up with the holding of land. When a change supervened in armament and methods of fighting, on the European Continent a new type of royal army took the place of feudal levies, and the administrative structure of Continental countries was adjusted to the requirements of the new military organization. Rank and caste were not eliminated, but they were no longer bound up with property in land. An army is necessarily built up on gradations of rank, and universal military service has imbued the Continental nations with hierarchical conceptions; even posts in the civil service were in many countries assimilated to ranks in the army. Society became sharply divided into those who were trained for officers and those who could not claim commissioned rank; and "honor," implying the right to fight duels, was restricted to members of the officer-class.

If the compelling, uncompromising exigencies of military organization are sufficient to override tradition, war is in itself revolution; it results in a destruction of existing forms, carried out by military organizations in accordance with an accepted code. Regard for property and law can hardly be maintained in war; invasion and conquest do away with prescriptive rights. The fine growth of English Conservatism is due, in a high degree, to the country having been free from the revolutionary action of war within its borders, and of militarism within its social organization. The true Conservative is not a militarist.

Feudalism in England, divested of its military purpose, and

not supplanted by any new military establishment on a national scale, survived in local government and social relations, continuing to rest on property in land; but as there was no sharp division of classes, based on the use of arms, and no subject of the King was debarred from holding land, the new civilian feudalism—a peculiarly English product—necessarily bore a plutocratic imprint. Primogeniture, feudal in origin, survived, and titles retained a territorial character, with the result that there can be but one holder of a title. This restriction has allowed more room for new creations, while the position of younger sons has similarly worked against a sharp division of classes.

The younger sons of country gentlemen, and even of peers, went into trade without thereby losing caste; the eldest son inherited the family estates, the second, third, or even fourth, were placed in the Church, in the army or navy, at the bar, or in some government office; but the next had usually to be apprenticed to a merchant, and, however great the name and wealth of the family, the boy baptized Septimus or Decimus was almost certain to be found in a counting-house; only courtesy lords were precluded by custom from entering trade. "Trade in England," wrote Defoe in 1726, "neither is or ought to be levell'd with what it is in other countries; or the tradesmen depreciated as they are abroad. . . . The word tradesman in England does not sound so harsh, as it does in other countries; and to say a gentleman-tradesman is not . . . nonsense. . . ."[3] "Were it not for two articles, by which the numbers of the families of gentlemen are recruited . . . when sunk and decayed . . . this nation would, in a few years, have very few families of gentlemen left; or, at least, very few that had estates to support them."[4] But "the gentry are always willing to submit to the raising their families, by what they call City fortunes,"[5] while "the rising tradesman swells into the gentry."

> Trade is so far here from being inconsistent with a gentleman, that in short trade in England makes gentlemen, and has peopled this nation with gentlemen; for . . . the tradesmen's children, or at least their grand-children, come to be as good gentlemen, statesmen, Parliament-men, privy-counsellors, judges, bishops, and noblemen, as those of the highest birth and the most antient families. . . .

> *We see the tradesmen of England, as they grow wealthy, coming every day to the Herald's Office, to search for the coats of arms of their ancestors, in order to paint them upon their coaches, and engrave them upon their plate, embroider them upon their furniture, or carve them upon the pediments of their new houses; and how often do we see them trace the registers of their families up to the prime nobility or the most antient gentry of the Kingdom?*
>
> *In this search we find them often qualified to raise new families, if they do not descend from old....*[6]

The first Lord Craven, whose father had been a wholesale grocer, "being upbraided with his being of an upstart nobility, by the famous Aubrey, Earl of Oxford, who was himself of the very antient family of the Veres, Earls of Oxford," replied that he would "cap pedigrees with him"; "he read over his family thus; I am William Lord Craven, my father was Lord Mayor of London, and my grandfather was the Lord knows who...."[7]

If anyone about 1760 could be named as prototype of the country gentleman it would be the Tory squire, Sir John Hinde Cotton, M.P., of Madingley Hall, Cambridgeshire, 4th baronet. The Cottons had been settled for centuries at Madingley and had sat in Parliament in the fourteenth and sixteenth centuries; the father of Sir John had represented the County and so did he himself. But his paternal grandmother was Elizabeth, daughter of John Sheldon, Lord Mayor of London; and his mother, Lettice, daughter of Sir Ambrose Crowley, the famous Durham ironmaster, whose warehouse in Upper Thames Street bore the sign of the "Leathern Doublet," to commemorate the dress in which he had come to London. "No gent., nor any pretence to arms" was the description given of his Quaker father,[8] and Ambrose Crowley himself, as Jack Anvil, transformed into Sir John Enville, appears in Addison's *Spectator* (No. 299) as the type of the self-made man, "bent upon making a family" with "a dash of good blood in their veins." Sir John Hinde Cotton married his cousin Anne, daughter of Humphrey Parsons, Lord Mayor of London, by Sarah, another daughter of Sir Ambrose Crowley; and his sister Mary married Jacob Houblon, the son of a merchant and a descendant of the *Pater Bursae Londoniensis*. Elizabeth, a third daughter of Crowley, married John, 10th Lord St. John of Bletso; one of Crowley's granddaughters married Sir William

Stanhope, M.P., brother of the famous Lord Chesterfield, and another, "with fortune of 200,000 pounds," John, 2nd Earl of Ashburnham.

Illustrations of this kind could be multiplied indefinitely, but even a dozen examples, though, in their accumulation, subconsciously reassuring to the reader, do not prove a thesis, and the subject is too vast and complex for an exhaustive statistical examination; an analysis of the House of Commons, that invaluable microcosmic picture of England, will, however, supply a certain amount of evidence.

Wealth amassed in trade was laid out in landed estates and used to secure seats in the House of Commons, for both helped to lift their holders into a higher social sphere.

> *A merchant may be Member of Parliament . . . and shall sit in the House of Commons, with the sons of peers. . . . This equality it is . . . which can alone preserve to commerce its honor, and inspire to those who profess it, an esteem for their condition. . . . The lords can have no contempt for the usefull professions of their fellow subjects, who are their equals, when assembled to regulate the public affairs of the nation.*[9]

Naturally purchases of landed estates by men enriched in trade were most frequent in the neighborhood of London, though the process is noticeable also around secondary centers such as Bristol, Liverpool, Norwich, or Hull, and in industrial districts, e.g., the wool-manufacturing counties of the West and the iron districts of the Western Midlands; "new men rooted themselves upon old acres."

As early as 1576, William Lambard wrote in his *Perambulation of Kent:*

> *The gentlemen be not heere (throughout) of so auncient stockes as else where, especially in the partes nearer to London, from whiche citie (as it were from a certeine riche and wealthy seedplot) courtiers, lawyers, and merchants be continually translated, and do become new plants amongst them.*[10]

And Defoe in 1728:

> *I dare oblige my self to name five hundred great estates, within one hundred miles of London, which within eighty years*

past, were the possessions of the antient English gentry, which are now bought up, and in the possession of citizens and tradesmen, purchased fairly by money raised in trade; some by merchandizing, some by shopkeeping, and some by meer manufacturing; such as clothing in particular.[11]

In the local histories of the home counties published between 1760 and 1830, such as Lysons, Hasted, Manning and Bray, Horsfield, Dallaway, Clutterbuck, Morant, etc., one can watch this process continue and expand, though it is no longer specifically mentioned, having become obvious and ordinary. The following account appears in the genealogical volume of the *Victoria County History* dealing with *The Landed Houses of Hertfordshire*:[12]

In some counties the origin of their modern landed houses can be traced in many cases to great local industries; Hertfordshire, rather an agricultural and residential than an industrial county, is not without its distinctive note, though this is of a different character. Banking and brewing, chiefly in London, are responsible for the rise and wealth of a quite exceptional proportion of families in this county.

To pursue this county, as an example, in the microcosmos of the House of Commons—these were the six Hertfordshire Members returned at the general election of 1761: *Hertford County*: Thomas Plumer Byde—a squire in Hertfordshire and a merchant in London,[13] descended on both sides from families aldermanic in origin, subsequently parliamentary; and Jacob Houblon, the owner of large landed estates, son of Charles Houblon, a Portugal merchant, by Mary, daughter of Daniel Bate, London merchant and vintner.[14] *Hertford Town*: John Calvert, a London brewer possessed of an estate in Hertfordshire;[15] and Timothy Caswall, an officer in the Guards, grandson of Sir George Caswall, a London banker of South Sea notoriety, nephew of John Caswall, also a London banker, and, on his mother's side, nephew of Nathaniel Brassey, another London banker, who had preceded Timothy Caswall as Member for Hertford, and had in 1761 secured his nephew's election for the borough.[16] *St. Albans*: James West, barrister and civil servant, the Duke of Newcastle's faithful Secretary to the Treasury, of a Warwickshire family, married to Sarah, daughter and heiress of Sir

James Steavens, a Bermondsey timber merchant;[17] and George Simon, Lord Nuneham, eldest son of Simon, 1st Earl Harcourt, by Rebecca, daughter of Charles Samborne Le Bas, and granddaughter of Sir Samuel Moyer, 1st bart., a Turkey merchant.[18]

In short, the representation of this county, even though it had neither rotten boroughs, pocket boroughs, nor boroughs under government management, fills in the detail of the picture given above of social amalgamation between the landed nobility or gentry and those who, as a class, have to be described by a foreign term—the big *bourgeoisie*.

The Upper Classes

Trade was not despised in eighteenth-century England—it was acknowledged to be the great concern of the nation; and money was honored, the mystic, common denominator of all values, the universal repository of as yet undetermined possibilities. But what was the position of the trader? There is no one answer to this question. A man's status in English society has always depended primarily on his own consciousness; for the English are not a methodical or logical nation—they perceive and accept facts without anxiously inquiring into their reasons or meaning. Whatever is apt to raise a man's self-consciousness—be it birth, rank, wealth, intellect, daring, or achievements—will add to his stature; but it has to be translated into the truest expression of his subconscious self-valuation: uncontending ease, the unbought grace of life. Classes are the more sharply marked in England because there is no single test for them, except the final, incontestable result; and there is more snobbery than in any other country, because the gate can be entered by anyone, and yet remains, for those bent on entering it, a mysterious, awe-inspiring gate. The Chinese used to ennoble a great man's ancestors; Menelaus greeted Telemachus as a son of "god-born kings," for no man who was "low born" could have been his father; and Sir James Barrie's "Admirable Crichton," when master of the lonely island, remembered that he had been " a king in Babylon." All stars appear higher to man than they are in the skies; for while the line of light curves, the human eye follows the tangent to the last short span of the distant road which the ray has traversed; the past is always seen on the line of the present. No "Admirable Crichton," Beau Nash, or Brummel is asked for his genealogical credentials; they are taken for granted (or dispensed with) even in the leisurely life of ease, where there is more scope for fastidiousness and distinctions than in the serious work of the nation. In the phylogenetic history of the Englishman the Oxford undergraduate of my own time corresponded to the eighteenth-century man, and with him nearly foremost among social qualifications was that a man should be amusing. Anyone can enter English society provided he can live, think, and feel like those who have built up its culture in their freer, easier hours.

English civilization is essentially the work of the leisured classes. We have no word to render the German idea of *Wissenschaft*, and we restrict the term of "science" to branches in which (alas!) the necessary labor and laboratories cannot be hidden. The German prefaces his monumental work by long chapters on methodology, and hesitates ever to take down the scaffolding which he has erected, for fear people might think the building had grown by itself. We prefer to make it appear as if our ideas came to us casually —like the Empire—in a fit of absence of mind. *Literæ Humaniores*, the most English of schools, goes back to the all-round man of the Renaissance. For specialization necessarily entails distortion of mind and loss of balance, and the characteristically English attempt to appear unscientific springs from a desire to remain human. It is not true that Englishmen have little respect for mental achievements. Whereas on the Continent scholarships rank as poor relief, at Oxford or Cambridge the scholar holds a privileged position, coveted as a distinction. More intellectual work is done by aristocrats in England than anywhere else, and, in turn, scientists, doctors, historians, and poets have been made peers—to say nothing of the discipline most closely connected with the State, law, where peerages have for centuries been the regular and almost unavoidable prizes for the leaders of the profession; but no German *Gelehrter* was ever made a baron or a count. What is not valued in England is abstract knowledge as a profession, because the tradition of English civilization is that professions should be practical and culture should be the work of the leisured classes.

The English landowners, for centuries past, have not tilled their land; they had no serfs to work it, nor did they do so with hired labor; they leased it out to small farmers. In the eighteenth century, in some Continental countries estates were measured by the number of "souls" (serfs attached to their soil), in others by the number of "smokes" (chimneys–homesteads), yet in others by their acreage; in England alone they were described in terms of their rental. The work of the owner on an English landed estate was, and remains, primarily administrative; but, though more exacting than it may seem to outsiders, it has always left the owners a fair amount of leisure for social administration and for political work, for literary and scientific pursuits, for agricultural experiments on the home farm, for "improvements" (the building of mansions, the laying out of gardens, the developing of mines and various industrial enterprises on their estates, the making of roads and canals, etc.), for outdoor sports and recreations, for social intercourse, for life in town, and for foreign travel. The one thing never mentioned in the sketch of Sir Roger de Coverley or of Squire Western is agricultural work, such as was done until recently on big estates in Central and Eastern Europe under the immediate supervision of their owners; nor is it obvious nowadays in the life of the average English country house. But primarily on the rental of England were raised her political system and lore, and her civilization.

This civilization is neither urban nor rural; the English ruling classes have for centuries been amphibious. In Germany there has always been a sharp division between the towns and the "land" outside; many towns for a long time preserved an independence which emphasized still more the division, but the political power in the big Germanic States was in the hands of the "agrarians," who, except for a small circle of Court aristocracy, lived on their land. In Italy during the Renaissance, the cities were dominant, and the big landowners inhabited them, as they did in ancient Greece and Rome; in some places (e.g., at Treviso) they were even forbidden by law to live outside the city walls. In eighteenth-century England the ruling classes lived neither in fortified castles nor in agrarian manorhouses nor in town palaces, but in palatial mansions planted out on their estates (the suburban system of our time is merely a replica of that amphibious life, democratized and rendered accessible to a large part of the nation). Few attempts at outside architecture have been made by the English aristocracy in their town houses; no Chatsworth or Longleat or Harewood was ever built in Bloomsbury, Piccadilly, or

Mayfair. But in the country the atmosphere and character of town civilization clings to their houses; they certainly are neither primitive nor rustic.

In style the English country house is not the product of the English countryside; some old Tudor or Jacobean mansions may still pass as autochthonous; the Georgian house bears witness to the classicism of the English mind; the pseudo-Gothic "castle," or a mansion Palladian in front and Gothic at the back, to a "grand tour" gone wrong. The English country house dominates its surroundings; no old forest reaches its doors, as in America; nor does it, like an Ukrainian manorhouse, hide in a "yar" (cañon), from fear of the endless steppes above, and of the sharp winds which sweep them. Its civilizing influence spreads over the lawns which surround it, over the turf and trees in the park; they are not much interfered with nowadays, and yet bear such a peculiarly well-groomed appearance.

But the eighteenth century, with its exuberant zeal and ingenious conceit, did not allow parks to live their own lives; the *furor hortensis*, the passion for landscape gardening, reigned supreme. Chatham on one occasion, when summoned on urgent business to London, mapped out a garden for a friend by torchlight; and Thomas Whately, M.P., Secretary to the Treasury, who had a prominent share in drafting the American Stamp Act, was best known to his own generation as the author of *Observations on Modern Gardening*— he could not leave things alone. England offers exceptional facilities for landscape gardening; no dominant natural features, "absolutely vertical" or "absolutely horizontal"—high mountains, wide plains, or great rivers—interfere with the fancies of men. Within the limited space, closed in by hills and mists, noble views can be opened up and pointed with pleasing objects. Here is the story of William Shenstone, an eighteenth-century poet, and of rural taste as then conceived:

> *In 1745 he took possession of his paternal estate, when his delight in rural pleasures, and his ambition of rural elegance was excited; he began from this time to point his prospects, to diversify his service, to entangle his walks, and to wind his waters; which he did with such judgement, and such fancy, as made his little domain the envy of the great and the admiration of the skilful; a place to be visited by travellers and copied by designers. . . .*

He spent his estate in adorning it, and his death was proba-
bly hastened by his anxieties. He was a lamp that spent its oil in
blazing.[19]

The zeal and conceit of the upper classes of eighteenth-century
England, which spent much of its best oil "in blazing," have
been paid for heavily, in matters small and great; but it was thus that
Englishmen learned to leave things well alone—to refrain from
drawing up elaborate, artificial, naïve schemes for parks or Empires.
The self-restraint and conscious rectitude of a neo-Puritanism,
"undemonstrative, gentlemanlike, and reasonable" had to be superim-
posed on the curious, voracious, acquisitive, utterly egotistic, and
amoral energy of the eighteenth century, before the Englishman
could change from a rover into a ruler. The eighteenth century was
the childhood of Imperial Britain.

The Land as Basis of Citizenship

The relations of groups of men to plots of land, of organized communities to units of territory, form the basic content of political history. The conflicting territorial claims of communities constitute the
greater part of conscious international history; social stratifications
and convulsions, primarily arising from the relationship of men to
land, make the greater, not always fully conscious, part of the
domestic history of nations—and even under urban and industrial
conditions ownership of land counts for more than is usually supposed. To every man, as to Brutus, the native land is his life-giving
Mother, and the State raised upon the land is his law-giving Father;
and the days cannot be long of a nation which fails to honor either.
Only one nation has survived for two thousand years, though an
orphan—my own people, the Jews. But then in the God-given Law
we have enshrined the authority of a State, and in the God-promised
Land the idea of a Mother-Country; through the centuries from
Mount Sinai we have faced Arets Israel, our land. Take away either,
and we cease to be a nation; let both live again, and we shall be ourselves once more.

When a tribe settles, membership in the tribe carries the right
to a share in the land. In time the order becomes inverted: the holding of land determines a man's position in the community. There is
some well-nigh mystic power in the ownership of space—for it is

not the command of resources alone which makes the strength of the landowner, but that he has a place in the world which he can call his own, from which he can ward off strangers, and in which he himself is rooted—the superiority of a tree to a log. In land alone can there be real partimony, and he who as freeman holds a share in his native land—the freeholder—is, and must be, a citizen. Wealth consists of an accumulation, or the command, of goods and chattels; the idea of inalienable property, cherished beyond its patent value, arises from the land. Throughout the centuries rich English businessmen have therefore aimed at acquiring landed estates and founding "county families"—they have commuted wealth into property, be it at a loss of revenue. Even the tiny garden at the back of the workman's house is a "corner of his own," for which the clean courtyard of model buildings is no compensation; and in the most reduced, impoverished form the "corner of one's own" still appeared until recently, as a qualification for full citizenship, in the latchkey franchise. It was not in rental and leisure alone that the superiority of the landed classes was grounded in eighteenth-century England, but even more in the ease of the well-balanced existence of men who had their share in the land and the State.

In the eighteenth century this connection between ownership of land and a share in the State was acknowledged and upheld by Tories and Whigs alike. Swift claimed that "law in a free country is, or ought to be, the determination of the majority of those who have property in land,"[20] while Defoe considered that in case of a dissolution of government the power would devolve on the freeholders, "the proper owners of the country," the other inhabitants being "but sojourners, like lodgers in a house." "I make no question but property of land is the best title to government in the world."[21] And on the very eve of the American Revolution, constitutional right, as arising from the ownership of land, was pleaded by the Continental Congress in the address *To the People of Great Britain*, voted at Philadelphia on 5 September 1774: "Are not the proprietors of the soil of Great Britain lords of their own property? Can it be taken from them without their consent? . . . Why then are the proprietors of the soil of America less lords of their property than you are of yours?"

English history, and especially English Parliamentary history, is made by families rather than by individuals; for a nation with a tradition of self-government must have thousands of dynasties, partaking of the peculiarities which in other countries belong to the royal family alone. The English political family is a compound of "blood," name, and estate, this last, as the dominions of monarchs, being the most important of the three; that is why mansions instead of families are so often the subject of monographs dealing with the history of the English upper classes. The name is a weighty symbol, but liable to variations; descent traced in the male line only is like a river without its tributaries;[22] the estate, with all that it implies, is, in the long run, the most potent factor in securing continuity through identification, the "taking up" of the inheritance. The owner of an ancestral estate may have far less of the "blood" than some distant relative bearing a different name, but sprung from a greater number of intermarriages between descendants of the founder of the family; still, it is he who in his thoughts and feelings most closely identifies himself, and is identified by others, with his predecessors. Primogeniture and entails psychologically help to preserve the family in that they tend to fix its position through the successive generations, and thereby favor conscious identification.

There is a curious interplay between men and land in British history; interlocked, they seem to compete for dominion. Which will stamp the name upon the other? In eighteenth-century Scotland, the individual was practically nameless between his clan and his land; men were called by their estates.[23] In England, after a man had founded a family on an estate, the estate would often convey the name of its founder to heirs receiving it through a woman and sometimes even to heirs unconnected by blood. Thomas Brodnax (M.P. for Canterbury), on inheriting Rawmere in 1727, changed his name to May, but in 1738, on inheriting Chawton in Hampshire, to Knight;[24] William Evelyn (M.P. for Hythe), on marrying Frances, daughter and heiress of William Glanville, assumed her name, but when in 1742, after his wife's death, their only daughter married Admiral Boscawen, and thereby "carried her estate to that family," William Evelyn "resumed his original name";[25] and Percy Wyndham, M.P., the second son of the famous Tory leader, William Wyndham, on inheriting estates under the will of Lord Thomond, the husband of his mother's sister, assumed the name of O'Brien, though in no way descended from that family.[26]

Landed property of any kind is called "realty," all other property being "personalty." Under most legal systems the rules of inheritance with regard to "realty" are determined by its location—it has its own "nationality"; "personalty" follows the law and nationality of its owner. British citizenship itself can be derived from men or from land, from the nationality of the parents or the land of birth. The pre-eminent rights of landowners have often been explained by their having "the greatest stake in the country," and certainly *qua* landowners they cannot withdraw themselves from the burdens which weigh on the permanent territorial framework of the nation—for instance, the national debt or misgovernment; as Locke put it, there was "always annexed to the enjoyment of land a submission to the government of the country of which that land is a part."[27] By a logical equation, if one's thinking inclines that way, one may therefore conclude that the men who are most intimately affected by the government have a primary claim to a share in it; in reality this conclusion is based on instincts and modes of thinking much deeper and much more cogent than any conscious reasonings, but into which it is not necessary here to enter.

For centuries a freehold in England has carried with it the most signal mark of citizenship, a vote; estates carried with them seats in the Great Council of the nation; and these connections were pressed so far that at times the land of England, rather than her people, seemed to be represented in her Parliament. This was the avowed doctrine when the *barones majores* personally attended it in right of their fiefs. But the interplay between men and land soon attached the writ to the heirs of "the body," rather than of the land. The House of Lords lost its original basis, but the leading landowners, if not of baronial rank, reappeared in the House of Commons as well-nigh hereditary, though not immovable, representatives of the shires and boroughs in which they held "the best property." Still, in the Commons they formed one element only, and in the elections their property was one factor only, supremely important but not exclusive or statutory. The House of Commons became the dominant assembly because it was the most comprehensive; it did not suffer from any rigid, logical rules, which the English mind abhors, and it had, what Englishmen always try to find, a common practical denominator. "The Commons in Parliament are not the representative body of the whole Kingdome," wrote Sir Robert Filmer in 1648; "they do not represent the King, who is the head and principall member of the Kingdome, nor do they represent the Lords. . . ."[28] Whatever the position had been in 1648, Filmer's dictum was patently untrue in the eighteenth century; through patronage, borough influence, and territorial predominence, both King and Lords were well represented in the Commons, but in terms commensurable with those of the rest of the nation.

This is not the place to discuss the mutual relations of the two Houses, their personnel, and the intimate connections which existed between them in the eighteenth century; what primarily concerns us here is their connection with the land of Great Britain. Although the writ to the "heirs male of the body" had been made the basis of most peerages, the idea of attachment to certain lands continued even in the eighteenth century—witness the revival of numerous peerages in heirs to peers' estates who had no claim to the title; occasionally a peerage was revived even in an heir who was in no way connected by blood with his predecessors—Percy (Wyndham) O'Brien, mentioned above, was in 1756 created Earl of Thomond in the peerage of Ireland, thus succeeding even to the title of the husband of his mother's sister, whose estates he had inherited and whose name he had adopted. The possession of estates which had belonged to peers was still always considered to carry with it a certain claim to a peerage; this is shown, *e.g.*, by the curious phrase which, on 19 May 1756, the Duke of Newcastle used, when conveying to Lord Chetwynd (an Irish peer) the refusal of an English peerage: "The King makes very few peers at present, and one who is most nearly allied to me, and has, I may say, better pretensions than any body, having the estates of two peers in him, whose peerages are, in a manner, sunk, will not be of the number."[29]

It is but natural that in the absence of a secret ballot the possession of land in counties or boroughs should have carried with it considerable influence in parliamentary elections through the pressure which its owners were able to exert on their tenants. But in eighteenth-century England this element of crude pressure shades off by almost imperceptible degrees into a tradition which connected a claim to the representation of certain constituencies even with specific estates, not because of their size or location only, but because of some mysterious tradition which seemed to attach to them and to be conveyed to their owners. To uphold such a tradition was well-nigh a duty incumbent on their possessor. To give one example: the Newport family had long been predominant in Shropshire, and Lord Bath, having purchased the reversion of part of their estates from the mother of the illegitimate son of Henry, 3rd Earl of Bradford, put up his son for Shrewsbury in 1759, pleading that this was his "duty to the Bradford interest"[30] (a conception of duty extraordinary, even as an "explanation," when professed to an estate which Lord Bath did not as yet own, and of which, indeed, neither he nor his son lived to acquire possession).[31] But an even more striking "example of the abiding nature of political tradition which could be furnished only in England"—and one should add, of territorial tradition in politics—was given in a letter from Alfred Robbins in *The Times* on 4 November 1924, after the general election of that year: "Mr. A. M. Williams, who has won the seat for the Northern Division of Cornwall, is a son of Mr. John Charles Williams . . . who holds the estate of Werrington"; this, for more than two centuries, "was considered by electoral managers to carry with it the representation of Launceston, which is the chief town of the Northern Division of Cornwall. . . ." From 1650 till 1865 the estate of Werrington and the Parliamentary representation of Launceston were held in succession by Sir Francis Drake, the Morices, and the Percys; in 1865, a Manchester cotton merchant, who had bought Werrington, "was promptly returned for Launceston"; in 1874, its next owner, a Cheshire brewer, explicitly claimed that Launceston ought to be represented by him or his nominee—which it was, till disfranchised in 1885; "the long spell of 'Werrington influence,' politically dominant in the district since 1650, was then broken, only to be revived in 1924."

In our days a case of this kind, if not accidental, would at least be treated as incidental—interesting but not important. In the eighteenth century the superiority of property, especially of landed property, over men was an acknowledged fact, and to neglect it would be to miss one of the main factors in the political thinking and practice of the age. The following letter from "Solomon See-well," in the *London Chronicle* of 2–4 April 1761, discussing the expected creation of new peers, has a peculiar flavor in its naïve and matter-of-fact treatment of the subject:

> *It is said many millions of property is going to be added to the weight of the upper house of parliament. If so, it may be proper to consider how much it is likely to weaken the scale of power to the Commons. . . .*
>
> *Property in counties, as well as boroughs, commands the choice of representatives; and if the bulk of property should once more get into the hands of members of the upper house, that will secure to them the appointment of the representatives of the people, when their own children and dependents will become the disposers at their pleasure of our liberties and fortunes.*

Did then the eighteenth-century Parliament represent the men or the land of Great Britain? One might as well ask to whom the child owes its life, to the father or the mother? It represented both; or to put it more accurately, it represented British men rooted in the soil of Great Britain. Those roaming beyond its borders were not (and are not) represented, while all those within its borders (even if they had no votes) were considered to have been represented, "virtually" at least, through the land on which they lived.[32] The very definition of "virtual representation" implicitly declared its character: there was "not a blade of grass in Great Britain" which was unrepresented in Parliament. But because territorial rather than tribal, the British Parliament could not (and cannot) cover those definitely rooted in other soil, nor "virtually" represent the "blades of grass" of other lands, even if inhabited by men of the same stock. The first British Empire suffered disruption because Englishmen failed as yet to distinguish between a "Mother Country" and a "native land"; and between the distant, sublimated authority of the Crown, symbolically "paternal," and the direct governmental power which in a free country is wielded by the sons of the soil. A tribal sovereignty can be common to members of the race scattered through various countries; the supreme power in a self-governing country must be in those acknowledging it as the mother who gave them birth.

The State

Beginning with God—*abhinu, malkenu* ("our Father, our King")
—all authority is paternal, and therefore all authority was
deemed to be "of God." Kings, as incarnation of authority, have
been termed fathers, in Eastern Europe down to our own days; and
the great seventeenth-century English champion of absolute monarchy, "the learned Sir Robert Filmer, Baronet," summed up his doctrine in *Patriarcha, or the Natural Power of Kings.* "Even the power
which God himself exerciseth over mankind," wrote Filmer, "is by
right of fatherhood; he is both the King and Father of us all."[33]
"The subjection of children to their parents is the fountain of all
regal authority."[34] "It is true, all kings be not the natural parents of
their subjects . . . yet in their right succeed to the exercise of
supreme jurisdiction."[35] "All power on earth is either derived or
usurped from the fatherly power."[36] "The law which enjoyns obedience to kings is delivered in the terms of Honour thy father."[37]
Similarly John Winthrop, the Puritan Governor of Massachusetts, a
contemporary of Sir Robert Filmer, but who could not have been
acquainted with Filmer's works and certainly would not have
accepted his conclusions, declared, when arguing against democracy,
that to allow it in Massachusetts would be "a manifest breach of the
5th Commandment."[38]

From the paternal and quasi-divine character of authority,
Filmer drew conclusions to suit his own instincts and inclinations:
that government should be monarchical and absolute. These conclusions he fortified with twisted biblical quotations and a mass of cum-
brous learning. John Locke destroyed Filmer's superstructure in his
famous *Two Treatises of Government,* in fine language and with
irresistible logic, both, so far as Filmer was concerned, misdirected to
a futile purpose. Were one roughly to sum up the essence of their
respective arguments, one might describe Filmer's thesis as a postu-
late that the "political child" should never grow up at all—and in
fact vast numbers of individuals and even whole nations never do
grow up; while Locke's fundamental assumption is that the "political
child," having attained manhood, discards all the memories and
instincts of its childhood, which, though possibly desirable, never is,
nor can be, achieved. Still, after having destroyed Filmer's arguments

and made great play with the inclusion of the mother in the Fifth Commandment, Locke finished by admitting the paternal origin, and implicitly the paternal character, of government:

> . . . *it was easy, and almost natural for children by a tacit and scarce avoidable consent to make way for the father's authority and government. They had been accustomed in their childhood to follow his direction, and to refer their little differences to him; and when they were men, who fitter to rule them? . . . 'Tis no wonder that they made no distinction betwixt minority and full age; nor looked after one-and-twenty or any other age that might make them the free disposers of themselves and fortunes, when they could have no desire to be out of their pupilage. . . .*
>
>   *Thus the natural fathers of families by an insensible change became the politic monarchs of them too. . . .*[39]

Whether the theory of an actual paternal origin of government is a correct phylogenetic or logical inference, or merely a psychological delusion, we shall probably never know; but this much is certain, that it is an assumption natural to us all. Correct perception of a psychological fact underlay Sir Robert Filmer's theory: all authority is to human beings paternal in character, for they are born, not free and independent as some of Filmer's opponents would have it, but subject to parental authority; in the first place, to that of their fathers. The development of every man, in his individual life, obviously proceeds from subjection to freedom, and it proves arrested growth if full freeedom is never reached, and if inwardly he carries on the revolutionary (or counter-revolutionary) struggle long after he himself should have attained uncontending authority. For in the life of every man comes a night when at the ford of the stream he has to strive "with God and with men"; if he prevails and receives the blessing of the father-spirit, he is henceforth free and at peace.

     Above individual men rises the community, the State. There the struggle is repeated, on an infinitely wider stage, in terms similar to those of man's individual life, and yet in dimensions which are beyond the understanding of the average man. For man is able in a quasi-mechanical, agglutinative manner to construct monstrous Leviathans which exceed his consciously regulated norms and his comprehension. A sudden expansion of the State, whether in territorial size or in the numbers of individuals which it comprises as active members, is frequently, and even usually, accompanied by a retrograde movement in matters of self-government; at every stage in social development freedom has to be reconquered.

In absolute monarchies the political child never outgrows its nonage, and at the utmost changes into a revolutionary. But there is still a long way from revolution to active self-government. The essence of our own present system is that the idea and symbols of authority are raised above the gerents of power and made inaccessible to them. The fact that the "paternal" authority of the State centers in the Crown, whose bearer does not, and must not, in any way personally exercise it, establishes a psychological equality between the actual rulers of the State and those governed by them, and between the winning and the losing side in the political struggle; it secures both the idea of authority and the unity of the nation.

Royalty, as the embodiment of the paternal idea, supplies the most natural and most appropriate expression to tribal unity, and as such is unrestricted by territorial limits. A compact and centralized national State can form a republic, and a State comprising vast or diversified but contiguous territories, a federal republic; the British Empire, united in its origins, racial and ideological, but scattered over various continents, must have for its bond the great royal symbol of paternal authority, divested, however, of executive power, which in free communities has to be with the grown-up children of each land. Benjamin Franklin declared: ". . . the British empire is not a single state; it comprehends many . . . We have the same King, but not the same legislatures";[40] ". . . the Parliament has no right to make any law whatever binding on the colonies; . . . the king, and not the king, lords, and commons collectively, is their sovereign."[41] And he objected to "a claim of subjects in one part of the King's dominions to be sovereigns over their fellow-subjects in another part of his dominions."[42] "Every man in England seems to consider himself as a piece of a sovereign over America; seems to jostle himself into the throne with the King, and talks of *our subjects in the Colonies*."[43]

Franklin's thesis was correct, but the constitutional ideas and practice of Great Britain hardly allowed as yet of its application. The King in Parliament and the King as first magistrate—the head of the executive—had to become well-nigh a fiction, a shadow, before he could acquire a free symbolic existence, outside the British Parliament and apart from it. But in eighteenth-century England, the King was still a real factor in Administration.

Government and Trade

A State must have a territorial basis, but government can exist without it, for example, in migrating tribes or in armies engaged on distant expeditions, which, having to face new and changing circumstances, require, if anything, more government than a settled nation. Though the State primarily belongs to the owners of the land, it is the circulating part of the nation which is most directly concerned with government; and governments, as all human institutions, are influenced and shaped by those who are willing to work and pay for them, *i.e.*, those who need them most. The merchant who moves among strangers requires organized assistance more than the agricultural laborer or the landowner; moreover, trade is, in its very nature, social, while agriculture starts with self-sufficiency and always retains a considerable measure of it; consequently, trade is at all times much more the subject of legislation than agriculture. The constitutional distinction between internal and external taxation, still accepted in England about 1630, in America about 1760, and in Hungary about 1840, testifies to the direct connection between the government and the merchant trading with foreign countries. The frontiers are the King's, they belong to the government and to the whole tribe, rather than to the fraction settled within them (the Dominions, as distinguished from the Empire, until recently had no jurisdiction beyond their coastline). The desert, the sea, and the towns have developed the purest, strongest types of male religion and governments apart from territory. The urban, trading element was for centuries over-represented in the House of Commons; and even after most of the borough representation had passed into the hands of the aristocracy and landed gentry, trade nonetheless continued to hold a most conspicuous place in British political thought and action.

Trade is the natural form for the acquisitive endeavors of islanders. But for purposes of trade all shores border on the ships of a seafaring nation; and water is the earliest high-road in history for the transport of bulky objects, not merely of luxuries. The idea, at one time current among economists, that the profits of trade depended upon the distance covered and the time consumed, crudely expressed facts of common experience. Trade depends on a diversity of produce, which is more likely to be found between distant than between neighboring countries; and trade between distant countries is a venture not to be attempted on a small scale, so that it requires considerable capital, and consequently results in more than average profits—up to a certain point the very rate of profits increases with the size of the capital. Trade at great distance and on a considerable scale leads to capitalism with its peculiar "trading" ideology, very different from, and indeed opposed to, that of militarism. As ships, the carriers of trade, are at the same time the "wooden walls" of an island, the trading spirit of its population is not checked and countered by militarism, which in France, Italy, and Germany, ultimately engulfed and destroyed the spirit and enterprise of the seaboard. The rise of powerful monarchies on the Continent had by the beginning of the sixteenth century interlocked them in rivalry and war, riveting their attention to the European Continent at the very time when their superior strength expelled England from it. England was forced to remain an island, which Venice and Holland could be only in a very imperfect manner.

Naval power and commerce, "like twins," are "born together, and not to live asunder,"[44] and oversea trade is a venture never to be despised by an island nation. In the Anglo-Saxon laws it was written that "if a merchant thrived, so that he fared thrice over the wide sea by his own means [craft], then was he thenceforth of thaneright worthy."[45] Trade with distant countries, across oceans, along untrodden paths, is something very different from keeping a booth at a country fair. George Cartwright rejoiced when in Labrador he exchanged "a small ivory comb," which had cost him "no more than twopence half-penny" in England, against a silver fox "worth four guineas";[46] but the hardships braved in the polar region, his refusal of a fine offered by Eskimos in atonement for an attempted theft,[47] in fact, the general character of his ventures, shows that he, the brother of Edmund Cartwright, the inventor, and Major John Cartwright, the reformer, was no mere trader. Continental nations engaged in wars for loot and talked of glory; the English went out for adventures and talked of trade. But Horace Walpole, a sentimental and unemotional pacifist, shrewdly suspected that "trade" was often a mere excuse for things which other men explained in different terms.

> *I am a bad Englishman, because I think the advantages of commerce are dearly bought for some by the lives of many more. . . . But . . . every age has some ostentatious system to excuse the havoc it commits. Conquest, honour, chivalry, religion, balance of power, commerce, no matter what, mankind must bleed, and take a term for a reason.*[48]

Still, the terms in which men try to account for their actions are of supreme importance; every country and every age has dominant terms, which seem to obsess men's thoughts. Those of eighteenth-century England were property, contract, trade, and profits. Locke, its teacher, declared that "government has no other end but the preservation of property,"[49] but under the term "property" he included a man's "life, liberty, and estate";[50] this was not the narrow "nightwatchman conception of the State" as developed in the nineteenth century, but a terminology dominated by the sense of ownership.[51] However much Mandeville explained away his *Fable of the Bees*, it was significant that he should have placed moral and economic values, to say the least, on one level. Possibly the reducing of all values to one common money denominator was to some extent stimulated by the discovery of the atom, a common unit in an infinitely diversified creation—social and moral disciplines, having no exact measures of their own and yet trying to simulate precision, are singularly liable to be influenced by terms and conceptions borrowed from science. The quantitative theory of happiness of the English "utilitarians" was, no doubt, psychologically connected with this habit of reducing moral values to the money unit.

Does this common money denominator signify a peculiarly materialistic turn of mind in the eighteenth century? It might perhaps be fairer to give the matter a broader basis. The later eighteenth century in England was an eclectic and inquisitive age, inventive in material production and mechanics, in time- and labor-saving devices; primarily an age of collectors, with a passion for accumulating no matter what—books, prints, manuscripts, shells, pictures, old coins, or the currency of the realm. For at bottom it does not matter much what a man collects—money, buttons, or irrelevant knowledge —it denotes the same stage in development. But when the collecting habit gets hold of a whole community, the apparent result is materialism; and trade becomes the great watchword in politics.

The Duke of Newcastle, a year before his death, summed up the record of his life by speaking of his

> *zealous endeavours to promote, at all times, the true interest of my country, and the security of our religious and civil liberties; to support the Protestant Succession in His Majesty's Royal Family . . . ; and to contribute all that was in my power to the encouragement and extension of the trade and commerce of these kingdoms.*[52]

Lord Hervey wrote in 1734 of "our trade, which is so much the vital breath of this nation that the one cannot subsist whenever the other is long stopped";[53] and George Grenville in 1764 felt flattered when the Spanish ambassador said about him that he "would lose all he has in the world rather than suffer diminution of the honour of the King his master, or of the commerce of the kingdom"[54]—a juxtaposition typical of eighteenth-century England. Lecky notes with some surprise the mental outlook of the eighteenth-century Parliament:

> *In very few periods in English political history was the commercial element more conspicuous in administration. The prevailing spirit of the debates was of a kind we should rather have expected in a middle-class Parliament than in a Parliament consisting in a very large measure of the nominees of great families. . . . The questions which excited most interest were chiefly financial and commercial ones. The increase of the National Debt, the possibility and propriety of reducing its interest, the advantages of a Sinking Fund, the policy of encouraging trade by bounties and protective duties, the evils of excise, the reduction of the land-tax, the burden of Continental subsidies, were among the topics which produced the most vehement and the most powerful debates.*[55]

His description is accurate. Young, ambitious members of the gentry class eagerly engaged in the study of trade and finance, and someone in an official position, in 1779, put the following marginal remark on a paper dealing with trade: "No man sho'd be elligible to sit in the H[ouse] of C[ommons] that has not a competent knowledge in geography and the trade and manufacturers of Great Britain."[56] Edward Eliot, of Port Eliot, applied to Newcastle for a place at the Board of Trade, because he hoped there to obtain "such information as may enable some of us young people who act together to put in execution the resolution we have formed, of endeavouring to speak in the House of Commons upon points of business."[57] When in 1759 Hans Stanley asked to be made a Lord of the Treasury, he declared to Newcastle: "The chief employment of my studies has been the revenue and the commercial interests of this country," an assertion amply confirmed by his memoranda on financial subjects. To Charles Jenkinson's studies of these subjects, his papers, now in the British Museum, bear witness. In fact, in the eighteenth century detailed economic information and sound economic speculation is found even in quarters where one would hardly have expected them. In 1754 Newcastle transmitted to William Murray (subsequently Lord Mansfield) two papers on financial matters "from two country gentlemen, Mr. Campion and Mr. Page . . . the one from an old man of seventy-four who never was above one year and half in busyness and that forty years ago, the other from a clerk in the South Sea House in the year 1720, retired, and settled in the country, now for near thirty years; the last is a master piece."[58] Adam Smith was not a lonely figure in his time, least of all in "that part of Britain usually called Scotland," as can be seen from the correspondence of James Oswald, Gilbert Elliot, or William Mure, all three Members of Parliament. The "trading" spirit was abroad, and men took pride in the record figures of British trade (unless they tried to make the flesh of their fellow-subjects creep with tales of its decay). When, in 1753, Sir George Savile was put up as candidate for Yorkshire, Mr. Thornhagh (subsequently Hewett), M.P. for Nottinghamshire, in supporting his nomination, argued that he was "the properest candidate for this trading county, as the situation of his property makes the prosperity of trade more immediately his concern";[59] and Lord Ducie, when resigning the Lord Lieutenancy of Gloucestershire, spoke of it with pride as "this great trading county."[60] The picture which eighteenth-century Englishmen had of their country, and their view of commerce as the dominant factor in its existence, is reflected in a memorandum drawn up about 1772 by George III, who in many ways was a typical exponent of the doctrines of his time. He thus envisaged an *entente* between Great Britain and France, and distinguished their relative positions:

> *Commerce the foundation of a marine can never flourish in an absolute monarchy therefore that branch of grandeur ought to be left to England whilst the great army kept by France gives her a natural preeminence on the continent.*[61]

The Imperial Problem

No great historic problem has ever been settled by means of a brilliant idea—an invention in the sphere of politics—when its solution was not latent in circumstances, but many a problem has found settlement by not being pressed at such a moment. "Indolence, when it is not the result of weakness or vice, is a very great virtue," wrote Shelburne in 1801.[62] Restraint, coupled with the tolerance which it implies and with plain human kindness, is much more valuable in politics than ideas which are ahead of their time; but restraint was a quality in which the eighteenth-century Englishman was as deficient as most other nations are even now.

By the conquests of the Seven Years' War, the British Empire in America had been enlarged and consolidated, and it was generally felt that the time had come for settling it on a more regular basis; but all conceptions regarding its future turned around questions of trade and finance. "Happily for this country," wrote in 1764 Thomas Whately, M.P., Joint Secretary to the Treasury, "the real and substantial, and those are the commercial interests of Great Britain, are now preferred to every other consideration: and the trade from whence its greatest wealth is derived, and upon which its maritime power is principally founded, depends upon a wise and proper use of the Colonies."[63] These, as Comptroller Weare explained, were not "planted with a view to founding new empires, but for the sake of trade,"[64] for England's "profit, not her glory."[65] Although British administrative practice was not nearly as callous as British political theory, and sympathetic concern for the Colonies was shown in hundreds of ways, it was not an article of conscious political thinking. "Nations have affections for themselves, though they have none for one another," wrote an Irish pamphleteer in 1779;

"the body politic has no heart. . . . There is no such thing as political humanity, or, if the sentiment did exist, it is not likely to be found in a country of commerce."[66]

Thus economic considerations impelled British statesmen to take action with regard to the Empire at a time when, even for constitutional reasons, a true settlement could not be attained. In 1760 Great Britain had not reached a stage at which it would have been possible to remodel the Empire as a federation of self-governing States under a Crown detached from the actual government of any of its component parts. Royalty, which is now the bond of the Empire, was still an active factor in British politics, and to eighteenth-century Englishmen any exercise of its attributes apart from the British Parliament would have seemed a dangerous and unconstitutional reversion to "prerogative." This junction between King and Parliament in Great Britain was by itself bound to carry the supremacy of the British Parliament into the Colonies; and the very fact that George III so thoroughly and loyally stood by the constitutional principles of the time rendered a conflict inevitable—had he entertained any idea of power or authority apart from the British Parliament, he might have welcomed the conception of a separate sovereignty in the Colonies. The necessary limitations to the authority of the British Parliament, a territorial assembly, were not as yet understood.

A social contrast is often drawn between an aristocratic or oligarchic Great Britain and democratic Colonies, but the true contrast was not altogether what it seemed. English society was never exclusive, in the sense of adhering to standardized ranks—had it been so, it might have been remembered that many of the Colonists were of the best blood of England; nor were the Colonies by any means as democratic as American orators would make them appear.[67] But the social structure of England, the product of many centuries of close organic growth, was compact and complex, and outsiders, of whatever rank, could not easily fit themselves into it; while that of the Colonies was comparatively simple, as it always must be in new countries with a vast, empty hinterland and a moving "frontier." Nor was the conception of British superiority over the Colonies based on social distinctions, but much rather on the fetishism of places, which ascribes a certain superiority to the inhabitants of the old country over those who have left it, while preserving its language, customs, traditions, and ideas; and on that curious family hierarchy of Mother Country and "children" which appears whenever one part of a nation continues in the old country while another forms a new community, leaving its own past in the custody of those who inherit the land of their common ancestors. The eighteenth-century British claim to superiority over the Colonies was largely the result of thinking in terms of personified countries.[68]

Almost the only men who about 1770 held the modern British view of the Empire were the English Dissenters; to them alone, who knew no hierarchy either in religion or politics, the Colonists were so many "congregations of brethren beyond the seas." In their own depressed condition, they followed the growth of those communities with a sincere and active love, and with a hope that the new England would some day right the wrongs of the old. That friendship was requited by the American Dissenters, and though sympathy with English Nonconformity naturally did not in any way soften their feelings towards Anglicanism, political or religious, it made them think in terms of the British Empire. Ezra Stiles (subsequently president of Yale University) wrote to the Rev. Dr. Fordyce, a Dissenting minister in London, on 22 November 1763:

> *Our infant churches from their original plantation in the deserts of America have ever retained an affectionate esteem and respect for their brethren the Dissenting Churches in England and Ireland, and the Established Church of Scotland. The similitude of our doctrines and forms of worship make our cause one, which if cemented by harmonious intercourse might render us at length into a much more respectable body in the British Empire and the Protestant world, than if we continue to subsist disunited, disconnected.*[69]

The disruption of the First British Empire, next to the downfall of the Puritan Commonwealth in Great Britain, was the greatest disaster for British Dissent, and the greatest setback for British democracy; and it is by no means certain that it was conducive to a healthy growth of democracy even in America, where French ideas, adaptable in their rootless superficiality, warped the further growth of the New England Puritan community, intellectually the strongest group on the continent. In the spirit of the Dissenters alone could a solution of the Imperial problem have been found in 1770, and it seems extremely doubtful whether Burke and his friends, if in power, would have succeeded in saving the First British Empire. Their ideas were no less hierarchical and authoritarian than those of George III and Lord North, and to them, too, trade was the soul of Empire; had Burke been in office during the American Revolution, we might merely have had to antedate his counter-revolutionary Toryism by some twenty years.

Why was not representation in the British Parliament—a British Union—offered to the Colonies? or why, alternatively, was not an American Union attempted, such as had been proposed at the Albany Congress in 1754? This might have freed Great Britain from burdens, responsibilities, and entanglements, and paved the way to Dominion status. Both ideas were discussed at great length and with copious repetition, but mechanical devices, though easily conceived on paper, are difficult to carry into practice when things do not, as it were, of their own accord, move in that direction. There is "the immense distance between planning and executing" and "all the difficulty is with the last."

> It requires no small labour to open the eyes of either the public or of individuals, but when that is accomplished, you are not got a third of the way. The real difficulty remains in getting people to apply the principles which they have admitted, and of which they are now so fully convinced.[70]

In the end statesmen hardly ever act except under pressure of "circumstances," which means of mass movements and of the mental climate in their own circles. But about 1770, the masses in Great Britain were not concerned with America, and the mental and moral reactions of the political circles were running on lines which, when followed through, were bound to lead to disaster.

The basic elements of the Imperial problem during the American Revolution must be sought not so much in conscious opinions and professed views bearing directly on it, as in the very structure and life of the Empire; and in doing that the words of Danton should be remembered—*on ne fait pas le procès aux révolutions.* Those who are out to apportion guilt in history have to keep to views and opinions, judge the collisions of planets by the rules of road traffic, make history into something like a column of motoring accidents, and discuss it in the atmosphere of a police court. But whatever theories of "free will" theologians and philosophers may develop with regard to the individual, there is no free will in the thinking and actions of the masses, any more than in the revolutions of planets, in the migrations of birds, and in the plunging of hordes of lemmings into the sea. At the moment of supreme crisis, in March 1778, Governor Thomas Hutchinson, a loyalist refugee in England, wrote in despair: "It's certain the political clock stands still." He was wrong; the political clock of Great Britain was ticking the seconds and striking the hours, as it always does, no slower and no quicker; it was a clock, and not a seismograph.

NOTES

IX. *The Social Foundations*

[1] J. J. Alexander, "Devon County Members of Parliament," *Reports and Transactions of the Devonshire Association*, Vol. 49, p. 368.

[2] *The Parisians*, Vol. i, p. 120.

[3] *The Complete English Tradesman* (1726), p. 380.

[4] Daniel Defoe, *A Plan of the English Commerce* (1728), p. 81.

[5] *Ibid.*, p. 13.

[6] Defoe, *The Complete English Tradesman*, pp. 376–377.

[7] *Ibid.*, pp. 377–378.

[8] See Peter Le Neve's *Pedigrees of Knights*, ed. by G. W. Marshall, *Harleian Society Publications* (1873), p. 495. See further "Pedigree of the Family of Crowley," by G. W. Marshall, in *The East-Anglian* (1867), Vol. iii, pp. 95–98; about Ambrose Crowley and his ironworks, see also William Hutchinson, *History of Durham* (1787), Vol. ii, pp. 441–443, and Surtees, *History of Durham* (1820), Vol. ii, pp. 272–273.

[9] See Sir John Nickolls, *Remarks on the Advantages and Disadvantages of France and of Great Britain with respect to Commerce* (1754), p. 110. "Sir John Nickolls" is a pseudonym—the author was a Frenchman, Plumard de Dangeul.

[10] *Ibid.*, p. 10.

[11] *A Plan of the English Commerce*, pp. 83–84.

[12] *Ibid.*, p. 4.

[13] T. P. Byde unsuccessfully contested Cambridge as an opposition candidate in 1774 and 1776 and became bankrupt in 1779 (see *Gentleman's Magazine*, 1779, p. 272); he died at Naples in 1789 "reduced to the most abject condition, after all his visionary speculations in his own country, and the unjustifiable means he pursued to realise them" (*Gentleman's Magazine*, 1789, Vol. i, p. 575, and Vol. ii, p. 669). William Baker, M.P., wrote to his mother-in-law, Lady Juliana Penn, on 13 November 1778: "By the folly and knavery of my neighbour Mr. Byde our whole county, and particularly his own district, is involved in the utmost confusion and distress. . . . Hardly a farmer in his neighbourhood, but has suffered by placing money in his hands. . . . In short it is easier to conceive than describe all the distress which this impudent and wicked man has occasioned" (Baker MSS.).

¹⁴ About Jacob Houblon and his ancestry, see Lady A. Archer Houblon, *The Houblon Family* (1907).

¹⁵ About the Calvert family, see *The Landed Houses of Hertfordshire* in the *V.C.H.*

¹⁶ See letter from Nathaniel Brassey to the Duke of Newcastle, 5 October 1760, Add. MSS. 32912, f. 387; and from T. Caswall to the same, 3 November 1760, Add. MSS. 32914, f. 56: "Mr. Brassey has serv'd long in Parliament and may continue so to do, or his substitute for him." Caswall was brought in at the general election of 1761 as that "substitute." The daughter and heiress of N. Brassey married Thomas Dimsdale, doctor and subsequently banker, M.P. for Hertford, 1780–90, the founder of a well-known Hertford parliamentary "dynasty"; see Clutterbuck, *History of Hertfordshire*, Vol. ii, p. 35.

¹⁷ The Duke of Newcastle, in a letter to Lord Rockingham, put her fortune at £100,000; see Add. MSS. 32968, f. 264.

¹⁸ Lord Nuneham's maternal grandfather, Charles Samborne Le Bas, was descended from John Le Bas, of Caen, Normandy, who in the beginning of the seventeenth century had married Anne, daughter of Richard Samborne, an English merchant settled at Caen (see *The Genealogist*, Vol. i, pp. 218–219.

¹⁹ A MS. note on William Shenstone by Elizabeth Gulston (presumably the sister of Joseph Gulston, M.P., the print collector), inserted in a copy of his letters to Lady Luxborough, now in the British Museum.

²⁰ *Thoughts on Various Subjects*, first edition of his *Works*, 1735, Vol. i, p. 306.

²¹ Daniel Defoe, *The Original Power of the Collective Body of the People of England* (3rd ed., 1702), p. 16.

²² Ten generations back, which means, as a rule, less than three centuries, a man has (barring the inevitable repetitions which result from intermarriages) more than a thousand progenitors; at the time of the Norman Conquest, this would make about a thousand millions! The mathematical probability is therefore distinctly in favor of every Englishman being descended from every person who was in this country at the time of the Conquest and has left descendants.

²³ Scotsmen did not even necessarily impose their names on their wives, and their own designation varied with their residence or estate. Gilbert Elliot, in June 1742, thus concluded a letter to William Mure of Caldwell, M.P.: "Dear Glanderston, adieu"; to which the editor has added the following explanation: "Glanderston was an old estate, and frequent residence of the Caldwell family about this period. Hence occasionally preferred to Caldwell as the title of the proprietor." See *Caldwell Papers* (1854), Part ii, Vol. i, p. 29.

[24] See W. A. Leigh and M. G. Knight, *Chawton Manor and its Owners* (1911), pp. 142–143.

[25] See Helen Evelyn, *History of the Evelyn Family* (1915), pp. 561–562.

[26] See G. E. C., *Complete Peerage*, under "Thomond."

[27] *Of Civil Government*, § 73.

[28] *The Anarchy of a Limited or Mixed Monarchy*, p. 14.

[29] Add. MSS. 32865, f. 51. The same case is mentioned in Newcastle's letter to Sir Jacob Downing (22 May 1756; Add. MSS. 32865, f. 87): "I was forc'd to submit the pretensions of my nephew Watson (who has the estates and, in some measure, the peerages of two peers, who are as it were sunk in him) to His Majesty's favour upon some other occasion." Lewis (Monson) Watson, second son of John, 1st Lord Monson, inherited the estates of his maternal grandfather, Lewis, 1st Earl of Rockingham. He was Newcastle's nephew by marriage, his wife being a daughter of Henry Pelham. He was created Lord Sondes in 1760.

[30] Lord Bath to Robert More, some time in June 1759; MS. Top. Salop, c. 3, in the Bodleian Library, at Oxford.

[31] Possession of these estates was acquired by Lord Bath's distant collateral heirs in 1783. About them see *The Grenville Papers*, Vol. i, p. 17; Edward Lloyd, *Antiquities of Shropshire* (1844), p. 243; H. E. Forrest, "Some Old Shropshire Houses and their Owners," in the *Transactions of the Shropshire Archaeological Society*, 4th Series, Vol. vii, Part ii (1920), p. 110.

[32] "Virtual representation" is no purely British invention, still less a mere ingenious fiction to palliate the absurdities of the unreformed House of Commons. In the seventeenth and eighteenth centuries the Lithuanian Jews had a communal Parliament of their own, called in Hebrew "Vaad" (Council). Its members were elected by the capital towns alone of the five territorial divisions into which Lithuanian Jewry was divided, but the members of each were deemed to represent all the other communes in their division, even though these had no share in returning them. See article on "The Lithuanian Vaad" by M. Wischnitzer, in the *Istorya Yevreyskavo Naroda* (*History of the Jewish People*), Moscow, 1914, Vol. xi.

[33] "Directions for Obedience to Government in Dangerous and Doubtful Times," published as an appendix to *Observations touching Forms of Government*, edition of 1696, p. 159.

[34] *Patriarcha*, p. 12.

[35] *Ibid.*, p. 19.

[36] *Observations*, p. 158.

[37] *Patriarcha*, p. 23.

³⁸ See R. C. Winthrop, *Life and Letters of John Winthrop* (1867), p. 430.

³⁹ *Of Civil Government*, §§ 75 and 76.

⁴⁰ To Barbeu Dubourg, 2 October 1770; *The Life and Writings of Benjamin Franklin*, edited by A. H. Smyth (1905–07), Vol. v, p. 280.

⁴¹ To William Franklin, 6 October 1773, Vol. vi, p. 144.

⁴² To Samuel Cooper of Boston, 8 June 1770, Vol. v, p. 260.

⁴³ To Lord Kames, 11 April 1767, Vol. v, p. 17.

⁴⁴ Defoe, *A Plan of the English Commerce*, 3rd ed. (1749), p. 150.

⁴⁵ *Ancient Laws and Institutes of England*, ed. by B. Thorpe (1840), p. 81.

⁴⁶ George Cartwright, *A Journal of Transactions and Events, during a Residence of nearly Sixteen Years on the Coast of Labrador* (1792), Vol. i, p. 145.

⁴⁷ "The man . . . returned with a beautiful seal-skin as a present to me; but I would by no means accept of it, making him and the rest understand, that I did not quarrel with him, that he should make me a present to be reconciled; but because he had been guilty of a dishonest action; and that as he now seemed to be sensible of his crime, I was perfectly satisfied" (*op. cit.*, Vol. i, p. 240).

⁴⁸ To Sir H. Mann, 26 May 1762.

⁴⁹ *Of Civil Government*, § 94.

⁵⁰ *Ibid.* § 87.

⁵¹ Similarly with the Americans "property" stood in the center of their thinking, and "liberty" itself was merely a function and safeguard of "property." It is thus that Abel Stiles, a New Englander, wrote to Ezra Stiles on 18 April 1766 about resistance to the Stamp Act (Stiles MSS., in the Yale College Library, New Haven, Conn.):

Shall Revelation say stand fast and contend earnestly for the Faith —and doth not the God of Nature, the God of Civil Liberty and property say stand fast. . . . Pray what forbids us to resist even unto blood, where that freedom is in question, the death of which is the death of property, as the pregnant mother's death is fatal to the infant unborn.

⁵² Add. MSS. 32987, f. 204. See also his letter to the Archbishop of Canterbury, 2 February 1766 (Add. MSS. 32973, ff. 342–344): "I have been bred up to think, that the trade of this nation is the sole support of it."

⁵³ *Memoirs* (ed., Romney Sedgwick), Vol. ii, p. 351.

⁵⁴ *The Grenville Papers*, Vol. ii, p. 516.

⁵⁵ *England in the Eighteenth Century*, Vol. i, pp. 433–434.

⁵⁶ This remark, in the margin of Roberts's MS. "Observations on

the Trade to Africa," appears against a complaint that the "gentlemen of the landed interest," and others, "desert the House when Africa is mentioned," though they attend "many days to late hours, on a dispute about a road, navigation or inclosure bill" (Eg. MS. 1162 A. ff. 55–56).

[57] 5 October 1756; Add. MSS. 32868, ff. 96–97.

[58] Add. MSS. 32736, ff. 591–594 and 477–481. There is another paper on revenue in the Newcastle MSS. from John Page, M.P. for Chichester, drawn up in October 1757 (Add. MSS. 32875, ff. 340–357), which, too, is very sound; he argues in it, e.g., in favor of taxing property and not production, and the rental of houses, not their windows.

[59] Andrew Wilkinson to Newcastle; Add. MSS. 32732, ff. 313–314.

[60] Ducie to Newcastle, 13 September 1758; Add. MSS. 32883, f. 442.

[61] *The Correspondence of King George III*, edited by Sir John Fortescue, Vol. ii, p. 429.

[62] In his autobiography; Lord Fitzmaurice, *Life of William, Earl of Shelburne* (1912), Vol. i, p. 25.

[63] In his pamphlet on *The Regulations lately made concerning the Colonies;* this pamphlet, ascribed in the British Museum catalogue to John Campbell, LL.D. was by Thomas Whately (see *Bowdoin-Temple Papers, Collections of the Massachusetts Historical Society*, Series vi, Vol. ix, p. 77). Whately, who was largely responsible for the Stamp Act and was one of the "men of business" of the Grenville group, was often represented as hostile to America; he was not. He wrote to J. Temple, surveyor-general of the customs for the Northern District of America, on 8 December 1764, while that act was being prepared: "I always loved the Colonies, I am, I always was, curious about them, and very happy when I am employed in any business that relates to them. The present circumstances of affairs gives me a great deal in my office, and the House of Commons must be full of the subject. Tho' much is done, much is still to do before that important and now vast object can be properly settled; but I am confident it will be done right at last. I know that those who are at present in administration are anxious for the prosperity of the Colonies; and highly sensible of their importance" (*ibid.*, p. 38). W. S. Johnson, agent for Connecticut, wrote to Jared Ingersoll about Whately from London on 18 February 1767, that he "unhappily . . . entertains mistaken principles and ill opinions with respect to the Colonies though I really think him sincere and that he in truth thinks he is aiming at the real interest of both countries" (Bancroft Transcripts in the New York Public Library, *Connecticut Papers*, pp. 95–96).

[64] "A letter to the Right Honorable Earl of —" in the *Collections of the Massachusetts Historical Society*, Series i, Vol. i (1792), pp. 66–67.

[65] See Van Schaack's diary, under 8 October 1779, in H. C. Van Schaack, *The Life of Peter Van Schaack* (New York, 1842), p. 243. He was at that time a loyalist refugee in England.

[66] *Considerations on the Expediency*, etc., Dublin, 1779.

[67] The following case, recorded in a letter from G. Lyman to J. Tyng, 23 May 1759, throws a curious light even on New England "democracy." When a certain Mr. Phelps of Hadley was appointed to the Commission of Peace of Northampton County in Massachusetts, the other magistrates wrote to the governor that they "beg His Excellency's pardon in their desire of resigning their commissions, in case he sets with them," and alleged that he had been put in "not for any benefit to him; but to reflect upon the Justices; because he, the said Phelps, was not a magistrate's son, etc., but a bricklayer till a few years past." Lyman indignantly repudiated this allegation, pointing out that Phelps was a lawyer (see the *New England Historical and Genealogical Register*, Vol. xi (1857), p. 79). In England no one made any fuss over Sir Robert Darling being returned to Parliament (in 1768), though "when a boy he used to keep cows," and afterward had been "apprentice to a lapidary" (see O. Marsh, *Biography of Bedfordshire*; Add. MSS. 21067, f. 62). And even the case of "Bob" Mackreth, who had been a waiter and billiard-marker at White's, but in 1774 became an M.P., caused amusement rather than indignation.

[68] I cannot enter here at length into this matter, with which I shall deal in a later volume, if ever I write it. For the present, see my article on "The Disinheritance of America" in the London *Nation*, 26 January 1929.

[69] A draft of this letter is among the Stiles MSS. (Yale College Library), in a leather-bound volume marked "Letters. IV."

[70] Shelburne in his autobiography; Fitzmaurice, *Shelburne*, Vol. i, p. 18.

A Bibliographical Introduction to Eighteenth-Century England

This bibliography is designed chiefly to provide "access routes" to further reading and research. It stresses modern scholarship. This is not done out of some perverse preference for recent and sometimes insubstantial contributions, but rather out of recognition of the most intractable problem of bibliographical searching—discovering recent publications. As a rule, biographies, autobiographies, and memoirs have been omitted. Undeniably, some of the finest modern scholarship in the field has been biographical, but the mass of such books is overwhelming, and it may reasonably be hoped that the entry points suggested here will bring the important ones to light.

Note: The place of publication is omitted if one of the original places of publication is London.

BIBLIOGRAPHIES

The standard bibliography on eighteenth-century Britain is Stanley Pargellis and D. J. Medley, *Bibliography of British History: The Eighteenth Century, 1714–1789* (Oxford, 1951). In the same series there is, for the period before 1714, Godfrey Davies and Mary Frear Keeler, *Bibliography of British History: Stuart Period, 1603–1714* (Oxford, 1970). There are useful bibliographical essays, organized by subjects, in the volumes of the Oxford History of England by Sir George Clark, Basil Williams, and J. Steven Watson (full citations below, under General Histories). The simplest way of updating the foregoing is to consult G. R. Elton, *Modern Historians on British History: A Critical Bibliography, 1945–1969* (1970), which divides works published between 1945 and 1969 by periods and subjects. A. Taylor Milne, ed., *Writings on British History* began publication in 1937, listing publications in the year 1934; the latest volume (1973), by Donald James Munro, brings the coverage down to 1948. These volumes are comprehensive and well-indexed, and are arranged by periods and subjects. The above series has recently been extended backwards by *Writings on British History, 1901–1933*. Volume IV, *The Eighteenth Century, 1714–1815*, appeared in 1969; because it necessarily omits a good deal, the prefatory note should be read carefully. Every student of eighteenth-century England should know about *English Literature, 1600–1800* (Princeton, 1950–1972; additional volumes in progress). It encompasses publications since 1926; indexes are found in every other volume. Volume VI (1972) reaches 1970. This collection covers much more than English literature, and from its inception it included a good deal on history. It notices articles as well as books and mentions locations of book reviews. Its indexes are the best places to begin a needle-in-the-haystack sort of search.

For keeping track of very recent work "The Eighteenth Century: A Current Bibliography," published annually in *Philological Quarterly*, offers the most advantages. It is restricted to the period from 1660 to 1800, is not restricted as to place of publication, and cites both articles and books. It has recently expanded its scope to include virtually all aspects of the history, culture, and social life of the period, but remains especially rich with respect to England. *English Literature, 1660–1800*, cited above, is an indexed compilation of these annual bibliographies from *Philological Quarterly*. The *Annual Bulletin of Historical Literature*, published by The Historical Association, London, is up-to-date within two or three years and contains a chapter on the eighteenth century in which English history is well represented. Also useful for finding recent work is *The British Humanities Index*, published by the Library Association, London; a subject index of articles, it encompasses scholarly as well as popular periodicals published in Britain. A new *Annual Bibliography of British and Irish History* is to be published by the Royal Historical Society, starting in 1976.

GENERAL HISTORIES

J. H. Plumb, *England in the Eighteenth Century* (Harmondsworth and Baltimore, 1950; repr. with revised bibliography 1963) and William B. Willcox, *The Age of Aristocracy, 1688–1830*, 2nd ed. (Lexington, Mass.,

1971) are concise, authoritative introductions. Derek Jarrett, *Britain, 1688–1815* (1965) is a more detailed, nicely balanced text. Christopher Hill's *Reformation to Industrial Revolution: A Social and Economic History of Britain, 1530–1780* (1967) is an inspired attempt to link social, economic, and political history. Dorothy Marshall, *Eighteenth Century England* (1962) is chiefly concerned with the political narrative. BEFORE 1714: Sir George Clark, *The Later Stuarts, 1660–1714*, 2nd ed. (Oxford, 1955) in the Oxford History of England series, is the standard work. The analytical arrangement of Christopher Hill, *The Century of Revolution, 1603–1714* (Edinburgh, 1961) puts the key developments in perspective. The essays collected in Geoffrey Holmes, ed., *Britain after the Glorious Revolution, 1689–1714* (1969), each accompanied by a bibliographical note, offer convenient introductions to the major features of the history of the period. FROM 1714 TO 1760: Basil Williams, *The Whig Supremacy, 1714–1760*, 2nd ed. (Oxford, 1962), Oxford History of England. FROM 1760 TO 1815: J. Steven Watson, *The Reign of George III, 1760–1815* (Oxford, 1960), Oxford History of England, is outstanding—expert, thoughtful, well wrought. The opening chapters of Asa Briggs, *The Making of Modern England, 1783–1867* (New York, 1965), originally published as *The Age of Improvement* (1959), also provide a penetrating synthesis. In a class by itself, though not suited to most beginners, is the first volume, *England in 1815*, of Elie Halévy's *History of the English People in the Nineteenth Century*, trans. rev. ed. (1949). It was originally published in French in 1913.

POLITICS

The mass of work in this field is awesome. Perhaps the most convenient and up-to-date guide is Robert A. Smith, *Eighteenth-Century English Politics: Patrons and Place-hunters* (New York, 1972), which offers a good bibliography as well as a concise account of the elements of politics and their evolution during the century. Politics are the concern of so many of the best works of modern scholarship on eighteenth-century England that it is appropriate to mention at least some of them. The ordering is chronological.

J. R. Western, *Monarchy and Revolution: The English State in the 1680s* (1972). J. R. Jones, *The Revolution of 1688 in England* (1972). J. H. Plumb, *The Growth of Political Stability in England, 1675–1725* (1967), U.S. edition, and *The Origins of Political Stability, England, 1675–1725* (Boston, 1967). Geoffrey Holmes, *British Politics in the Age of Anne* (1967). W. A. Speck, *Tory and Whig: The Struggle in the*

Constituencies, 1701–1715 (1970), a detailed study of electoral politics. J. H. Plumb, *Sir Robert Walpole: The Making of a Statesman* (1956); *The King's Minister* (1960). Archibald S. Foord, *His Majesty's Opposition, 1714–1830* (Oxford, 1964). John B. Owen, *The Rise of the Pelhams* (1957), an intensive study of politics in the 1740s. Sir Lewis Namier, *The Structure of Politics at the Accession of George III*, 2nd ed. (1957), and *England in the Age of the American Revolution*, 2nd ed. (1961). George Rudé, *Wilkes and Liberty: A Social Study of 1763 to 1774* (Oxford, 1962). Herbert Butterfield's *George III, Lord North, and the People, 1779–80* (1949, repr. New York, 1968) is appreciated by both beginners and experts. Richard Pares, *King George III and the Politicians* (Oxford, 1953) is more difficult but masterly. John Norris, *Shelburne and Reform* (1963) is a detailed study of aspects of the early reform movement that are too often forgotten. On a related theme see Ian R. Christie, *Wilkes, Wyvill and Reform: The Parliamentary Reform Movement in British Politics, 1760–1785* (1962). John Ehrman, *The Younger Pitt: The Years of Acclaim* (1969) offers a penetrating view of parties and issues during Pitt's early career. Early developments in party history may be traced in Donald E. Ginter's introduction to his *Whig Organization in the General Election of 1790* (Berkeley and Los Angeles, 1967). F. O'Gorman, *The Whig Party and the French Revolution* (1967) describes how the Whigs split. John Cannon, *Parliamentary Reform, 1640–1832* (Cambridge, 1973) is a recent survey with bibliography. The following collections of articles and essays concentrate chiefly on political matters: Geoffrey Holmes, ed., *Britain after the Glorious Revolution, 1689–1714* (1969). Sir Lewis Namier, *Crossroads of Power: Essays on Eighteenth-Century England* (1962). Rosalind Mitchison, ed., *Essays in Eighteenth-Century England from the English Historical Review* (1966). Ian R. Christie, *Myth and Reality in Late-Eighteenth-Century British Politics and Other Papers* (1970).

THE CONSTITUTION

E. Neville Williams, *The Eighteenth-Century Constitution, 1688–1815* (Cambridge, 1960) is the best guide, and has a good bibliography. Chapters 5, 6, and 7 of Sir David Lindsay Keir, *The Constitutional History of Modern Britain since 1485*, 8th ed. (1966) offer a concise and judicious commentary. The following also focus on constitutional matters: Jennifer Carter, "The Revolution and the Constitution," in G. Holmes, ed., *Britain after the Glorious Revolution* (1969); Richard Pares, *Limited Monarchy in Great Britain in the Eighteenth Century*, Historical Association pamphlet (1957); John Brooke, *The House of Commons, 1754–1790: Introductory Survey* (Oxford, 1968); Betty Kemp, *King and Commons, 1660–1832* (1957).

LAW

Nothing surpasses the thorough investigation of the eighteenth century in Volumes X, XI, and XII of Sir William Holdsworth, *A History of English Law*, 17 vols. (1903–72). Leon Radzinowicz, *A History of English Criminal Law and its Administration from 1750: The Movement for Reform, 1750–1833* (1948) is an important specialized study. The profession is treated by Holdsworth, but see also Robert Robson, *The Attorney in Eighteenth-Century England* (Cambridge, 1959).

CROWN ADMINISTRATION

The scholarly studies are monographic: John M. Beattie, *The English Court in the Reign of George I* (Cambridge, 1967); M. A. Thomson, *The Secretaries of State, 1681–1782* (Oxford, 1932); David B. Horn, *The British Diplomatic Service, 1689–1789* (Oxford, 1961); Franklin B. Wickwire, *British Subministers and Colonial America, 1763–1783* (Princeton, 1966); Ronald R. Nelson, *The Home Office, 1782–1801* (Durham, N.C., 1969). Elizabeth E. Hoon, *The Organization of the English Customs System, 1696–1786* (New York, 1938, repr. 1968), Edward Hughes, *Studies in Administration and Finance, 1558–1825* (Manchester, 1934), which considers the salt and excise offices, and W. R. Ward, *The English Land Tax in the Eighteenth Century* (Oxford, 1953) are the standard works on the revenue departments. The note on sources for Chapter 8 of John Ehrman, *The Younger Pitt* (1969) is a sound bibliographical guide to administration in the second half of the century. See below for the treasury, army, and navy.

THE TREASURY AND FINANCE

Henry Roseveare, *The Treasury: The Evolution of a British Institution* (1969). Stephen B. Baxter, *The Development of the Treasury, 1660–1702* (1957). P. G. M. Dickson, *The Financial Revolution in England: A Study in the Development of Public Credit, 1688–1756* (1967).

THE ARMY

Rex Whitworth, *Field Marshall Lord Ligonier: A Story of the British Army, 1702–1770* (Oxford, 1958) explains, along the way, the army's organization and fighting techniques. An excellent brief account, drawing chiefly on the regiments in America, is found in Chapter 8 of John Shy, *Toward Lexington: The Role of the British Army in the Coming of the American Revolution* (Princeton, 1965). R. E. Scouller, *The Armies of Queen Anne* (Oxford, 1966) is detailed, but not easily digested. The standard work on the militia is J. R. Western, *The English Militia in the Eighteenth Century: The Story of a Political Issue, 1660–1802* (1965).

THE NAVY

For bibliography see the relevant chapters in Robin Higham, ed., *A Guide to the Sources of British Military History* (Berkeley and Los Angeles, 1971). John Creswell, *British Admirals of the Eighteenth Century: Tactics in Battle* (1972) is an important study. The navy's performance as a department of government is considered in Daniel A. Baugh, *British Naval Administration in the Age of Walpole* (Princeton, 1965). For shipboard life at the end of the century see Michael Lewis, *A Social History of the Navy, 1793–1815* (1960). G. J. Marcus, *A Naval History of England, I: The Formative Centuries* (1962) and *A Naval History of England, II: The Age of Nelson* (1971) offer a comprehensive naval history in the traditional mold.

IMPERIAL ADMINISTRATION

On America see I. K. Steele, *Politics of Colonial Policy: The Board of Trade in Colonial Administration, 1696–1720* (Oxford, 1968) and James A. Henretta, *Salutory Neglect: Colonial Administration under the Duke of Newcastle* (Princeton, 1972). On India see Holden Furber, *John Company at Work* (Cambridge, Mass., 1948) and Bankey B. Misra, *The Central Administration of the East India Company, 1773–1834* (Manchester, 1959). T. H. Beaglehole, *Thomas Munro and the Development of Administrative Policy in Madras, 1792–1818* (Cambridge, 1966).

FOREIGN POLICY

David B. Horn, *Great Britain and Europe in the Eighteenth Century* (Oxford, 1967) is a good survey, and contains good bibliographies. For the earlier period Ragnhild Hatton and J. S. Bromley, eds., *William III and Louis XIV: Essays, 1680–1720, by and for Mark A. Thomson* (Liverpool and Toronto, 1968) and G. C. Gibbs, "The Revolution in Foreign Policy," in *Britain after the Glorious Revolution*, ed. by G. Holmes (1969) may be consulted. The main outlines of foreign policy at the end of the century are discussed in John M. Sherwig, *Guineas and Gunpowder: British Foreign Aid in the Wars with France, 1793–1815* (Cambridge, Mass., 1969).

IMPERIAL POLICY

Klaus E. Knorr, *British Colonial Theories, 1570–1850* (Toronto, 1944, repr. 1963) is comprehensive and scholarly. Kate Hotblack, *Chatham's Colonial Policy: A Study in the Fiscal and Economic Implications of the Colonial Policy of the Elder Pitt* (1917) still offers the briefest comprehensive view of an important problem. In respect to North America, Carl Ubbelohde, *The American Colonies and the British Empire, 1607–1763* (New York, 1968) and Ian R. Christie, *Crisis of Empire: Great Britain and the American Colonies, 1754–1783* (1966) are brief introductions with ample bibliographical leads. Thomas C. Barrow, "The Old Colonial System from an English Point of View" in *Anglo-American Political Relations, 1675–1775,* ed. by Alison G. Olson and Richard M. Brown (New Brunswick, 1970) is a short lucid essay on a key question. Commercial policy in the British Caribbean is treated in Frank W. Pitman, *The Development of the British West Indies, 1700–1763* (New Haven, 1917) and Richard Pares, *War and Trade in the West Indies, 1739–1763* (Oxford, 1936, repr. London, 1963). A rich up-to-date bibliography of colonial policy in America and the West Indies may be found in Michael Kammen, *Empire and Interest* (Philadelphia, 1970). As for India, P. J. Marshall, *Problems of Empire: Britain and India, 1757–1813* (1968) provides an introduction. Lucy S. Sutherland, *The East India Company in Eighteenth-Century Politics* (Oxford, 1952) is the major work. Everyone interested in imperial policy should be aware of the collection of bibliographical essays edited by Robin W. Winks, *The Historiography of the British Empire-Commonwealth* (Durham, N.C., 1966).

IMPERIAL WARS

There is a good bibliographical guide in Glyndwr Williams, *The Expansion of Europe in the Eighteenth Century* (1966). Notable area studies are: Gerald S. Graham, *Empire of the North Atlantic: The Maritime Struggle for North America,* 2nd ed. (Toronto, 1958); Richard Pares, *War and Trade in the West Indies, 1739–1763,* cited above; Henry Dodwell, *Dupleix and Clive: The Beginning of Empire* (1920); and Sir Herbert Richmond, *The Navy in India, 1763–1783* (1931). Piers Mackesy, *The War for America, 1775–1783* (1964) is an excellent account which views the problems posed by the struggle from a British perspective.

ECONOMIC HISTORY

The best modern general work on the earlier period is Charles Wilson, *England's Apprenticeship, 1603–1763* (1965); on the later, Peter Mathias,

The First Industrial Nation: An Economic History of Britain 1700–1914 (1969). Mathias's treatment of the eighteenth century is arranged thematically; he provides excellent bibliographies. T. S. Ashton, *An Economic History of England: The 18th Century* (1955) remains a valuable survey. There is vast literature on the industrial revolution. T. S. Ashton, *The Industrial Revolution, 1760–1830*, rev. ed. (1962) is thoughtful, concise, and readable. Phyllis Deane, *The First Industrial Revolution* (Cambridge, 1965) divides the subject into digestible segments. In tracing the progress of innovation nothing surpasses Paul Mantoux, *The Industrial Revolution in the Eighteenth Century*, English trans. (1928. rev. ed. 1961). Recent titles in the Debates in Economic History series exhibit the major concerns of current research: R. M. Hartwell, ed., *The Causes of the Industrial Revolution in England* (1967); Francois Crouzet, ed., *Capital Formation in the Industrial Revolution* (1972); A. E. Musson, ed., *Science, Technology, and Economic Growth in the Eighteenth Century* (1972). The state of recent scholarship on economic thought is briefly considered in Mark Blaug's review article, "Economic Theory and Economic History in Great Britain, 1650–1776," *Past and Present*, No. 28 (1964).

AGRICULTURE

Among recent works J. D. Chambers and G. E. Mingay, *The Agricultural Revolution, 1750–1880* (1966) offers the best survey. Recent scholarship is assembled in E. L. Jones, ed., *Agriculture and Economic Growth in England, 1650–1815* (1967) and G. E. Mingay's pamphlet, *Enclosure and the Small Farmer in the Age of the Industrial Revolution* (1968); both have good bibliographies. Chapters 7 and 8 of H. C. Darby, ed., *A New Historical Geography of England* (Cambridge, 1973) are excellent for reference.

TRANSPORTATION

Ralph Davis, *The Rise of the English Shipping Industry in the Seventeenth and Eighteenth Centuries* (1962). Charles Hadfield, *British Canals: An Illustrated History*, 2nd ed. (1959). William Albert, *The Turnpike Road System in England, 1663–1840* (Cambridge, 1972). B. F. Duckham, *The Transport Revolution, 1750–1830*, The Historical Association, London, rev. ed. (1972), is a brief introduction to later eighteenth-century developments.

FOREIGN TRADE

Ralph Davis, *A Commercial Revolution: English Overseas Trade in the*

Seventeenth and Eighteenth Centuries, The Historical Association, London (1967) is a brief essay by an expert. W. E. Minchinton, ed., *The Growth of English Overseas Trade in the Seventeenth and Eighteenth Centuries* (1969) is the best starting point for further research. For a more extensive bibliography dealing with colonial trade, especially in the Atlantic, see Michael Kammen, *Empire and Interest* (Philadelphia, 1970).

POPULATION

There are two excellent introductory collections: Michael Drake, ed., *Population in Industrialization* (1969) and M. W. Flinn, *British Population Growth, 1700–1850* (1970). H. J. Habakkuk, *Population Growth and Economic Development since 1750* (Leicester, 1972) is as clear and concise an account of a rather technical subject as one can hope to find. J. D. Chambers, *Population, Economy, and Society in Pre-Industrial England* (Oxford, 1972) is more difficult reading, but encompasses a wider range of considerations. E. A. Wrigley, *Population and History* (1969) is the best novice's guide to historical demography.

SOCIAL HISTORY

E. N. Williams, *Life in Georgian England* (1962) and Dorothy Marshall, *English People in the Eighteenth Century* (1956) are popular surveys. J. H. Plumb, *Men and Places* (1963) contains a number of relevant essays. The most important books are G. E. Mingay, *English Landed Society in the Eighteenth Century* (1963) and M. Dorothy George, *London Life in the Eighteenth Century* (1925, repr. New York, 1962). Any study of the workers in the era of the industrial revolution should take account of M. Dorothy George, *England in Transition: Life and Work in the Eighteenth Century* (Harmondsworth and Baltimore, 1953) and E. P. Thompson, *The Making of the English Working Class* (1964), which has gone through many printings. Harold Perkin, *The Origins of Modern English Society, 1780–1880* (1969) begins with a useful analysis of eighteenth-century society that looks forward to the nineteenth-century transformations.

LOCAL HISTORY

Two especially rich, comprehensive, and thoughtful works stand out: J. D. Chambers, *Nottinghamshire in the Eighteenth Century: A Study of Life and Labour under the Squirearchy* (1932, repr. 1966) and Edward Hughes, *North Country Life in the Eighteenth Century*, 2 vols. (1952–

65). On the metropolis see George Rudé, *Hanoverian London, 1714–1808* (1971). For regional industrial and agricultural development see H. C. Darby, ed., *A New Historical Geography of England* (Cambridge, 1973), Chapters 7 and 8. Geoffrey H. Martin and Sylvia McIntyre, *A Bibliography of British and Irish Municipal History, Vol. I: General Works* (Leicester, 1972) is not strictly confined to municipal history. Persons contemplating archival research might begin by consulting W. V. Stephens, *Sources for English Local History* (Manchester, 1973), the relevant volumes of the Victoria County History, and county record office published guides.

INSTITUTIONS AND CULTURE

A. S. Turberville, ed., *Johnson's England*, 2 vols. (Oxford, 1933, repr. 1952) brings together expert essays on institutions, culture, and daily life. F. G. Emmison, ed., *English Local History Handlist*, The Historical Association, London, 4th ed. (1969) is a bibliography, not of local studies, but of works touching practically every feature of English life.

EDUCATION

A good introductory survey may be found in chapters 3, 4, and 5 of W. H. G. Armytage, *Four Hundred Years of English Education*, 2nd ed. (Cambridge, 1970). John Lawson and Harold Silver, *A Social History of Education in England* (1973) is a valuable recent survey. The most important book dealing with elementary education in the eighteenth century remains M. G. Jones, *The Charity School Movement: A Study of Eighteenth Century Puritanism in Action* (Cambridge, 1938). But the recent writings by Joan and Brian Simon in Brian Simon, ed., *Education in Leicestershire, 1540–1940: A Regional Study* (Leicester, 1968) and by Michael Sanderson, "Social Change and Elementary Education in Industrial Lancashire, 1780–1840," *Northern History*, III (1968), are of great interest, although they treat both ends of the century rather than the middle. There are two recent books on the grammar schools: W. A. L. Vincent, *The Grammar Schools: Their Continuing Tradition, 1660–1714* (1969), an important inquiry into the question of decline; and Richard S. Tompson, *Classics or Charity? The Dilemma of the 18th Century Grammar School* (Manchester, 1971). Both are solid studies with good bibliographies. On literacy see Michael Sanderson, "Literacy and Social Mobility in the Industrial Revolution in England," *Past and Present*, No. 56 (1972) and Lawrence Stone, "Literacy and Education in England, 1640–1900," *Past and Present*, No. 42 (1969).

THE UNIVERSITIES

The anatomy of the ancient universities is displayed in A. D. Godley, *Oxford in the Eighteenth Century* (1908) and D. A. Winstanley, *Unreformed Cambridge* (Cambridge, 1935). For the political aspect see Winstanley's *The University of Cambridge in the Eighteenth Century* (Cambridge, 1922) and W. R. Ward, *Georgian Oxford: University Politics in the Eighteenth Century* (Oxford, 1958). A fresh assessment of Oxford as a center of learning may be found in Dame Lucy Sutherland's lecture, *The University of Oxford in the Eighteenth Century: A Reconsideration* (Oxford, 1973).

THE PRESS

G. A. Cranfield, *The Development of the Provincial Newspaper, 1700–1760* (Oxford, 1962). Ian R. Christie, "British Newspapers in the Later Georgian Age," in his collection of essays entitled *Myth and Reality* (1970).

THE POOR LAW

The up-to-date introduction, with a good bibliography, is J. D. Marshall's pamphlet, *The Old Poor Law, 1795–1834*, 2nd ed. (1973). The standard work remains Sidney and Beatrice Webb, *History of English Local Government. English Poor Law History. Part 1: The Old Poor Law* (1927, repr. 1963).

CRIME

John M. Beattie, "The Pattern of Crime in England, 1600–1800," *Past and Present* No. 62 (1974).

SPORTS AND RECREATION

Robert W. Malcolmson, *Popular Recreation in English Society, 1700–1850* (Cambridge, 1973).

TRAVELLERS' IMPRESSIONS

There is a good bibliography, which distinguishes historical periods, in Francesca M. Wilson, ed., *Strange Island: Britain through Foreign Eyes, 1395–1940* (1955).

RELIGION

Norman Sykes, *Church and State in England in the Eighteenth Century* (Cambridge, 1934, repr. Hamden, Conn., 1962) remains the indispensable study of the established church. G. V. Bennett, "Conflict in the Church," in *Britain After the Glorious Revolution, 1689–1714*, ed. by G. Holmes (1969) emphasizes the impact of politics. Bernard Semmel, *The Methodist Revolution* (New York, 1973) places Methodism near the center of eighteenth- and early-nineteenth-century English social thought. Rupert Davies and Gordon Rupp, eds., *A History of the Methodist Church of Great Britain*, Vol. I (1965) is useful in a different way; vol. I covers the eighteenth century. Bibliographical leads to material on the dissenting sects may be found in two complementary books on the problem of toleration: Richard B. Barlow, *Citizenship and Conscience: A Study in the Theory and Practice of Religious Toleration in England during the Eighteenth Century* (Philadelphia, 1962), and Ursula Henriques, *Religious Toleration in England, 1787–1833* (1961). Richard T. Vann, *The Social Development of English Quakerism, 1655–1755* (Cambridge, Mass., 1969) is a useful monograph. The third volume of Horton Davies's general history, *Worship and Theology in England: From Watts and Wesley to Maurice, 1690–1850* (Princeton, 1961), is a fine survey and has a massive bibliography.

SOCIAL AND POLITICAL THOUGHT

Gerald R. Cragg, *Reason and Authority in the Eighteenth Century* (Cambridge, 1964) is a useful recent survey with a bibliography. There are of course many good recent studies of individual thinkers. The best introduction to political thought in the earlier part of the century is Isaac Kramnick, *Bolingbroke and his Circle: The Politics of Nostalgia in the Age of Walpole* (Cambridge, Mass., 1968). For the later part see Anthony Lincoln, *Some Political and Social Ideas of English Dissent, 1763–1800* (Cambridge, 1938). Caroline Robbins, *The Eighteenth-Century Commonwealthman* (Cambridge, Mass., 1959, repr. New York, 1968), considers the connection between eighteenth-century radicalism and its seventeenth-century inspiration. There is a penetrating essay on the impact of eighteenth-century English political culture on American revolutionary thought: Bernard Bailyn, *The Origins of American Politics* (New York, 1968).

SCIENCE

Robert E. Schofield, *Mechanism and Materialism: British Natural Philosophy in an Age of Reason* (Princeton, 1970) mainly concerns scientific thought and has a bibliography. Arnold Thackray, *Atoms and Powers: An Essay on Newtonian Matter—Theory and the Development of Chemistry* (Cambridge, Mass., 1970), is somewhat specialized, but contains a wide-ranging bibliography. For the relation of science to industrial innovation see A. E. Musson, ed., *Science, Technology, and Economic Growth in the Eighteenth Century* (1972).

MEDICINE

Lester S. King, *The Medical World of the Eighteenth Century* (Chicago, 1958) focuses on medical knowledge in Britain. King offers a brief account which refers to more recent work in "Medical Theory and Practice at the Beginning of the 18th Century," *Bulletin of the History of Medicine*, XLVI (1972). There is a fine four-volume study, begun by J. J. Keevil, of *Medicine and the Navy, 1200–1900* (Edinburgh, 1957–63); Christopher Lloyd and Jack L. S. Coulter wrote *Volume III, 1714–1815* (1961). See also William R. Le Fanu, "The Lost Half-Century in English Medicine, 1700–1750," *Bulletin of the History of Medicine*, XLVI (1972). Medical practitioners are briefly studied in Bernice Hamilton, "The Medical Professions in the Eighteenth Century," *Economic History Review*, 2nd ser. IV (1951). Any study of the medical professions should also involve Cecil Wall, H. Charles Cameron, and E. Ashworth Underwood, *A History of the Worshipful Society of Apothecaries of London. Vol. I: 1617–1815*, and Sir George Clark, *A History of the Royal College of Physicians of London*, 3 vols. (Oxford, 1964- in prog.). Vol. II of the latter encompasses the period from 1675 to 1858. Scotland supplied eighteenth-century England with a large portion of its doctors. In this connection Vern and Bonnie Bullough, "The Causes of the Scottish Medical Renaissance of the Eighteenth Century," *Bulletin of the History of Medicine*, XLV (1971) is of interest. On the social history of insanity see Kathleen Jones, *Lunacy, Law, and Conscience, 1744–1845: The Social History of the Care of the Insane* (1955) and William L. Parry-Jones, *The Trade in Lunacy: A Study of Private Madhouses in England in the Eighteenth and Nineteenth Centuries* (1972). The latter mainly concerns the nineteenth century, but its bibliography is useful for the eighteenth as well.

LITERATURE

The mass of recent scholarship is immense. The best survey and reference tool is George Sherburn and Donald F. Bond, *The Restoration and Eighteenth Century, 1600–1789*, Volume III of *A Literary History of England*, ed. by Albert C. Baugh, 2nd ed. (New York, 1967). More detailed treatment may be found in the Oxford History of English Literature: James Sutherland, *English Literature of the Late Seventeenth Cen-*

tury (Oxford, 1969) and Bonamy Dobrée, *English Literature in the Early Eighteenth Century, 1700–1740* (Oxford, 1959). Two books of particular interest to historians are John W. Saunders, *The Profession of English Letters* (1964), Chapters 6 and 7 of which deal with the eighteenth century, and John Loftis, *The Politics of Drama in Augustan England* (Oxford, 1963).

ART, ARCHITECTURE, AND MUSIC

There are brief essays on the artist and the composer in James L. Clifford, ed., *Man Versus Society in Eighteenth-Century Britain* (Cambridge, 1968, New York, 1972). Ellis K. Waterhouse, *Painting in Britain, 1530 to 1790*, 2nd ed. (Harmondsworth and Baltimore, 1962) is a fine illustrated introduction. A concise interpretation of mid-century painting may be found in the same author's *Three Decades of British Art, 1740–1770* (Philadelphia, 1965). The standard illustrated survey of architecture is John Summerson, *Architecture in Britain, 1530 to 1830*, 5th ed. (Harmondsworth and Baltimore, 1969). Morris Brownell's forthcoming book on Alexander Pope and the arts of Georgian England takes note of the recent work on English painting, landscape gardening, architecture, and sculpture to mid-century. On music, Percy M. Young, *A History of British Music* (1967) is a readable account that gives the eighteenth century its due. See also Roger Fiske, *English Theatre Music in the Eighteenth Century* (1973). Of particular interest to historians is Eric D. Mackerness, *A Social History of English Music* (1964).

SCOTLAND, IRELAND, AND WALES

This bibliographical note concerns England, but some mention of general works dealing with the rest of the British Isles may be helpful. SCOTLAND: Both George S. Pryde, *Scotland from 1603 to the Present Day* (Edinburgh, 1962) and William Ferguson, *Scotland: 1689 to the Present* (Edinburgh, 1968) devote considerable attention to the eighteenth century and have good bibliographies. The former is somewhat easier reading; the latter, a better path to further research. T. C. Smout, *A History of the Scottish People, 1560–1830*, 2nd ed. (1970) is a good social history; the notes contain suggestions for further reading. Henry Hamilton, *An Economic History of Scotland in the Eighteenth Century* (Oxford, 1963) is the indispensable work in its field. IRELAND: The leading modern survey is J. C. Beckett, *The Making of Modern Ireland, 1603–1923* (1966). William E. H. Lecky, *A History of Ireland in the Eighteenth Century* is still one of the most readable and informative works; there is a recent abridged edition by L. P. Curtis, Jr. (Chicago, 1972). For a good brief bibliography see Edith M. Johnston, *Irish History: A Select Bibliography*, The Historical Association, London (1969). WALES: David Williams, *A History of Modern Wales* (1950) is a good general history. There are leads to further reading on social and economic topics in David J. V. Jones, *Before Rebecca: Popular Protests in Wales, 1793–1835* (1973). *A Bibliography of the History of Wales*, 2nd ed. (Cardiff, 1962) is a useful research tool; section J concerns the period from 1714 to 1789.

Index

Dancing masters, 185
Danes, 30
Danton, George Jacques, 236
Darling, Sir Robert, 243
Dartmouth, William Legge, 2nd Earl of, 155
Deane, Phyllis, 73, 89
Defoe, Daniel, 76, 95, 160, 179, 210, 212
Denbigh, William Feilding, 3rd Earl of, 153
Derby, 67
Devon, 109, 121, 132, 206–207
Devonshire, William Cavendish, 4th Duke of, 109
Devonshire-Pitt administration, 160
Dialogus de Scaccario, 208
Diet, 36
Dimsdale, Thomas, 239
Diplomacy. *See* Foreign affairs
Diseases, 39, 114
Dispensary, The, 184, 196
Disraeli, Benjamin, 112
Dissenters (religious), 34–35, 120, 138, 141–142, 235
Divine right of kingship, 118, 141
Doomsday Book, 185
Dorset, 121–122, 132, 148
Dorset, Lionel Cranfield Sackville, 7th Earl (later created 1st Duke) of, 152
Douglas, Dr. James, 197
Dover, Henry Jermyn, 1st Baron, 152
Dowlais ironworks, 106
Drake, Sir Francis, 223
Droitwich, 153
Ducie, Matthew Moreton, 2nd Baron, 232, 242
Dudley family, 101
Dunning, John (later 1st Baron Ashburton), 164
Durham, 75, 101, 128, 142, 186–187, 189–190, 193, 211
Durham, Bishop of, 42, 189
Dutch aristocracy, 110

Dutch people, 1, 33, 66, 176. *See also* Holland

Earle, Gyles, 147
East Anglia, 71, 83
East India Company, 15, 26, 156, 158
East Indies, 9, 207
Economic Reform, 22
Economic thought, 16, 23, 229, 232
Edinburgh, 199
Edward III, King of England, 49
Egmont, John Perceval, 1st Earl of, 135–136, 150
Egremont, Charles Wyndham, 2nd Earl of, 112
Egremont, Earls of, 109
Elections, 20, 126–127, 131–139, 142, 163, 171–172, 181, 186, 205–206, 213, 222
Electorate, 2, 21, 133, 135–136, 138, 156, 205–206
Eliot, Edward, 232
Ellingham (Norfolk), 144, 154
Elliot, Sir Gilbert, 232, 239
Elliot, Sir Walter, 105
Ellison, Robert, 188
Empire, 6, 20, 218, 224, 227–228, 233–236. *See also* American colonies; Colonies
Entrepreneurship, 78–79
Eskimos, 229
Esquires, 10, 43, 45–46
Essex, 138
Estate agent, 186
Estate management, 190
Estates, landed, 8, 9, 11–12, 14, 19, 42, 51, 71, 98–101, 103–106, 107–108, 110–111, 123, 189–190, 210, 212–213, 216–218, 220–223, 230. *See also* Landowners
Eton, 186, 188–189
Evelyn, William, 220
Everitt, Alan, 71
Exchequer, 102, 208